A TEXT BOOK OF

EMBEDDED SYSTEMS

FOR

Semester – I

Final Year (B.E.) Degree Course in
Computer Science & Engineering

As Per New Revised Syllabus of
Dr. Babasaheb Ambedkar Marathwada University,
Aurangabad,
2009 - 2010

DEEPA S PANDIT
B.E. (E & TC)
Assistant Professor, Electronics and Telecommunication Dept.
Institute of Knowledge, College of Engineering,
Pimple Jagtap, Pune.

NIRALI PRAKASHAN

EMBEDDED SYSTEMS

ISBN: 978-93-83525-85-0

First Edition : October, 2013

© : Author

The text of this publication, or any part thereof, should not be reproduced or transmitted in any form or stored in any computer storage system or device for distribution including photocopy, recording, taping or information retrieval system or reproduced on any disc, tape, perforated media or other information storage device etc., without the written permission of Author with whom the rights are reserved. Breach of this condition is liable for legal action.

Every effort has been made to avoid errors or omissions in this publication. In spite of this, errors may have crept in. Any mistake, error or discrepancy so noted and shall be brought to our notice shall be taken care of in the next edition. It is notified that neither the publisher nor the author or seller shall be responsible for any damage or loss of action to any one, of any kind, in any manner, therefrom.

Published By :
NIRALI PRAKASHAN
Abhyudaya Pragati, 1312, Shivaji Nagar,
Off J.M. Road, PUNE – 411005
Tel - (020) 25512336/37/39, Fax - (020) 25511379
Email : niralipune@pragationline.com

Printed at
Repro Knowledgecast Limited
India

DISTRIBUTION CENTRES
PUNE

Nirali Prakashan
119, Budhwar Peth, Jogeshwari Mandir Lane
Pune 411002, Maharashtra
Tel : (020) 2445 2044, 66022708, Fax : (020) 2445 1538
Email : bookorder@pragationline.com

Nirali Prakashan
S. No. 28/25, Dhyari,
Near Pari Company, Pune 411041
Tel : (020) 24690204 Fax : (020) 24690316
Email : dhyari@pragationline.com
bookorder@pragationline.com

MUMBAI
Nirali Prakashan
385, S.V.P. Road, Rasdhara Co-op. Hsg. Society Ltd.,
Girgaum, Mumbai 400004, Maharashtra
Tel : (022) 2385 6339 / 2386 9976, Fax : (022) 2386 9976
Email : niralimumbai@pragationline.com

DISTRIBUTION BRANCHES

NAGPUR
Pratibha Book Distributors
Above Maratha Mandir, Shop No. 3, First Floor,
Rani Jhanshi Square, Sitabuldi, Nagpur 440012,
Maharashtra, Tel : (0712) 254 7129

BENGALURU
Pragati Book House
House No. 1, Sanjeevappa Lane, Avenue Road Cross,
Opp. Rice Church, Bengaluru – 560002.
Tel : (080) 64513344, 64513355,
Mob : 9880582331, 9845021552
Email:bharatsavla@yahoo.com

JALGAON
Nirali Prakashan
34, V. V. Golani Market, Navi Peth, Jalgaon 425001,
Maharashtra, Tel : (0257) 222 0395
Mob : 94234 91860

KOLHAPUR
Nirali Prakashan
New Mahadvar Road,
Kedar Plaza, 1st Floor Opp. IDBI Bank
Kolhapur 416 012, Maharashtra. Mob : 9855046155

CHENNAI
Pragati Books
9/1, Montieth Road, Behind Taas Mahal, Egmore,
Chennai 600008 Tamil Nadu, Tel : (044) 6518 3535,
Mob : 94440 01782 / 98450 21552 / 98805 82331, Email : bharatsavla@yahoo.com

RETAIL OUTLETS
PUNE

Pragati Book Centre
157, Budhwar Peth, Opp. Ratan Talkies,
Pune 411002, Maharashtra
Tel : (020) 2445 8887 / 6602 2707, Fax : (020) 2445 8887
Pragati Book Centre
Amber Chamber, 28/A, Budhwar Peth,
Appa Balwant Chowk, Pune : 411002, Maharashtra,
Tel : (020) 20240335 / 66281669
Email : pbcpune@pragationline.com

Pragati Book Centre
676/B, Budhwar Peth, Opp. Jogeshwari Mandir,
Pune 411002, Maharashtra
Tel : (020) 6601 7784 / 6602 0855
PBC Book Sellers & Stationers
152, Budhwar Peth, Pune 411002, Maharashtra
Tel : (020) 2445 2254 / 6609 2463

MUMBAI
Pragati Book Corner
Indira Niwas, 111 - A, Bhavani Shankar Road, Dadar (W), Mumbai 400028, Maharashtra
Tel : (022) 2422 3526 / 6662 5254, Email : pbcmumbai@pragationline.com

www.pragationline.com info@pragationline.com

Preface to the First Edition ...

It gives me an immense pleasure to present this book on **"EMBEDDED SYSTEMS** to the students of final year (B.E.) Degree in Computer Science & Engineering of Dr. Babasaheb Ambedkar Marathwada University, Aurangabad.

Embedded System is an important and advanced subject for all E&TC, Electronics, Computer and IT Engineering students. So a sincere effort has been made in this book to present design procedures using simple language, neat sketches and programs wherever necessary. Previous university questions and exercises are included at the end of each unit.

I take this opportunity to express my sincere thanks to Mr Dinesh Furia of Nirali Publication, a pioneer in the field of publication. I would like to express our gratitude to Mr Manav Verma for giving a new look to this edition and stressing on quality. I am also thankful to Mr Jignesh Furia who has been instrumental in publishing this book. I specially appreciate the efforts taken by Mr MP Munde, Ms Pallavi Kumari, Mr Ilyas Shaikh, Ms Chaitali Takle and the entire staff of Nirali Prakashan for bringing this edition to the students and faculty in a timely manner.

My special thanks goes to my husband Mr S S Pandit for his constant support and help and my daughter Akshata for her patience.

Despite my best efforts, it is possible that some errors have escaped my attention.

I would gratefully acknowledge of these and also welcome any suggestions and comments for further improvement of the book.

Mahatma Gandhi Jayanti 2013   **Deepa S Pandit**
Pune   dipasp@yahoo.co.in

SYLLABUS

1. 8051 Microcontroller (08 Hrs.)

Introduction, Comparison with Microprocessor, Evolution of Microcontroller, Microcontroller and embedded systems, Microcontroller selection criteria, Architecture and Block Diagram of 8051, Flag bits and PSW, ROM memory space allocation, RAM memory space allocation, Pin diagram of 8051, Addressing modes, Memory organization of 8051.

2. 8051 Programming in C (08 Hrs.)

Bit addresses of I/O and RAM, Data types in 8051 C, Time delay in 8051 C, I/O Programming, Logic operations, Data conversion, Accessing Code ROM Space, Data Serialization, Registers for Timer Programming, Modes of Timers, Counter Programming, Programming Timers of 8051.

3. Serial Communication and Interrupt Programming (08 Hrs.)

Basic of Serial Communication, Registers of 8051 used for Serial Communication, Programming 8051 for receiving and transmitting serial data, 8051 Interrupts, Programming Timer Interrupts, Programming External Hardware Interrupts, Programming and communication interrupt, Interrupt priority in 8051.

4. Interfacing of 8051 (08 Hrs.)

LCD Interfacing, Keyboard Interfacing, ADC 0804 and 0808/09 Interfacing, DAC 0808 interfacing, Interfacing and Accessing External data memory, Stepper motor interfacing using 8255, RTC Interfacing, DC Motor control and PWM.

5. Real Time Operating Systems (08 Hrs.)

Real Time Operating System Concept, Architecture of kernel, Schedule management, Task scheduler, Interrupt routines, Semaphores, Mailbox, Message queues, Pipes, Events, Timers, Memory management, RTOS services in contrast with traditional OS, Overview of commercial RTOS like Vxworks, RT Linux, µcos, QNX.

CONTENTS

1. 8051 Microcontroller — 1.1 – 1.60

2. 8051 Programming in C — 2.1 – 2.28

3. Serial Communication and Interrupt Programming — 3.1 – 3.34

4. Interfacing of 8051 — 4.1 – 4.100

5. Real Time Operating system — 5.1 – 5.46

Appendix — A.1 – A.6

Unit - I
Chapter 1

8051 MICROCONTROLLER

SECTION (A)

1.1 INTRODUCTION

The microprocessor or "computer on chip" became a commercial reality in 1971 when the 4 bit 4004 microprocessor was introduced by the Intel Corporation. Other semiconductor companies also followed the footsteps of Intel so that dozens of microprocessors were available to choose a microprocessor.

Later microcontroller which is also called as the byproduct of microprocessor was developed. It uses the same fabrication techniques and programming concepts.

1.1.1 Microprocessor

A microprocessor is a general purpose central processing unit of a digital computer. Fig. 1.1 shows the block diagram of a microprocessor CPU which consists of an arithmetic and logical unit (ALU), a program counter (PC), a stack pointer (SP), working registers, clock circuits and interrupt circuits.

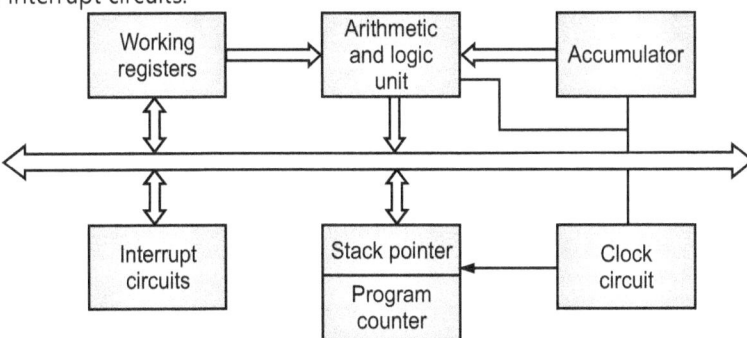

Fig. 1.1 : Block diagram of a microprocessor

To form a complete microcomputer one has to connect memory (both RAM and ROM), memory decoders, an oscillator, and a number of input/output (I/O) devices such as parallel and serial data ports externally. In addition special circuits such as interrupt handlers and counters, mass storage devices such as a floppy and hard disk drives and I/O peripherals such as a keyboard and a CRT display can be added to form a small computer.

The hardware design of a microprocessor CPU is arranged such that a small or very large system can be configured around the CPU as the application demands. The main use of a microprocessor is to read the data, perform the required calculations on the data and store the resultant data using storage device or display the result for further use. The microprocessor ROM stores the small fixed programs that can be operated by peripherals and other devices connected to the system. The design of the microprocessor is done with the desire to make it expandable and flexible as possible.

For a small application small size of memory and I/O devices must be connected to the CPU. This increases the hardware cost and the total cost of the system also increases. To avoid these drawbacks microcontrollers were developed.

1.1.2 Microcontrollers

The microcontroller which is the true computer-on-chip incorporates all the features which are found in a microprocessor CPU. It also adds the other features which makes the complete computer such as ROM, RAM, parallel I/O, serial I/O, counters and a clock circuit.

Fig. 1.2 shows the typical block diagram of a microcontroller. The main use of a microcontroller is to control the operation of a machine using a fixed program which is stored in ROM and that does not change over the life time of the system.

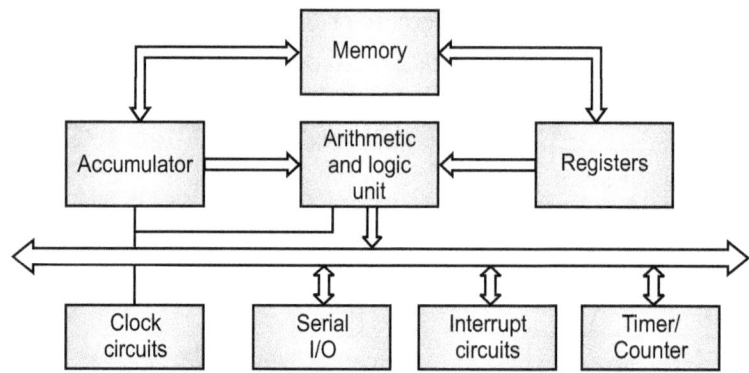

Fig. 1.2 : Typical block diagram of a microcontroller

The first 8 bit microcontroller 8048 was introduced by Intel in 1976. Gradually different high performance microcontroller families were developed such as MCS51, MCS96 etc.

The MCS51 family consists of microcontrollers ranging from 8031 to 8751. They are available in MOS or CMOS technology with different packages. They are designed for mathematical operations. These families provides separate program and data memory. They provide high speed.

1.2 COMPARISON OF MICRCOCONTROLLERS WITH MICROPROCESSORS

Q. Compare microcontroller with general purpose microprocessor.
[8 M] [May/June 2010, 2011]

Table 1.1

Microprocessors	Microcontrollers
1. Microprocessor depends on other devices for various functions.	1. Microcontroller has everything inbuilt on a single chip.
2. It consist of ALU, general purpose registers, stack pointer, program counter, timing and control circuit and interrupt circuits.	2. Microcontroller consists of ALL components of microprocessor and has inbuilt RAM, ROM, I/O devices, timers/counters etc.
3. It is used to process the information in computer systems.	3. It is used to control the I/O devices which requires minimum external components.
4. It has one or two bit manipulation instructions.	4. It has many bit manipulation instructions.
5. It has less multifunctioned pins.	5. It has many multifunctioned pins.
6. They have large memory address space and more data.	6. They have less address space and less data.
7. Design is simple and flexible.	7. Design is complex and less flexible.
8. It has a single memory map for code and data.	8. It has separate memory map for code and data.
9. It requires more hardware externally to form a small application.	9. It requires less hardware to form a small application.
10. Time required to access memory and I/O devices is more.	10. Time required to access memory and I/O devices is less because they are inbuilt.
11. The clock rates are very fast.	11. Clock rates are slow.
12. It has many instructions to move data between memory and CPU.	12. It has one or two instructions to move data between memory and CPU.
13. They are expensive.	13. They are cheap.

1.3 EVOLUTION OF MICROCONTROLLER

Each application demands a microcontroller with right amount of functionality at the minimum cost. Applications may be different from controlling an appliance to controlling an automobile. No single microcontroller design can meet these demands economically, so semiconductor manufacturers offers an array of microcontrollers to handle the data of 4 – 8 – 16 or 32 bit words.

Bits are not the only thing that increases the word length but additional functions are also added to meet the market needs and the popular additional functions are :
- Analog to digital converters
- Counter arrays
- Watchdog timers (WDTs)
- Serial data (UART)
- Pulse width modulation (PWM)
- Phase locked loops (PLLs)
- External bus controllers for static and dynamic memories.

1.3.1 Eight Bit Microcontrollers
- Texas instruments introduced its first microcontroller in 1974 with the name TMS 1000.
- Intel introduced its first microcontroller in 1976 as Intel 8048.
- When the ALU of the microcontroller performs the arithmetic and logical operations on 8-bit data, and when the internal bus of the microcontroller is 8-bit, such microcontroller is called as 8-bit microcontroller.
- Summary of 8-bit microcontrollers.

Table 1.2

Manufacturers	Model No.	No. of pins	I/O pins	ROM K Bytes	RAM K Bytes	No. of counters	Additional features
Intel	8048	40	27	1 KB	64	1	External memory 8 KB
Intel	8031	40	32	–	128	2	(1) External memory 128 KB (2) Serial port.
Intel	8051	40	32	4 KB	128	2	(1) External memory 128 KB (2) Serial port.

Manufacturers	Model No.	No. of pins	I/O pins	ROM K Bytes	RAM K Bytes	No. of counters	Additional features
Intel	8052 AH	40	32	8 KB	256	3	(1) External memory 128 KB (2) Serial port.
Microchip	P1C16C56	18	12	1 KB	25	0	(1) Watchdog timer (WDT) (2) Self reset (3) 25 mA/20 mA sinking and sourcing capability (4) Low cost.
National	COP820	28	24	1 KB	64	1	(1) Serial bit I/O
Motorola	6805	28	20	1 KB	64	1	–
Motorola	68HC11	52	40	8 KB	256	2	(1) Serial port (2) A/D converter (3) Watchdog timer (WDT)
Philips	87C552	68	48	8 KB	256	3	(1) Serial port (2) A/D converter (3) Watchdog timer (WDT)
Rockwell	6500/1	40	32	2 KB	64	1	–
TI	TMS 17500	40	32	2 KB	128	1	External memory 64 KB
TI	TMS 370C050	68	55	4 KB	256	2	(1) External memory 112 KB (2) A/D converter (3) Serial port (4) Watchdog timer (WDT)
Zilog	Z8	40	32	2 KB	128	2	(1) External memory 124KB (2) Serial port
Zilog	Z86C83	28	22	4 KB	256	2	8 channel A/D converter

1.3.2 Sixteen Bit Microcontrollers

Sixteen bit microcontroller are better suited for programming in high level languages, such as C. 16-bit microcontrollers are used in applications for calculation and data intensive and includes disk drives, modems, printers, scanners, pattern recognition, and automotive and servomotor control.

A typical example of 16-bit microcontroller is the Motorola 68HC16Z3 which has 4K RAM, 8K ROM, 2 counters, 24 I/O pins with additional features of counters, arrays, UART, A/D converter and watchdog timer (WDT).

1.3.3 Thirty-Two Bit Microcontrollers

Thirty-two bit microcontrollers are currently targeting for high end applications such as PDAs, GPS, automotive control, communication networks, robotics, entertainment/game boxes, digital cameras, cell phones etc.

For example, the sharp LH79520 housed in a 176 - pin LQFP package which offers the following features ;

- 32K RAM
- Colour LCD controller
- Three UARTs
- Synchronous serial
- Two PWMs
- 64 I/O pins
- Four counters
- Watchdog timer (WDT)
- Real time clock (RTC)
- Phase locked loop (PLL)
- Direct memory access (DMA)

1.4 MICROCONTROLLER AND EMBEDDED SYSTEMS

Microprocessors and microcontroller are widely used in embedded system products. A embedded system performs the dedicated task (one and only one task). The best example is printer. It perform only one task, accept the data and print it. Some of the examples of embedded systems designed using microcontrollers are intercom, cable TV tuner, camera, printers, telephones, fax machine, cell phones, video games, remote controls etc.

In recent years, many manufacturers of general purpose microprocessors such as Intel, and AMD (Advanced Micro Devices, Inc.) and Cyrix have targeted their microprocessors for high end applications in embedded market. Therefore, these microprocessors are called as **high end embedded processors.**

One of the critical requirement of an embedded system is to decrease power consumption and space. This can be achieved by integrating more functions on a CPU chip. All the embedded processors based on the X86 and 680X0 have low power consumption in addition to some forms of I/O, COM port, and ROM all on a single chip. In high performance embedded processors, the trend is to integrate more and more functions on the CPU chip. This trend is changing PC system design too. Normally, to design the PC motherboard, one need a CPU plus a chip-set consisting of I/O, a cache controller, a flash ROM, containing BIOS and a secondary cache memory.

Many embedded systems are using X86 PCs because in MS-DOS and Windows standardization. This reduces the cost as well as saves the development time.

Table 1.3 shows some embedded products using microcontrollers.

Table 1.3

Home	Office	Auto
Intercom		
Telephones	Telephones	Trip computer
Security systems	Computers	Engine control
Garage door openers	Security systems	Air bag
Answering machines	Fax machines	ABS (Anti breaking system)
Fax machines	Microwave	Instrumentations
Home computers	Copier	Security system
TV	Laser printer	Transmission control
Cable TV tuner	Colour printer	Entertainment
VCR	Paging	Climate control
Camcoders		Cellular phone
Remote controls		Keyless entry
Video games		
Cellular phones		
Musical instruments		
Sewing machines		
Lighting control		
Paging		
Camera		
Pinball machines		
Toys		
Exercise equipments		

1.5 SELECTION CRITERIA FOR A MICROCONTROLLER

Q. Explain the criteria used for choosing a microcontroller for embedded applications. [8 M] [Nov./Dec. 2011, May/June 2013]

Each microcontroller has a unique instruction set and register set. They are not compatible with each other, programs written for one microcontroller will not run on the other. These are variety of microcontrollers available in the market. So designers consider the following three criteria for choosing a microcontroller. These are as follows :

1. It should meet the computing needs of the task at hand efficiently and cost effectively.
2. Availability of software development tools such as compilers, assemblers, and debuggers.
3. Wide availability and reliable resources of the microcontrollers.

Among other considerations

(a) **Speed :** What is the highest speed it supports ?

(b) **Packaging :** It is important in terms of space, assembling and prototyping the end product.

(c) **Power consumption :** This is critical for battery operated products.

(d) RAM and ROM size on chip.

(e) The number of I/O pins and timer on the chip.

(f) **Upgrading capability :** Easy to upgrade to higher performance or lower power consumption versions.

(g) Cost per unit.

1.6 MICROCONTROLLER RESOURCES

1.6.1 Bus Width

The 8051 and 8096 families have an 8-bit internal bus width. The control and sequencing circuit activates the different sections and subsections at different times. Therefore, the same 8-bit bus is used for carrying all the data, addresses and the instruction codes. Therefore registers require only 8-bit addresses. If a 16 bit operation is required to perform, then two instruction cycles are required. The external address bus width is 16 bit in microcontrollers. Hence it can access 2^{16} = 64 KB address space externally. The external data bus is multiplexed with the lower order address bus using time division multiplexing.

By using a latch the address bus and data bus is separated from the multiplexed bus.

1.6.2 Program Memory and Data Memory

Program memory is mainly read only memory (ROM). ROM can be PROM/EEPROM or flash.

ROM area in a microcontroller consist of metal layer that is etched according to the mask to get 1's and 0's according to the ROM image which is burned in ROM.

In 8051 total memory is divided into program memory and data memory. Program memory stores the programs to be executed while data memory stores the data like intermediate results, variables and constants required for the execution of the program.

Data memory may be read from or written to and thus it is implemented using RAM.

1.6.3 Parallel Ports

Microcontroller based system has different types of ports :
- 8-bit port with a latch for input or output.
- 8-bit port with latch as well as bus buffers for address data and control busses.
- 8-bit port with data direction register.
- 8-bit input port with analog input capability.
- 8-bit port with handshaking signals.
- Open-drain port.
- Quasi - bidirectional port.

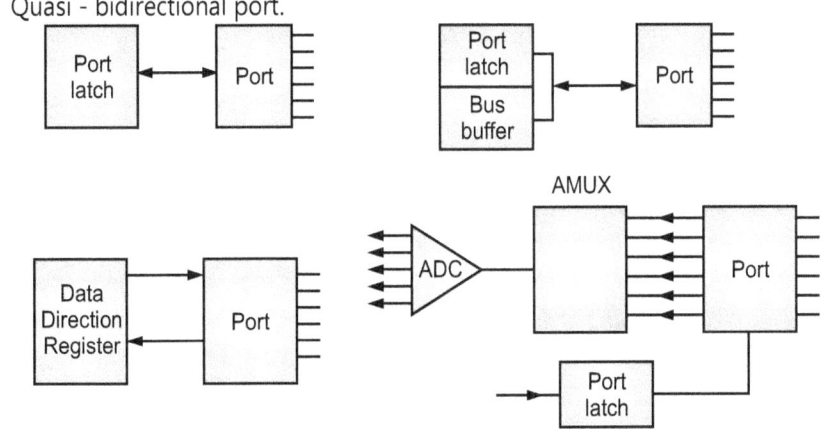

Fig. 1.3 : Microcontroller port types

1.6.4 Pulse Width Modulated Output (PWM)

Pulse width modulation is a digital-to-analog conversion method that changes the duty cycle of an output pulse from 0% to 100%. The output pulse is provided on a single output pin. PWM outputs are useful when they are used to drive DC motors.

The speed of the motor depends on three factors : (a) load, (b) voltage, (c) current. By changing the width of the pulse applied to the DC motor, we can increase or decrease the amount of power provided to the motor. Therefore the speed of the DC motor can be controlled.

1.6.5 On-chip A/D Converters (ADC)

Analog to digital converter converts the analog signals to digital numbers which can be read by the microcontroller and processed. The higher resolution ADC provides a smaller step size. An ADC has n-bit resolution where n can be 8, 10, 12, 16 or even 24 bits. In addition to resolution, conversion time is the another factor to judge an ADC. The ADC chips are either parallel or serial.

In parallel ADC 8 or more pins are dedicated to bringing out the binary data, but in serial ADC only one pin is available for data out.

1.6.6 Watchdog Timer (WDT) [May/June 2011]

Watchdog timer is a timing device that resets the system after a predefined timeout. After power-up it is activated within the first few clock cycles. In many embedded systems it is useful because it helps in rescuing the system if a fault develops and the program gets stuck. On restart, the system can function normally. Most microcontrollers have on-chip watchdog timers.

1.6.7 Reset

(Reset forces the system to begin the processing of instructions from a starting address.) The address is set by default on a power up. The program which is reset and runs on a power-up may of the following type :

1. A system program that executes from the beginning.
2. A system boot-up program.
3. A system initialization program.

In certain processors, there are two start-up addresses one is based on the power-up reset vector and the other on the reset vector after the reset instruction or after a time-out.

The reset circuit is activated for a fixed duration and then deactivated. The processor keeps the reset pin active and then deactivates. The reset can be activated by an external reset circuit that activates on power up, on switching-on reset of the system or on detection of a low voltage. This circuit output connects to a pin called the reset pin of the processor.

The circuit may be a simple RC circuit, an external IC circuit or a custom built IC. e.g. MAX 6314 and Motorola MC 34064. It can also be activated by (1) software instruction, (2) time-out by a programmed timer known as watchdog timer, (3) a clock monitor detecting a slowdown below certain frequencies.

1.6.8 Timers and Real Time Clocks

A timer circuit is mainly configured as the system clock, which ticks and generates system interrupts periodically.

A timer circuit is mainly configured as the real-time clock (RTC) that generates system interrupts periodically for the schedulers, real time programs and for periodic saving of time and date in the system. The RTC is used to obtain software-controlled delays and time-outs. RTC works as a driver for software timers (SWTs). Microcontrollers also provide internal timer circuits for counting and timing devices.

1.7 ARCHITECTURE OF 8051

Q. Draw and explain block diagram of 8051. [8 M] [May/June 2012]

8051 is an 8-bit microcontroller introduced by Intel Corporation in 1981. This microcontroller had 128 bytes of RAM, 4K bytes of on-chip ROM, two timers, one serial port and four ports all on a single chip.

8051 is a 8-bit processor means CPU works on only 8-bit data at a time. Data larger than 8-bit can be broken into 8-bit pieces and then processed.

The 8051 has a total of four I/O ports, of each 8-bits. The 8051 can have a maximum of 64 K bytes of on-chip ROM.

1.7.1 Features of 8051

Table 1.4

Feature	Quantity
ROM	4 K bytes
RAM	128 bytes
Timer	2
I/O pins	32
Serial port	1
Interrupt sources	6

- 8-bit CPU with registers A and B.
- 16-bit program Counter (PC) and Data Pointer (DPTR).
- 8-bit Program Status Word (PSW).
- 8-bit Stack Pointer (SP).
- Internal ROM or EEPROM of the 4K size.
- Internal RAM of 128 bytes :
  - Four register banks, each containing eight registers.
  - Sixteen bytes, which may be addressed at the bit level.
  - Eighty bytes of general purpose data memory.
- 32 input/output pins arranged as four 8-bit ports.
- Two 16-bit timer/counters : T_0 and T_1.
- Full duplex serial data receiver/transmitter : SBUF.
- Control registers : TCON, TMOD, SCON, PCON, IP and IE.
- Two external and three internal interrupt sources.
- Oscillator and clock circuits.

Fig. 1.4 shows the architecture block diagram of 8051.

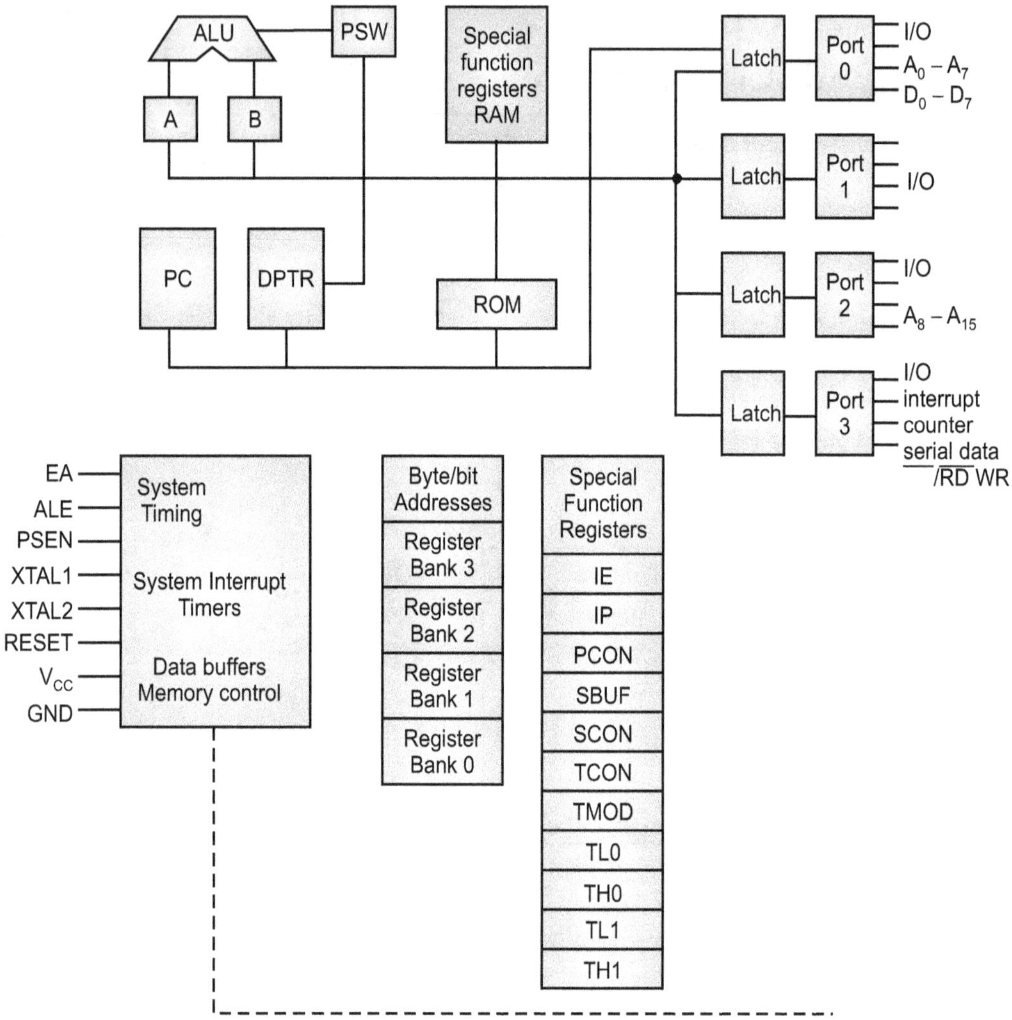

Fig. 1.4 : 8051 Architectural block diagram

1.7.2 8051 Oscillator and Clock

Pins XTAL1 and XTAL2 are provided for connecting a resonant network to form an oscillator. A quartz crystal and capacitors are used as shown in Fig. 1.5. The crystal frequency is the basic clock frequency of the microcontroller. 8051 run at specific maximum and minimum frequencies, typically 1 MHz to 16 MHz. Minimum frequency is required because some internal memories are dynamic and must always operate above a minimum frequency otherwise data will be lost.

Serial communication need the frequency of the oscillator because internal counters divide the basic clock frequency to decide the baud rate. If the basic clock frequency is not divisible without a remainder, then the resulting communication frequency is not standard.

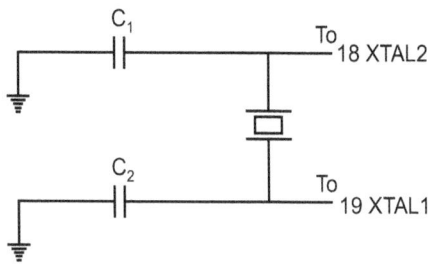

Fig. 1.5

Ceramic resonators are used as an alternative to crystal resonators. But for high speed serial data communication it provides less frequency stability and accuracy compared to crystal resonators.

1.7.3 Program Counter and Data Pointer

8051 contains two 16-bit registers: The Program Counter (PC) and the data pointer (DPTR). Each is used to hold the address of a byte in memory.

The Program Counter (PC) addresses the locations of program instruction bytes in memory. The PC is automatically incremented and may also be altered by certain instruction. This is the only register that does not have internal address.

The DPTR register is made of two 8-bit registers, DPH and DPL and are used to provide memory addresses to access internal and external code and external data. DPTR can be specified by in 16-bit name, DPTR, or by each individual byte name, DPH and DPL. This register is under the control of program instruction and does not have a single internal address, instead DPH and DPL are each assigned onaddress.

1.7.4 A and B CPU Registers

8051 consists of 34 general purpose registers. Register A is the accumulator which holds the results of many instructions, particularly mathematical and logical operations. The B register is used with register A for multiplication and division operations. It may be used as a scratch pad in other instructions.

The other 32 are arranged as a part of internal RAM in four banks, $B_0 - B_3$ of eight registers.

1.7.5 Program Status Word (PSW)

Q. Explain program states word register of 8051 in detail.. [8 M]
[May/June 2010, 2011, 2013]

This is a bit addressable register. It consists of set of flags. Flags are 1-bit registers used to store the result of certain program instructions.

The 8051 has four math flags and three general purpose user flags. The math flag includes carry (c) Auxiliary carry (AC), overflow (OV), and parity (P). User flags are named F_0, GF_0, GF_1. GF_0 and GF_1 are stored in PCON. They are general purpose flag used to record some event in the program. It also consists of register select bits that identify which of the register bank is currently in use by the program. Fig. 1.6 shows program status word (PSW).

D_7	D_6	D_5	D_4	D_3	D_2	D_1	D_0
CY	AC	F0	RS1	RS0	OV	—	P

Fig. 1.6

- D_7 Carry flag
- D_6 Auxiliary carry flag used for BCD arithmetic
- D_5 User flag 0 (F0)
- D_4 RS1 and RS0 register bank select bit 1 and 0.
- D_3

RS1	RS0	
0	0	Select register bank 0
0	1	Select register bank 1
1	0	Select register bank 2
1	1	Select register bank 3

- D_2 Overflow flag (OV)
- D_1 Reserved for future use
- D_0 Parity flag 1 for odd parity; 0 for even parity.

1.7.6 The Stack and Stack Pointer

Q. Explain stacks in 8051 with suitable example. [8 M] [May/June 2012]

The 8-bit stack pointer holds the address of the stack top. Stack is a separate memory location in RAM to store the data temporarily. When the data is stored on the stack, the SP increments increments before storing data on the stack. As data is retrieved from the stack then the SP decrements to point to the next available byte of the stored data. The data is stored and retrieved back using the two instructions : PUSH and POP.

The structure of the stack is same as the last in first out (LIFO) register. The stack can overwrite data in the register banks, bit addressable RAM, scratch pad RAM areas. Therefore, the stack is placed at a higher location in internal RAM to avoid conflict with the register and bit addressable internal RAM areas.

1.7.7 Memory Organization

> **Q. Explain RAM space allocation and register banks in 8051 microcontroller.** [8 M]
> [May/June 2013]

The total memory of an 8051 is logically divided into program memory and data memory. Program memory store the program to be executed whereas the data memory stores the data such as intermediate results, variables and constants required for the execution of the program. The program memory is usually implemented using EPROM whereas the data memory is implemented using RAM.

1.7.7.1 Program Memory

Both program memory and data memory may be categorized as on-chip (internal) and external memory. The 8051 can address 4 k bytes on-chip program memory whose map starts from 0000H and ends at 0FFFH. It can address 64 k bytes of external program memory under the control of $\overline{PSEN}$ signal, whose address map is from 0000H to FFFFH. Here internal program memory overlaps with that of the external program memory. These two memory spaces can be distinguished using the $\overline{PSEN}$ signal.

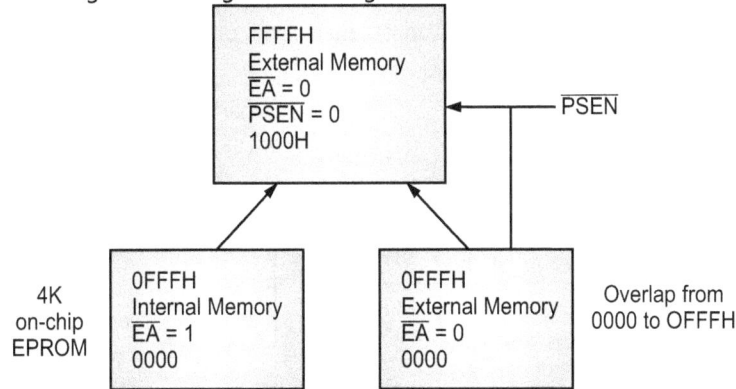

Fig. 1.7 : Program memory map of an 8051 system

1.7.7.2 Data Memory

8051 supports 64 k bytes of external data memory whose map starts at 0000H and ends at FFFFH. This external data memory can be accessed under the control of DPTR register. It stores the addresses for external data memory accesses. During the external memory access 8051 generates $\overline{RD}$ and $\overline{WR}$ signals. The chip select signal of the external data memory may be derived from the address lines.

Internal data memory of 8051 consists of two ports : First is the RAM of 128 bytes and the second is the set of addresses from 80H to FFH, which includes the addresses allotted the special function register.

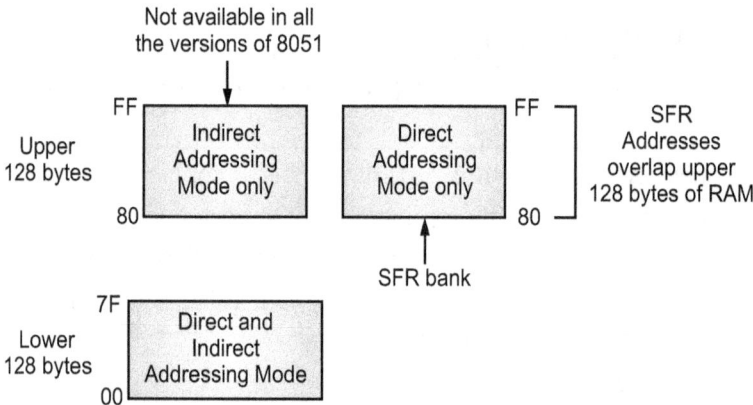

Fig. 1.8 : Internal data memory of 8051

The address map of the 8051 internal 128 bytes RAM starts from 00 and ends at 7FH. This RAM can be addressed by using direct or indirect mode of addressing. The special function register address map i.e. from 80H to FFH is accessible only with direct addressing mode.

In case of 8051 versions with 256 bytes on-chip RAM, the map starts from 00H and ends at FFH. In this case, the address map of special function registers i.e. 80H to FFH overlaps with the upper 128 bytes of RAM. Addressing mode differentiates between these two memory spaces.

The lower 128 bytes of RAM are organised in three parts. The address block from 00 to 1FH i.e. the lowest 32 bytes which form the first section is divided into four banks of 8-bit registers, denoted as bank 00, 01, 10 and 11.

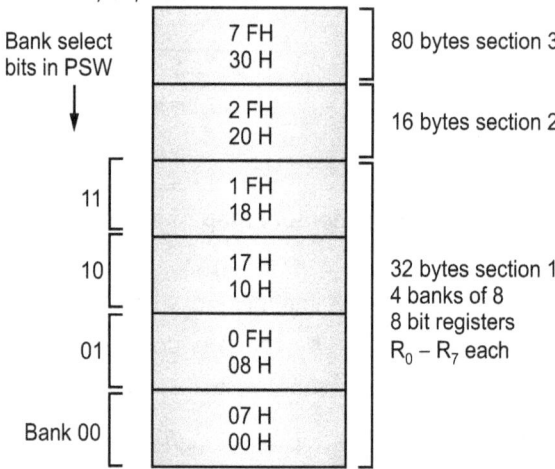

Fig. 1.9 : Internal organization of lower 128 bytes of RAM

Each of these banks contain eight 8-bit registers. After reset, bank 0 is selected by default. The stack pointer gets initialized at address 07H but actual stack data is stored from 08H onwards. These bank selection bits are present in program status word.

The second section extends from 20H to 2FH i.e. 16 bytes are bit addressable block of memory which contains 128 bits. Each of these bits can be addressed using the addresses 00 to 7FH. There are two methods to access these bits.

In the first it's bit number is directly mentioned in the instruction while in the second the bit is mentioned with it's position in the respective register byte.

The third block of internal memory occupies addresses from 30H to 7FH. This block of memory is byte addressable. In general, this third block of memory is used as stack memory. All the internal data memory locations are accessed using 8-bit addresses using appropriate mode of addressing.

1.7.8 Special Function Registers [May/June 2010]

The 8051 operates which does not require the use of internal 128 byte RAM addresses from 00 to 7FH are done by a group of specific internal registers, each called a special function register (SFR). Some SFRs are bit addressable. The SFR names and equivalent internal RAM addresses are given in Table 1.5.

Table 1.5 : SFR names and their RAM addresses

Name	Bit addressable	Function	Internal RAM address
A	Y	Accumulator	0E0
B	Y	Arithmetic	0F0
DPH	N	Addressing external memory	83
DPL	N	Addressing external memory	82
IE	Y	Interrupt enable control	0A8
IP	Y	Interrupt priority	0B8
P_0	Y	Input/Output port latch	80
P_1	Y	Input/Output port latch	90
P_2	Y	Input/Output port latch	A0
P_3	Y	Input/Output port latch	0B0
PCON	N	Power control	87
PSW	Y	Program status word	0D0
SCON	Y	Serial port control	98
SBUF	N	Serial port data buffer	99
SP	N	Stack pointer	81
TMOD	N	Timer/Counter mode control	89
TCON	Y	Timer/Counter control	88
TL0	N	Timer 0 low byte	8A
TH0	N	Timer 0 high byte	8C
TL1	N	Timer 1 low byte	8B
TH1	N	Timer 1 high byte	8D

1.7.9 Register Set of 8051

> **Q. Explain RAM space allocation and register banks in 8051.** [8 M] [May/June 2011]
> **Q. Explain register banks and stacks with suitable example.** [8 M] [May/June 2011]

8051 has two 8-bit register A and B, which can be used to store operands. Including these A and B registers, 8051 has a family of special function registers (SFRs). There are in total, 21 bit addressable, 8-bit registers. ACC (A), B, PSW, P_0, P_1, P_2, P_3, IP, IE, TCON and SCON are all 8-bit, bit - addressable registers. The remaining registers, SP, DPH, DPL, TMOD, TH0, TH1, TL0, TL1, SBUF, and PCON registers are to be byte addressable. The registers DPH and DPL are the higher and lower bytes of a 16-bit register DPTR, which is used for accessing external data memory. Starting 32-bytes of on-chip RAM may be used as general purpose registers. Their addresses lie in the range from 0000H to 001FH. These 32, 8-bit registers are divided into four groups of 8 registers each, called as register bank. Only one bank is accessible at a time. To select the register bank, RS0 and RS1 bits of the program status word are used.

The registers TH0 and TL0 form a 16 bit counter/timer register. Similarly, TH1 and TL1 form the 16-bit count for the timer T_1. The four port latches are presented by P_0, P_1, P_2 and P_3. Register SP is a stack pointer register. Register PSW is a flag register which contains the status information. Register IP can be programmed to control the interrupts priority. Register IE can be programmed to control interrupts. TCON is called Timer/Counter register. Some of the bits of these registers are used to turn OFF or ON of the timer. The register TMOD is used for programming the modes of operation of the timer/counters. The SCON register is a serial port mode control register and is used to control the operation of the serial port. The SBUF register acts as a serial data buffer for transmit and receive operations. The PCON register is called power control register. This register contains power down bit and idle bit which activate the power saving modes of operation provided in the CHMOS version called as idle mode and power down mode.

1.7.9.1 Idle Mode

In idle mode, the oscillator continuously runs and the interrupt, serial port and timer blocks are active but the clock to the CPU is disabled. The CPU status is stored. This mode can be terminated with a hardware interrupt. After this, the CPU resumes program execution from where it left OFF.

1.7.9.2 Power Down Mode

In power down mode, the on-chip oscillator is stopped. All the functions of the controller are held maintaining the contents of RAM. The only way to terminate this mode is hardware reset. The reset defines all the SFRs but the RAM contents are left unchanged. Both of these modes can be entered by setting the respective bit in an internal register called PCON register using software Fig. 1.10 shows the hardware required to implement idle and power down modes.

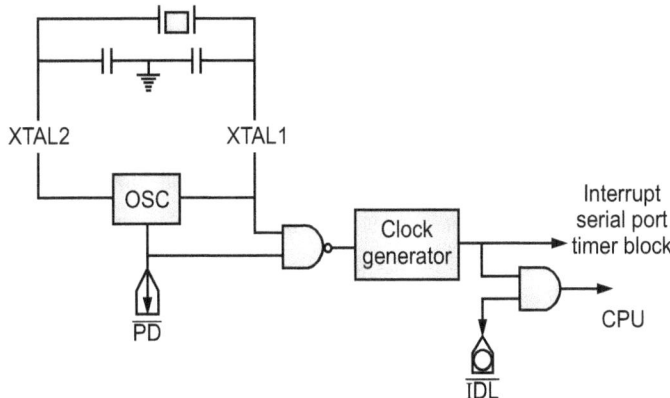

Fig. 1.10 : Hardware required to implement idle and power down modes

1.8 INPUT/OUTPUT PORT

Q. Explain bit addressability features of 8051 for I/O ports. [May/June 2013]

The 8051 microcontroller has four ports named as P_0, P_1, P_2 and P_3. Each port consist of 8-bits. All ports are bidirectional. The 8051 microcontroller DIP has 40 pins and out of 40 pins 32 pins are reserved for port functions. Each port has a D-type output latch for each pin. The SFR for each port is made up of these eight latches, which can be addressed at the SFR address for that port. Port latches are different from port pins.

After reset all ports are configured as input ports. When zero is written to a port, it acts as output port and when one is sent to a port, it acts as input port.

1.8.1 Port 0

Port 0 pins may serve as input, output or when used together, as a bidirectional low-order address and data bus for external memory.

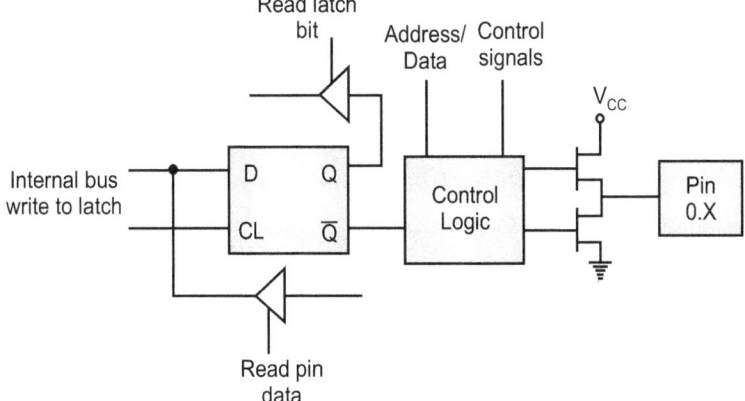

Fig. 1.11 : Port 0 pin configuration

1 must be written to the corresponding port 0 latch by the program when a pin is used as an input pin which makes both of the output transistors off. Therefore it causes the pin to float in a high impedance state and the pin is connected to the input buffer.

0 must be programmed to make the pin as output pin which makes the lower FET ON, grounding the pin. All latches that are programmed to a 1 still float. Therefore, external pull-up registers will be needed to supply a logic high when port 0 is used as output port.

When port 0 is used as an address but to external memory, the address lines are switched to gates of the Field Effect Transistors (FETs) by the internal control signals. When the address bit is logic 1, it turn ON the upper FET and turn OFF the lower FET which gives the logic high to output pin.

When address bit is logic 0, the lower FET is turned On and upper FET is turned OFF to give a logic low at the output pin. The bus becomes a data bus when the address is formed and latched into external circuits by the Address Latch Enable (ALE) pulse. Now port 0 reads data from the external memory and configures itself as an input port by writing logic 1 to all port 0 latches.

1.8.2 Port 1

Port 1 pins are not dual functioned. Therefore, the output latch is directly connected to the gate of the lower FET to which active pull-up load is connected. Fig. 1.12 shows the port 1 pin configuration.

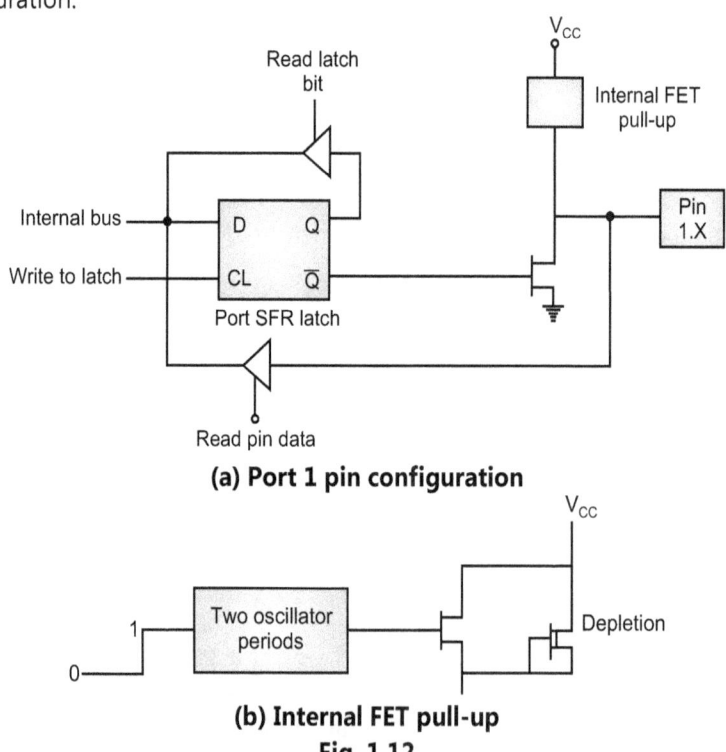

(a) Port 1 pin configuration

(b) Internal FET pull-up

Fig. 1.12

One is written to the latch, when used as input port which makes the lower FET OFF. Pin buffer input is pulled high by the FET load. An external circuit is used to overcome the high impedance pull-up and drives the pin low.

When it is used as an output port, the latches drive the input of an external circuit high through the pull-up if the latch contains 1. If 0 is written to the latch, the lower FET turns ON, the pull up turns OFF and the pin drive the input of the external circuit low.

Internal pull-up provides a low impedance path to the positive voltage supply to help reduce rise times in charging any parasitic capacitances in the external circuitry. The second FET is turned ON for two oscillator time periods during a low-to-high transition on the pin.

1.8.3 Port 2

Q. Explain dual role of port 2 with suitable example. [Nov./Dec. 2011]

Port 2 is used as an input/output port similar to port 1. Port 2 is used to supply a high order address byte in conjunction with the port 0 low-order byte to address external memory. Fig. 1.13 shows the port 2 pin configuration.

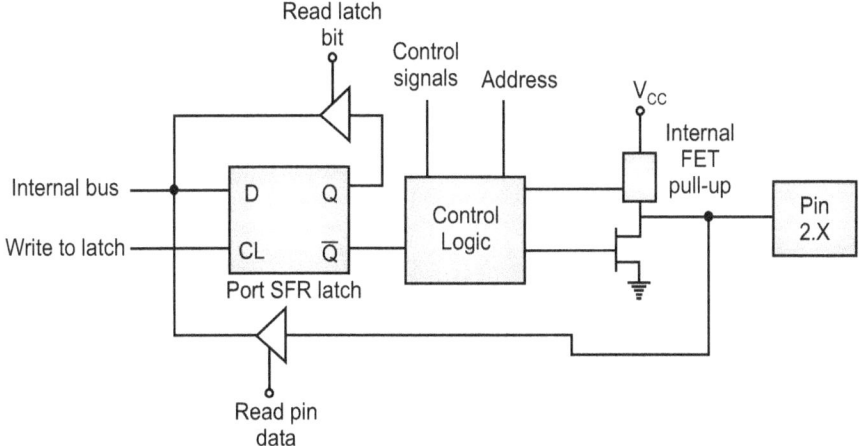

Fig. 1.13 : Port 2 pin configuration

Port 2 pins are changed momentarily by the address control signals when the high byte of a 16-bit address is supplied. During external memory addressing, port 2 latches remains stable. They need not to be turned around for data input as in case of port 0.

1.8.4 Port 3

Port 3 is used as input/output port as port 1. The input and output functions are programmed under the control of the P_3 latch or under the control of other special function registers. Fig. 1.14 shows port 3 pin configuration.

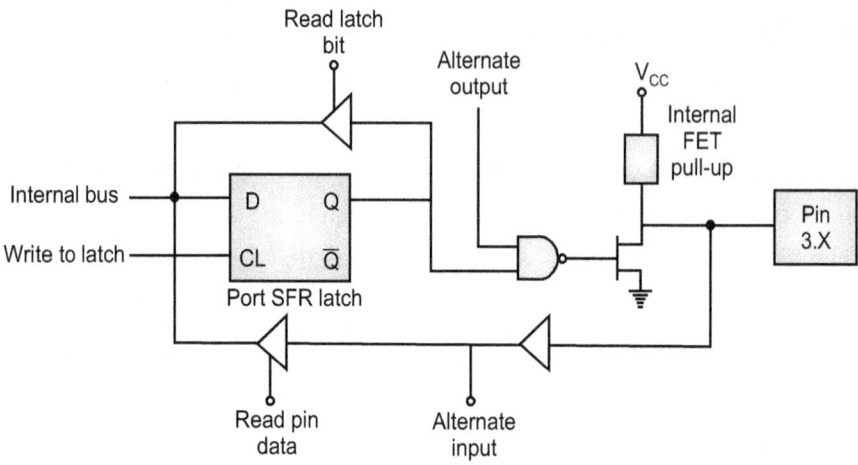

Fig. 1.14

Unlike port 0 and port 2, each pin of port 3 is individually programmed for alternate use or for external addressing functions. Table 1.6 shows the port 3 pin function and SFRs used by each pin.

Table 1.6

Pin	Alternate Use	SFR
P3.0 – RXD	Serial data input	SBUF
P3.1 – TXD	Serial data output	SBUF
P3.2 – $\overline{INT0}$	External interrupt 0	TCON.1
P3.3 – $\overline{INT1}$	External interrupt 1	TCON.3
P3.4 – T_0	External timer 0 input	TMOD
P3.5 – T_1	External timer 1 input	TMOD
P3.6 – $\overline{WR}$	External memory write pulse	–
P3.7 – $\overline{RD}$	External memory read pulse	–

1.9 COUNTERS AND TIMERS

Counting of external events such as the frequency of a pulse train, or the generation of precise internal time delays are required for the many microcontroller application. These tasks can be accomplished using software techniques. This makes the processor busy so to reduce the burden on processor, two 16-bit up counters named as T_0 and T_1 are provided for the use of the programmer.

Each counter is programmed to count internal clock pulses which also acts as a timer or programmed to act as a counter by counting external pulses.

The counters are divided into two 8-bit registers namely timer low (TL0 and TL1) and high (TH0, TH1) bytes. All counter action is controlled by timer mode control register (TMOD) and timer/counter control register (TCON).

When timer is used as a counter to count a certain number of internal pulses or external events, a number is placed in one of the counter. The number is nothing but the maximum countless the desired count plus 1. The counter then increments the number to the maximum and then again comes to 0 by setting a timer flag.

When a counter is programmed to be a timer it will count the internal clock frequency of the 8051 oscillator divided by 12d. For example, if oscillator frequency is 6 MHz then the timer clock will have 500 kHz frequency.

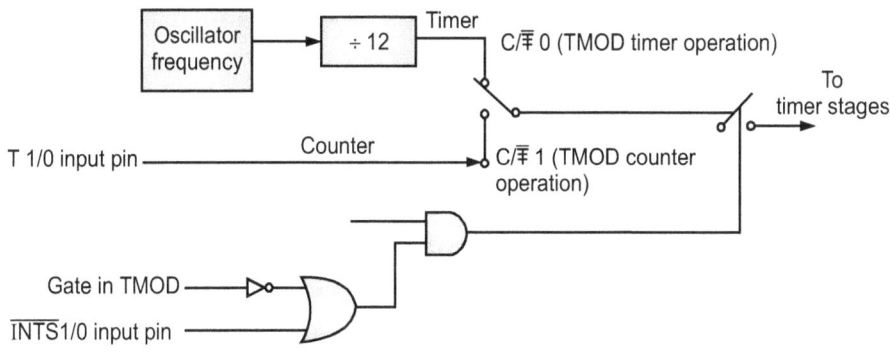

Fig. 1.15 : Timer/counter control logic

To act as a timer, the $C/\overline{T}$ bit in the TMOD register must be 0 and bit TRX in the TCON register must be 1 (timer run) and gate bit in the TMOD register must be 0 or external pin $\overline{INTX} = 1$.

1.9.1 TMOD Register

> **Q. Draw and explain the role of TMOD and TCON register of 8051, while programming 8051 microcontroller for embedded applications.**
> **[8 M] [May/June 2012]**

Fig. 1.16 shows Timer Mode Control (TMOD) special function register.

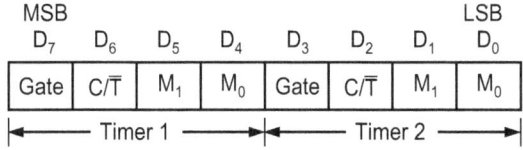

Fig. 1.16

Bit D_7 and D_3 : Gate

This is a OR gate to RUN/STOP time 1 or 0 with the help of program it is set to 1, to enable timer to run if bit TR0/1 in TCON register is set and signal on external interrupt $\overline{INT1/0}$ pin is high.

Bit D_6 and D_2 : $C/\overline{T}$

It is used to decide counter or timer operation, when it is set to 1 it is used as a counter by counting pulses from external input pins. When it is set 0, it acts as a timer by counting internal frequency.

Bits D_1 and D_5, M_1 and bits D_4 and D_0 : M_1 and M_0

It is used to select the timer mode of operation

Table 1.7 : TMOD is not bit-addressable

M_0	M_0	Mode
0	0	Mode 0
0	1	Mode 1
1	0	Mode 2
1	1	Mode 3

1.9.2 Timer Control (TCON) Special Function Register

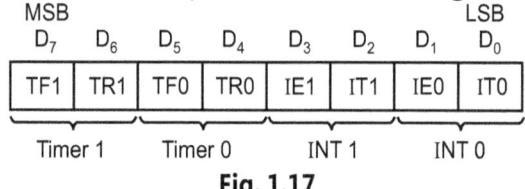

Fig. 1.17

Bit D_7 : Timer 1 overflow flag (TF1)

When it is set, timer 1 rolls from all 1's to all 0's and cleared by processor vectors to execute interrupt service routine located at 001BH program address.

Bit D_6 : Timer 1 run control bit (TR1)

This is set to enable the timer 1 to count and reset to halt the timer.

Bit D_5 : Timer 0 overflow flag (TF0)

When it is set timer 0 rolls from all 1's to all 0's and cleared by processor vectors to execute interrupt service routine located at 000BH program address.

Bit D_4 : Timer 0 run control bit (TR0)

This is set to enable timer 0 to count and reset to halt the timer.

Bit D_3 : External interrupt 1 Edge flag (IE1)

When a high to low edge signal is received on port 3, pin no. 3 ($\overline{INT1}$), it is set and cleared by processor vectors to execute interrupt service routine located at 0013H program address.

Bit D_2 : External interrupt 1 signal type control bit (IT1)

It is set by the program to enable external interrupt 1 during a falling edge of the signal and cleared by program to enable a low-level signal on external interrupt to generate an interrupt.

Bit D_1 : External Interrupt 0 Edge Flag (IE0)

When a high-to-low edge signal is received on port 3 pin 2, it is set to 1 and cleared to zero by processor vectors to interrupt service routine located at 0003H program address. It is not related to timer operation.

Bit D_0 : External interrupt 0 signal type control bit (IT0)

This is used to enable external interrupt zero by triggering at a falling edge of the signal when it is set to 1 and cleared to enable a low-level signal on external interrupt 0 to generate an interrupt.

This is a bit addressable.

1.10 TIMER OPERATION MODES

> **Q. Explain with suitable example mode 1 and mode 2 programming of 8051 timers.**
> **[8 M] [May/June 2010]**

Depending upon the mode selection control bits M_1 and M_0 in TMOD register the timer can operate in any one of the four modes :

1. Mode 0
2. Mode 1
3. Mode 2
4. Mode 3

1.10.1 Mode 0

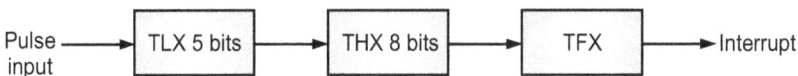

Fig. 1.18 : Timer/counter mode 0 : 13 bit counter

In this mode timer operates as a 13-bit register (TLX - 5 bits and THX - 8 bits). The pulse input is divided by 32d in TL so that TH counts the original oscillator frequency reduced by a total 384 d.

The timer is enabled by writing 00 in TMOD register. If the timer count exceeds 13 bits i.e. 1FFFH the next count will be zero. 0000H by generating an interrupt to inform to the programmer that one cycle is over. Also TF1 and TF0 timer overflow bit will be set. The timer interrupt is enabled using Interrupt Enable register (IE).

1.10.2 Mode 1

Operation in mode 1 is same as mode 0. The only difference is that mode 0 was a 13 bit time/counter register, but in mode 1 it is 16-bit timer/counter register.

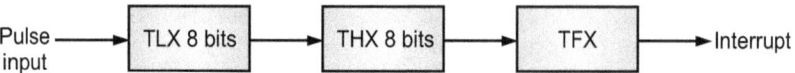

Fig. 1.19 : Time Mode 1 operation as 16 bit timer/counter

The mode is set by writing 01 in mode selection bits in TMOD register.

1.10.3 Mode 2

This mode is configured as the 8-bit timer/counter by using TLX only with auto-reload feature. THX is used to hold the value that is loaded into TLX every time TLX overflows from FFH to 00H, when TLX overflows, the timer flag is set.

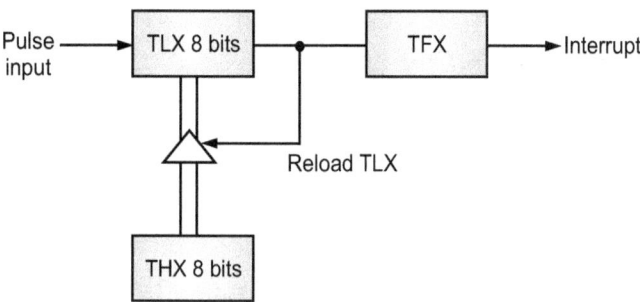

Fig. 1.20 : Timer mode 2 with auto-reload feature

Count is stored in THX. TLX will start count up from the number stored in THX, when TLX overflow interrupt is generated to indicate overflow and again initialized with the contents of THX.

1.10.4 Mode 3

In mode 3 timer 1 just holds the count whereas timer 0 registers TL0 and TH0 are configured as two separate 8-bit counters. TL0 is controlled by the gate arrangement as shown in Fig. 1.21 and sets timer flag TF0 whenever it overflows from FFH to 00H.

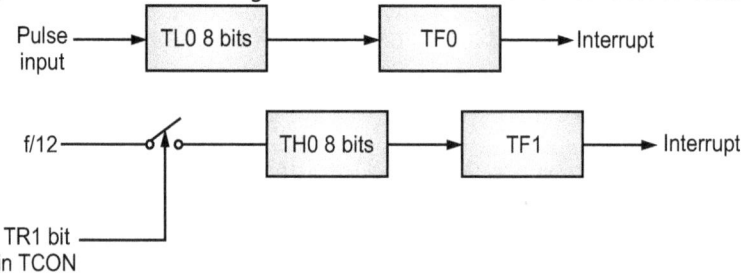

Fig. 1.21 : Timer mode 3 as two 8-bit timer/counter

The important point in this mode is no interrupt is generated by timer 1 while timer 0 uses the TF1 overflow flag. The important application of mode 3 is it is used for the baud rate generation for the serial port.

The difference between the counting and timing is that the source of the clock pulses to the counters. When it is used as a timer, the clock pulses are generated by dividing the oscillator frequency by 12. When it is used as a counter, pin T_0 (P3.4) supplies pulses to counter 0 and pin T_1 (P3.5) to counter 1. The $\overline{C/T}$ is used to control the timer/counter operation.

1.11 PROGRAMMING OF TIMERS AND COUNTERS USING ASSEMBLY LANGUAGE PROGRAMMING

Program 1.1

Write an assembly language program to generate a square wave of 2 kHz frequency if crystal frequency is 11.0592 MHz on pin 1.4.

Solution :

The time period of the square wave is $\frac{1}{2 \times 10^3}$ = 500 µs.

Assume that the duty cycle of the square wave is 50%. Therefore, the square wave will be high for 250 µs and it will be low for 250 µs.

Crystal frequency is 11.0592 MHz means the counter will count up every $\frac{1}{11.0592 \times 10^6}$ = 1.085 µs.

$$\frac{250 \text{ µs}}{1.085 \text{ µs}} = 230,$$

The values that should be loaded into TH and TL are

$$65536 - 230 = (65306)_{10} \approx \text{FF1AH}$$

$$\therefore \quad T_L = 1\text{AH and } T_H = \text{FFH}$$

Program

Comments	Instructions	Comments
Label 1 :	MOV TMOD, # 10H	Load TMOD register in time mode
	MOV TL1, # 1AH	Load TL
	MOV TH1, # 0FFH	Load TH
	SETB TR1	Start Timer 1
Label 2 :	JNB TF1, Label 2	Remain until overflow
	CLR TR1	Stop timer 1
	CPL P1.4	Clear port pin
	CLR TF1	Clear timer 1 flag
	SJMP Label 1	Reload timer

Program 1.2

Write an assembly language program for 8051 such that LED connected to port 1.5 will flash at a rate 0.5 sec., when line P2.1 goes high use timer 0 for generating delay.

Solution :

$$\text{Assume crystal frequency} = 12 \text{ MHz}$$

$$\therefore \quad \text{Timer clock frequency} = \frac{12 \text{ MHz}}{12} = 1 \text{ MHz}$$

$$\therefore \quad T = 1 \text{ μs}$$

Therefore, maximum delay = 65536×1 μs = 65.536 ms

To get a delay of 0.5 sec, program the timer for 10 times so that 0.5 sec delay is obtained i.e. 50 ms. To obtain a 50 ms delay 50,000 must be subtracted from 65536.

i.e. $\quad 65536 - 50000 = 15536$ or (3CB0)H

i.e. $\quad T_L = B0H$ and $T_L = 3CH$

Program for Delay Routine

Label	Instructions	Comments
Delay :	MOV R0, # 0AH	Initialize counter to 10
Label 1 :	MOV TL0, # B0H	Load TL
	MOV TH0, # 3CH	Load TH
	SETB TR0	Start timer 0
Label 2 :	JNB TF0 label 2	Remain until overflow
	CLR TR0	Stop timer 0
	CLR TF0	Clear timer 0 flag
	DJNZ R0, Label 1	Decrement and repeat if $R_0 \neq 0$
	RET	
	MOV TMOD, # 01	Timer 0 mode 1
	MOV P2, # 0FFH	Consider port 2 as input port
Label 3 :	JB P2.1, Label 3	Continue till P2.1 = 1
HERE :	CPL P1.5	Toggle P1.5
	ACALL DELAY	Call subroutine
	SJMP HERE	Repeat

Program 1.3

Write an assembly language program to switch ON or OFF a LED connected on P1.2 when external interrupt $\overline{INT0}$ is activated.

Program :

Label	Instructions	Comments
	ORG 0000H	Bypass interrupt vector table.
	LJMP main	
	ORG 0003H	Interrupt vector for interrupt 0
	SETB P1.2	Turn ON LED
Label 1 :	MOV R0, # 500	wait for sometime
	DJNZ R0, Label 1	
	RETI	Return to the main program
	ORG 0030H	
Main :	MOV IE, # 81H	Enable INT0
Label 2 :	SJMP label 2	
	END	end program

Program 1.4

Write an assembly language program to generate a square wave of 1 kHz and 75% duty cycle at pin P1.5. Assume microcontroller is operating at 6 MHz.

Solution : Time for one machine cycle = $\dfrac{12}{6 \text{ MHz}}$ = 2 µ sec.

Square wave of period = $\dfrac{1}{1 \text{ kHz}}$ = 1 m sec.

Hence, the delay required for ON period = $\dfrac{750 \text{ µs}}{2 \text{ µs}}$ = 375 and delay required for OFF period = $\dfrac{250 \text{ µs}}{2 \text{ µs}}$ = 125.

$\therefore$ Count = $(65536 - 375)_{10}$ = $(65161)_{10}$ = $(FE89)_{16}$

and $(65536 - 125)_{10}$ = $(65411)_{10}$ = $(FF83)_{16}$

Label	Instructions	Comments
	ORG 0000H	
	LJMP main	
	ORG 001BH	
	CPL P1.5	
	CLR TR1	
	MOV TL1, R1	
	MOV 00, R3	
	MOV R3, 01	
	MOV R1, 00	
	MOV TH1, R2	
	MOV 00, R4	
	MOV R4, 02	
	MOV R2, 00	
	SETB TR1	
	CLR TF1	
	RETI	
	ORG 0100H	
Main :	SETB P1.5	
	MOV IE, # 88H	
	MOV TMOD, # 10H	
	MOV R1, # 83H	
	MOV R2, # 0FFH	
	MOV R3, # 89H	
	MOV R4, # 0FEH	
	MOV TH1, R4	
	MOV TL1, R3	
	SETB TR1	
	SJMP TR1	
Here :	SJMP Here	
	END	

1.12 PROGRAMMING THE TIMERS/COUNTERS IN EMBEDDED C

Program 1.5

Write a C program to toggle all bits of port 1 continuously. Use timer 0 to generate delay of 10 sec. between each toggle.

Solution : Assume crystal frequency = 12 MHz

$$\therefore T = \frac{12}{12 \times 10^6} = 1\ \mu s$$

To obtain a 50 ms delay $\frac{50\ ms}{1\ \mu s}$ = 50,000 clocks are required

$\therefore$ Count = 65536 − 50000
= 15536 ≃ (3CB0)H

$\therefore$ TH1 = 3CH and TL1 = B0H

The delay loop is repeated 200 times to generate 10 sec. delay.

Program :

```
# include <reg 51.h>
void DELAY ( )
void main ( )
{
  while (1)
  {
    P1 = 0X00;
    DELAY ( );
    P1 = 0XFF;
    DELAY ( );
  }
}
void DELAY ( )
{
  unsigned char x;
  for (x = 0; x < 200; X++)
  {
    TMOD = 0X01;
    TL0 = 0XB0H;
    TH0 = 0X3CH;
    TR0 = 1
    while (TF0! = 1);
  }
}
```

Program 1.6

Write a C program for counting the pulses on P3.2 pin (T_1) and display the hex count on P_0(LSB) and P_1(MSB).

Program :

```c
# include <reg51.h>
Sbit in = P3^2;
void main ( )
{
  P0 = 0X00;
  P1 = 0X00;
  TMOD = 0X50;
  TL1 = 0X00;
  TH1 = 0X00;
  in = 1;
  TR1 = 1;
  while (1)
  {
    TF1 = 0;
    P0 = TL1;
    P1 = TH1;
  }
}
```

Program 1.7

Write an 8051C program to switch On or OFF a LED connected on P1.5 pin. Complement the LED whenever switch connected on P3.1 is pressed.

Program :

```c
# include <reg51.h>
Sbit mybit = P1^5;
void INTR( ) interrupt 0
{
  mybit = ~ mybit;
}
void main ( )
{
  IE = 0X81;
  while (1);
}
```

1.13 SERIAL DATA AND INPUT AND OUTPUT

In multiprocessor distributed systems, computers must be able to communicate with other computers, and the cheapest way to communicate is to send and receive data serially. The 8051 uses SBUF to hold data for serial communication. Register SCON controls the serial data communication whereas PCON controls data rates. Pins RXD (P3.0) and TXD (P3.1) are used for connection to the serial data network.

SBUF is divided into two registers physically, one is used to write and to hold data to be transmitted out of the 8051 via TXD. Other is used to read and holds received data from external sources via RXD. Both registers uses the same address 99H mutually exclusive.

There are four programmable modes for serial data communication that are chosen by setting the SMX bits in SCON. Modes decides the baud rate for serial communication. Fig. 1.22 and Fig. 1.23 shows the bit arrangement for SCON and PCON.

1.13.1 The Serial Port Control Register (SCON)

(MSB)							(LSB)
D_7	D_6	D_5	D_4	D_3	D_2	D_1	D_0
SM0	SM1	SM2	REN	TB8	RB8	TI	RI

Fig. 1.22

Bit D_7 and Bit D_6 : Serial port mode bit 0 and 1

These bits are used to select the mode of the serial communication.

SM0	SM1	Mode	
0	0	0	Used as shift register; baud = f/12
0	1	1	8-bit UART; baud = variable
1	0	2	9-bit UART; baud = f/32 or f/64
1	1	3	9-bit UART; baud = variable

Bit D_5 : Multiprocessor communication bit (SM2)

This is used to allow multiprocessor communication in modes 2 and 3. It is set to 1 an interrupt is generated if bit 9 of the received data is a 1. If the bit 9 is 0 then no interrupt is generated, when it is set to 1 for mode 1, no interrupt will be generated unless a valid stop bit is received. When mode 0 is used it is set to 0.

Bit D_4 : Receiver Enable bit (REN)

When it is 1, data is received

When it is 0, data is not received.

Bit D_3 : Transmitted bit 8 (TB8)

It is set/reset by the programmer in modes 2 and 3.

Bit D_2 : Received bit 8 (RB8)

It acts as a stop bit in mode 1 and bit 8 of received data in modes 2 and 3. It is not used in mode 0.

Bit D_1 : Transmit Interrupt flag (TI)

In mode 0 it is set to 1 at the end of bit 7 time and at the beginning of the stop bit for other modes.

Bit D_0 : Receive Interrupt flag (RI)

In mode 0, it is set to 1 at the end of bit 7 time and halfway through the stop bit for other modes.

It is a bit addressable means individual bits can be set or reset.

1.13.2 The Power Mode Control (PCON)

> **Q. What is the significance of SCON register of 8051? Explain all the bits of SCON register of 8051.** [8 M] [May/June 2013]
>
> **Q. Explain the role of TI and RI flags of 8051 for serial communications.** [8 M] [May/June 2013]
>
> **Q. Explain all bits of SCON register of 8051.** [8 M] [Nov./Dec. 2011]

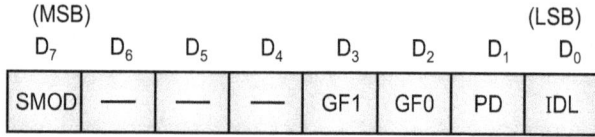

Fig. 1.23

Bit D_7 : Serial baud rate modify bit (SMOD)

When it is set to 1 baud rate is doubled using timer 1 for modes 1, 2 and 3. To use a timer 1 baud rate it is set to 0.

Bit D_6 to D_4 are reserved for future use.

Bits D_3 and D_2 : General purpose user flat bit 1 and 0.

It is set or reset by the programmer

Bit D_1 : Power down bit (PD)

For CHMOS processors, it is set to 1 to enter the power down configuration.

Bit D_0 : Idle mode bit (IDL)

For CHMOS processors it is set to 1 to enter idle mode configuration.

PCON is not bit addressable.

1.13.3 Data Transmission and Reception

When data is written to SBUF and TI is set to 1 the transmission of data starts. If the program fails to wait for the TI flag and overwrites SBUF when the previous data byte is in the process of being transmitted, the result will be shown as unpredictable.

If the receive enable bit (REN) is 1 in SCON for all modes the reception of data will start. For mode 0 RI bit must be cleared, when complete data is received, the receiver Interrupt Flag RI is set. The received data is not transferred to SBUF until the last data bit is received.

1.13.4 Serial Data Transmission Modes

Serial data transmission can be done in four different modes that can be set using SCON register.

      Mode 0 : Shift register with fixed baud rate.

      Mode 1 : 8-bit UART with variable baud rate.

      Mode 2 : 9-bit UART with fixed baud rate.

      Mode 3 : 9-bit UART with variable baud rate.

Modes 2 and 3 have special provision for multiprocessor communication. Baud rate is fixed for mode 0 whereas it is variable for modes 1, 2 and 3. Variable baud rates are calculated by the timer 1 overflow rate.

1.13.4.1 Mode 0

When SM0 and SM1 are set to 00, it configures SBUF to receive or transmit eight data bits using pin RXD for both functions. Pin TXD is connected to the internal shift frequency pulse source to supply shift pulses to external circuits.

The Baud rate for mode 0 is fixed and it is calculated as oscillator frequency divided by 12. Fig. 1.24 shows the timing for mode 0 shift register data transmission. It is also called as the shift register. It is used for left shift and right shift operation. The shifting operation is done sequentially.

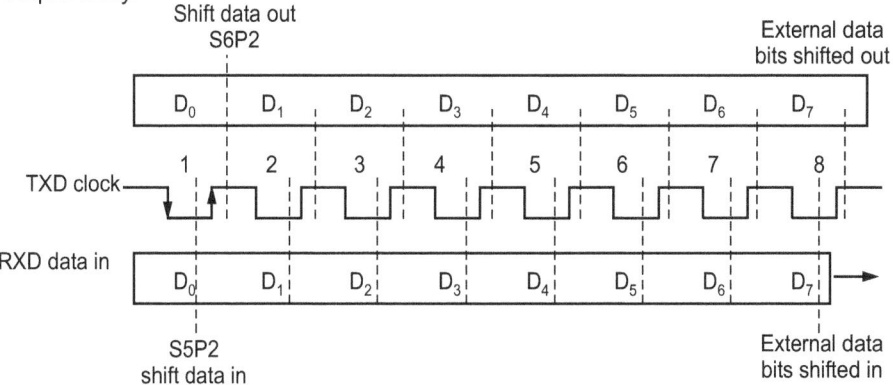

Fig. 1.24 : Mode 0 shift register timing

During transmission, data is shifted out of RXD, the data changes on the falling edge of S6P2 or one clock pulse after the rising edge of the output TXD shift clock. During reception, data comes on pin RXD. It should be synchronized with the shift clock produced at TXD. Data is sampled at the falling edge of S5P2 and stored in SBUF on the rising edge of the shift clock.

Mode 0 is not used for data communication between the two computers. But it is used as high speed serial data collection method using discrete logic to obtain high data rates.

1.13.4.2 Mode 1

It is a 10-bit full duplex receiver when SM0 and SM1 are set to 01. Here data may be transmitted and received simultaneously. Pin TXD is used to transmit the data and pin RXD is used to receive the data.

Data transmitted is of 10 bits, 1 start bit, 8 data bits, and one stop bit. When all the 10 bits are sent, the interrupt flag TI is set.

The received data is obtained in the same manner as data is received.

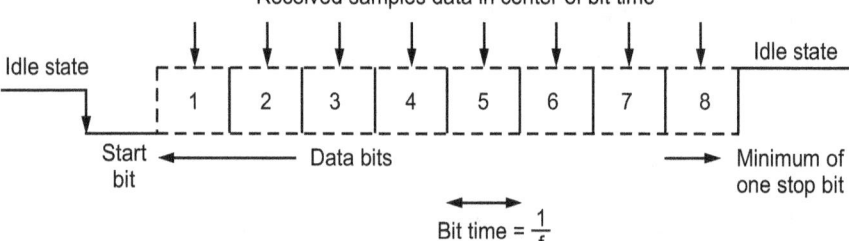

Fig. 1.25 : Standard UART data word

This mode is called as an anti-noise measurement. If the reception circuit is enabled by noise on the transmission line, then check for a low after half a bit interval which limits false data reception.

Mode 1 uses timer 1 to calculate baud rate by using the overflow flag of the time to determine the baud frequency. Generally, timer 1 is used in timer mode 2 as an autoload 8-bit timer that generates the baud frequency.

$$f_{baud} = \frac{2^{SMOD}}{32} \times \frac{\text{Oscillator frequency}}{12 \times [256 - TH1]}$$

SMOD is the bit in PCON which can be 0 or 1.

If timer 1 does not use mode 2 then the baud rate is

$$f_{baud} = \frac{2^{SMOD}}{32} \times (\text{timer 1 overflow frequency})$$

To obtain the standard baud rate 9600 then an 11.0592 MHz crystal frequency is selected.

1.13.4.3 Mode 2

Mode 2 is similar to Mode 1 except 11-bit transmission. It transmits a start bit, 9-bit data and a stop bit. The nineth data bit is copied from bit TB8 in SCON during transmission. When data is received, it is stored in bit RB8 of SCON register.

The baud rate is calculated as follows.

$$f_{baud\ 2} = \frac{2^{SMOD}}{64} \times \text{Oscillator frequency}$$

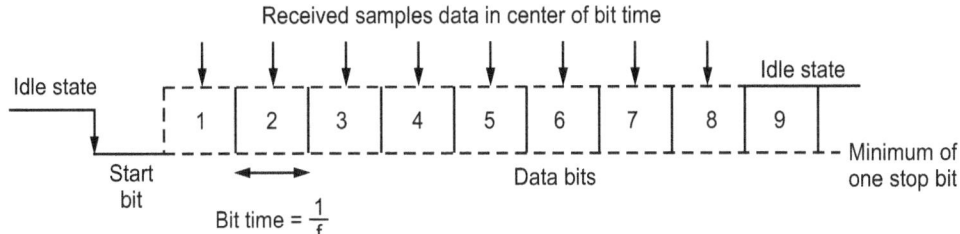

Fig. 1.26 : Multipurpose data word

Mode 2 gives very high data rate which is used in multiprocessor applications.

1.13.4.4 Mode 3

Mode 3 is similar to mode 2 except that baud rate is determined as in mode 1 using timer 1.

Table 1.8 : Summary of serial port operating modes

Mode	Transmission format	Baud rate
Mode 0	8 data bits	$\frac{1}{12} \times$ Oscillator frequency
Mode 1	10 data bit (1-start bit, 1 stop bit and 8 data bits)	Variable
Mode 2	11 data bit (1 start bit, 1 stop bit and 9 data bits)	$\frac{1}{32} \times$ Oscillator frequency
Mode 3	11 data bits (1start bit, 8 data bit, programmable 9th bit, 1 stop bit)	Variable

1.14 8051 INTERRUPTS

Q. Write short note on Interrupts in 8051   [6 M] [May/June 2010]
Q. Explain different interrupts in 8051. Explain how to set up interrupt priority.
    [8 M] [May/June 2013]
Q. Write short note on setting interrupt priority with IP register of 8051.
    [8 M] [Nov./Dec. 2011]

Interrupt is nothing but breaking the normal sequence of execution. Suppose microcontroller is executing some program and the user wants the service from microcontroller so to inform the microcontroller, the user give interrupt to the microcontroller. Then microcontroller executes its current instruction and suspend the program. Then it will service the user and resumes the program where it has been suspended. The external input applied to the microcontroller is known as **interrupt**.

Interrupts may be generated by internal chip operation or provided by external sources, whenever an interrupt is appeared, the microcontroller executes the interrupt service routine. Each interrupt has a fixed location in the memory that holds the address of ISR. 8051 supports five interrupts. Three of these are generated automatically by the internal operations like Timer Flag 0, Timer Flag 1 and the serial port interrupt. (RI or TI). Two interrupts are generated by external signals provided by circuitry that is connected to pin $\overline{INT0}$ and $\overline{INT1}$.

1.14.1 Timer Flag Interrupt

When a timer/counter overflows, the corresponding timer flat TF0 or TF1 is set to 1. The flag is cleared to zero when the resulting interrupt generates a program call to the appropriate timer subroutine in memory.

1.14.2 Serial Port Interrupt

When a data byte is received, an interrupt bit, RI is set to 1 in the SCON register. When a data byte is transmitted an interrupt bit TI is set to 1. These are ORed together to provide a single interrupt to the processor called as serial port interrupt.

1.14.3 External Interrupts

External circuits, use pins $\overline{INT0}$ and $\overline{INT1}$. These pins can be used to set interrupt flags IE0 and IE1 in the TCON register to 1.

1.14.4 The Interrupt Enable (IE) Register

Q. Explain use of EI register of 8051. [8 M] [Nov./Dec. 2012]

D_7	D_6	D_5	D_4	D_3	D_2	D_1	D_0
EA	--	ET2	ES	ET1	EX1	ET0	EX0

Fig. 1.27

Bit D_7 : Enable interrupt bit.

    When EA = 0 disable all interrupts

        EA = 1 individual interrupts to be enabled.

Bit D_6 : Reserved for the future use

Bit D_5 : Reserved for the future use

Bit D_4 : Enable serial port interrupt (ES)

    ES = 1 enable serial port interrupt

    ES = 0 disable serial port interrupt

Bit D_3 : Enable Timer 1 overflow interrupt (ET1)

    ET1 = 1 enable timer 1 overflow interrupt

    ET1 = 0 disable timer 1 overflow interrupt

Bit D_2 : Enable external interrupt 1 (EX1)

EX1 = 1 $\overline{INT1}$ is enabled

EX1 = 0 Clear $\overline{INT1}$

Bit D_1 : Enable timer 0 overflow interrupt (ET0)

when ET0 = 1 enable timer 0 overflow interrupt

ET0 = 0 disable timer 0 overflow interrupt

Bit D_0 : Enable external interrupt 0 (EX0)

EX0 = 1 enable $\overline{INT0}$ interrupt

EX0 = 0 disable $\overline{INT0}$ interrupt.

It is bit addressable.

1.14.5 The Interrupt Priority (IP) Register

D_7	D_6	D_5	D_4	D_3	D_2	D_1	D_0
–	–	PT2	PS	PT1	PX1	PT0	PX0

Fig. 1.28

Table 1.9

Bit	Symbol	Function
7	–	Not implemented
6	–	Not implemented
5	PT2	Reserved for future use
4	PS	Priority of serial port interrupt
3	PT1	Priority of timer 1 overflow interrupt. Set/cleared by program
2	PX1	Priority of external interrupt 1. Set/cleared by 1
1	PT0	Priority of timer 0 overflow interrupt. Set/cleared by program
0	PX0	Priority of external interrupt 0. Set/cleared by program

Note : It is bit addressable.

1.14.6 Reset Interrupt

It is a non-maskable interrupt and whenever a high level is applied to the RST pin, the 8051 will go into Reset mode. Note that the contents of the program counter is not stored for the further resumption. It is just a command which jumps to a address 0000h and starts running. On Reset register bank 0 is selected by default. After Reset the contents of the registers are given in Table 1.10.

Table 1.10

Register	Value (hex)
PC	0000
DPTR	0000
A	00
B	00
SP	07
PSW	00
P_{0-3}	FF
IP	XXX00000b
IE	0XX00000b
TCON	00
TMOD	00
TH0	00
TL0	00
TH1	00
TL1	00
SCON	00
SBUF	XX
PCON	0XXXXXXXb

1.14.7 Interrupt Control

To handle the interrupts the two registers are used IE and IP.

To enable or disable the single interrupt or group of interrupts Interrupt Enable (IE) register is used. To serve the more important interrupts, priorities are assigned to the interrupts. The priorities can be set by using Interrupt Priority (IP) register. The priorities of the interrupts are assigned according to table 1.11.

Table 1.11 : Interrupt priorities

Sr. No.	Interrupt source	Name	Priority Level
1.	External interrupt 0	$\overline{INT0}$	Highest
2.	Timer interrupt 0	TF0	
3.	External interrupt 1	$\overline{INT1}$	
4.	Timer interrupt 1	TF1	
5.	Serial communication	RI + TI	
6.	Timer 2 (for 8052)	TF2	Lowest

1.14.8 Interrupt Vector Table Addresses

On occurrence of interrupt, the contents of the program are saved 0 to the stack. Then appropriate memory location is called. The control goes to the particular location, performs the operation and at the end of the routine RETI instruction brings back PC to its original address where it was interrupted. The memory locations where the control is transferred is given in Table 1.12.

Table 1.12 : Interrupt vector

	Interrupt	Vector Address
1.	Reset	0000H
2.	External hardware interrupt 0(IE0)	0003H
3.	Timer 0 interrupt (TE0)	000BH
4.	External hardware interrupt 1	0013H
5.	Timer 1 interrupt	001BH
6.	Serial (TF1)	0023H

1.14.9 Nested Interrupts

When the 8051 is executing an interrupt service routine (ISR) and during service if another high priority interrupt wants the service then 8051 suspends the low priority interrupt service and attends the high priority interrupt service, when it completes the high priority interrupt service, then it completes low priority interrupt service and then returns to the main program. This is called as an interrupt inside an interrupt or **Nested Interrupt.**

1.14.10 Interrupt Programming

Program 1.8

Write an assembly language program to generate a square of 10 kHz with timer 0 in mode 2, at port pin P1.2 also display a value of 'Y' at port 0 and 'N' at port 2. Assume crystal frequency = 12 MHz.

$$\text{Timer clock frequency} = \frac{12 \times 10^6}{12} = 1 \text{ MHz}$$

For 10 kHz wave with 50% duty cycle.

On period is 0.05 m sec. and off period is 0.05 m sec.

∴
$$TH0 = 256 - 0.05 \times 10^{-3} \times 1 \times 10^6$$
$$TH0 = (206)_{10} = CEH$$

Program :

Label	Instructions	Comments
	ORG 0000H	By pass interrupt vector table,
	LJMP main	timer 0 interrupt vector
	ORG 000BH	
	CPL P1.2	
	RETI	
	ORG 0030H	
Main :	MOV TMOD, # 02H	Initialize both the timers in mode 2
	MOV TH0, # CEH	load count value into TH0.
	MOV IE, # 82H	Enable interrupt timer 0
	SETB TR0	Start timer 0
Label :	MOV P0, # 'Y'	Display 'Y' at port 0
	MOV P2, # 'N'	Display 'N' at port 2
	SJMP Label	Keep doing till interrupted
	END	

1.15 PIN DIAGRAM OF 8051

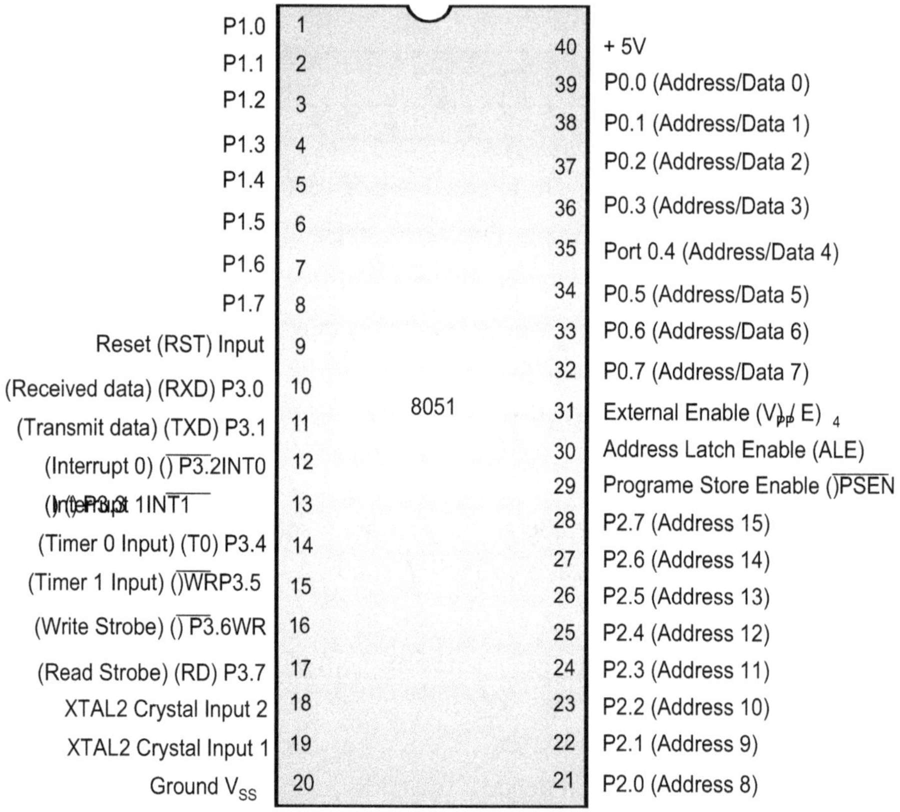

```
                        P1.0  | 1        40 |  + 5V
                        P1.1  | 2        39 |  P0.0 (Address/Data 0)
                        P1.2  | 3        38 |  P0.1 (Address/Data 1)
                        P1.3  | 4        37 |  P0.2 (Address/Data 2)
                        P1.4  | 5        36 |  P0.3 (Address/Data 3)
                        P1.5  | 6        35 |  Port 0.4 (Address/Data 4)
                        P1.6  | 7        34 |  P0.5 (Address/Data 5)
                        P1.7  | 8        33 |  P0.6 (Address/Data 6)
             Reset (RST) Input| 9        32 |  P0.7 (Address/Data 7)
       (Received data) (RXD) P3.0 | 10  8051  31 |  External Enable (Vpp E)
       (Transmit data) (TXD) P3.1 | 11       30 |  Address Latch Enable (ALE)
          (Interrupt 0) (/)P3.2INT0 | 12     29 |  Programe Store Enable (/)PSEN
          (Interrupt 1)INT1   | 13       28 |  P2.7 (Address 15)
          (Timer 0 Input) (T0) P3.4 | 14    27 |  P2.6 (Address 14)
          (Timer 1 Input) (/)WRP3.5 | 15    26 |  P2.5 (Address 13)
          (Write Strobe) (/) P3.6WR | 16    25 |  P2.4 (Address 12)
          (Read Strobe) (RD) P3.7 | 17      24 |  P2.3 (Address 11)
          XTAL2 Crystal Input 2 | 18        23 |  P2.2 (Address 10)
          XTAL2 Crystal Input 1 | 19        22 |  P2.1 (Address 9)
                Ground V_ss | 20             21 |  P2.0 (Address 8)
```

Fig. 1.29 : Pin diagram of 8051

8051 microcontroller is available in a standard 40 pin dual in line package.

1.16 ADDRESSING MODES

> Q. *Write short notes on different addressing modes of 8051.*
> [6 M] [May/June 2010, 2011]

The way of accessing data is called its addressing mode. There are various addressing modes of a microprocessor while designing. The 8051 provides a total of 5 different addressing modes :

(1) immediate,

(2) register,

(3) direct,

(4) register indirect,

(5) indexed.

1.16.1 Immediate Addressing Mode

In immediate addressing mode the data is directly specified in the instruction itself. Immediate data must be given with pound sign, #. This addressing mode is used to load any information into any of the registers. For example :

MOV A, # 25H

MOV R_4, # 62

MOV B, # 40H

MOV DPTR, # 4521H

1.16.2 Register Addressing Mode

Register addressing mode uses the registers to hold the data. Data may be in any of the registers.

For example :

MOV A, R0

1.16.3 Register Specific Addressing Mode

In this addressing mode the instruction refers to a specific register such as accumulator or data pointer, DPTR. For example :

    DAA

1.16.4 Direct Addressing Mode

In this mode, the operand is specified by an 8-bit address field in the instruction directly. All the 128 bytes of RAM can be accessed using direct addressing mode. In direct addressing mode, the data is stored in RAM location whose address is known and this address is given in the instruction. For example :

    MOV A, 40H   ; copy data from address 40H into accumulator

    MOV R0, 15H ; copy the contents of memory location whose address is 15H to register R0 of the selected bank.

1.16.5 Indirect Addressing Mode

In this addressing mode, a register is used as a pointer to the data. Here data is stored in RAM memory location whose address is specified by one of the registers (R_0 and R_1) and that register is mentioned in the instruction R_0 and R_1 of each register bank can be used as a pointer preceded by the '@' sign. For example :

    MOV A, @ R_0 ; Move contents of RAM location whose address is held by R_0 into A.

1.16.6 Indexed Addressing Mode

Indexed addressing mode is widely used in accessing data elements of look-up table entries located in the program ROM space of the 8051. MOVC A, @ A + DPTR instruction is used for this. The 16 bit register DPTR and register A are used to form the address of the data elements stored in on-chip ROM.

For example : MOV C A, @ A + DPTR; This instruction will load the accumulator with the byte from program memory. The byte from program memory is fetched from the sum of unsigned eight bit accumulator contents and contents of the DPTR.

SECTION (B)

Instruction set of 8051

The instruction set is divided into number of groups of functionally related instructions. The different groups are :

1. Data transfer group
2. Arithmetic group
3. Bit manipulation group
4. Program transfer instruction group
5. Processor control group.

1. Data Transfer Instructions :

(i) MOV (destination-byte) (source-byte)

Function : Move byte variable

Flags affected : None

Description : This instruction copies a byte from the source location to the destination. Total 15 combinations are possible for this instruction. They are as follows :

(a) Register A as the destination :

    MOV A, @ Ro

    MOV A, # data

    MOV A, Rn

    MOV A, direct

(b) Register A is the source

    MOV Rn, A

    MOV direct, A

    MOV @ Ri, A

(c) Rn is the destination

    MOV Rn, # immediate

    MOV Rn, A

    MOV Rn, direct

(d) The destination is a direct address

    MOV direct, # data

    MOV direct, @ Ri

    MOV direct, A

    MOV direct, Rn

    MOV direct, direct

(e) Destination is an indirect address

    MOV @ Ri, # data

    MOV @ Ri, A

    MOV @ Ri, direct

(ii) MOV (dest-bit), (source-bit)

Function : MOV bit data

Flags affected : CY flag

Description : This instruction copies the source bit to the destination bit. Here one of the operand must be the CY flag.

For example :

    MOV P1.2, C   ; Copy carry bit to port bit P1.2

    MOV C, P2.5   ; Copy port bit P2.5 to carry bit

(iii) MOV DPTR, # 16-bit value :

Function : Load data pointer

Flags affected : None

Description : This instruction loads the 16-bit DPTR (data pointer) register with a 16-bit immediate data. For example :

    MOV DPTR, # 456FH   ; DPTR = 456 FH

    MOV DPTR, # MYDATA   ; Load 16-bit address assigned to MYDATA

(iv) MOVC A, @ A + DPTR :

Function : Move code byte

Flags affected : None

Description : This instruction moves a byte of data located in program (code) ROM into register A. This allows to put string of data in the code space and read them into the CPU. The address of the desired byte is formed by adding the original value of the accumulator to the 16-bit DPTR register.

Example :

    MOV DPTR, # 2476H

    MOV A, R3

    MOVC A, @ A + DPTR

(v) MOVC A, @ A + PC :

Function : Move code byte

Flags affected : None

Description : This instruction moves a byte of data located in the program area to A. The address of the desired byte is calculated by adding the program counter (PC) register to the original value of the accumulator.

For example :

    MOV A, R3
    INC A
    MOVC A, @ A + PC
    RET

(vi) MOVX (dest-byte), (source-byte)

> **Q. Illustrate with example the use of MOVX instruction for external RAM.**
> **[8 M] [Nov./Dec. 2011]**

Function : Move external

Flags affected : None

Description : This instruction transfers data between external memory and register A. This instruction allows to access externally connected memory. The address of external memory being accessed can be 16-bit or 8 bit.

(a) The 16-bit external memory address is held by the DPTR register

    MOVX A, @ DPTR   ; Address of external memory is pointed by DPTR
    MOVX @ DPTR, A   ; Stores the contents of accumulator to the external
                            memory pointed by DPTR

(b) The 8-bit address of external memory is held by R0 or R,

    MOVX A, @ Ri   where i = 0 or 1.

This instruction moves a bytes from external memory whose 8-bit address is pointed to by Ro or Ri

(vii) PUSH direct :

Function : Push onto the stack

Flags affected : None

Description : This instruction copies the desired byte onto the stack and increments stack pointer by 1. This instruction supports only direct addressing mode.

For example : PUSH 0E0H where E0H is the RAM address belonging to register A.

(viii) Pop direct :

Function : POP from the stack

Flags affected : None

Description : This instruction copies the byte pointed by SP (stack pointer) to the location whose direct address is indicated in the instruction and decrements SP by one.

For example : POP 0E0H

(ix) XCH A, byte :

Function : Exchange A with a byte variable.

Flags affected : None

Description : This instruction exchanges the contents of register A and the source byte. The source byte can by any register of RAM location.

For example :

    MOV A, # 65H

    MOV R2, # 57H

    XCH A_1 R_2

after execution A = 57H and R_2 = 65H.

This instruction supports three addressing modes

1. Register   XCH A, Rn
2. Direct   XCH A, direct
3. Register-Indirect   XCH A, @ Rn

(a) XCHD A_1 @ Ri

Function : Exchange digits

Flags affected : None

Description : The XCHD instruction exchanges only the lower nibble of A with the lower nibble of the RAM location pointed to by Ri while leaving the upper nibbles in both places intact

    Memory location

    [40H] = 97H

For example :

    MOV A, # 12H

    MOV R_1, # 40H

    XCHD A, @ R1

after execution of XCHD instruction, A = 17H and RAM location 40H has 92H.

2. Arithmetic Instructions :

(i) ADD A, source byte

Function : Addition

Flags affected : OV, AC, CY

Description : This instruction adds the source byte to the accumulator (A) and stores the result in A. This instruction is used for both signed and unsigned numbers.

For example :

    MOV A, # 45H
    ADD A, # 4DH
            (45 + 4D)H = 92H

∴   CY = 0, AC = 1

This instruction supports following addressing modes

(a) Immediate   ADD A, # data
(b) Register   ADD A, Rn
(c) Direct   ADD A, direct
(d) Register-indirect   ADD A, @ Ri   where i = 0 or 1

(ii) ADDC A, source byte :

Function : Add with carry

Flags affected : OV, AC, CY

Description : This instruction adds the source byte to A in addition to the CY flags (A = A + byte + CY). This is used in multibyte additions.

For example :

    CLR C   ; CY = 0
    MOV A, # 89H   ; A = 89H
    ADDC A, # 0F2H   ; A = 89H + F2H + 0 = 17BH A = 7BH CY = 1
    MOV R3, A   ; Save A
    MOV A, # 31H
    ADDC A, # 25H   A = 31H + 25H + 1 = 57H.

(iii) DAA :

Function : Decimal adjust accumulator after addition.

Flags affected : CY

Description : This instruction is used after addition of BCD numbers to convert the result back to BCD. The data is adjusted in the following two possible cases.

(a) It adds 6 to the lower 4-bits of A if it is greater than 9 or if AC = 1.
(b) It also adds 6 to the upper 4-bits of A if it is greater than 9 or if CY = 1.

For example :
    MOV A, # 47H
    ADD A, # 38H   A = 47 + 38 = 7FH invalid BCD 7FH + 6 = 85H valid BCD
    DAA

(iv) DEC byte :

Function : Decrement

Flags affected : None

Description : This instruction subtracts 1 from the byte operand. The instruction supports four addressing modes.

    (i)   Accumulator   DEC A
    (ii)   Register   DEC Rn
    (iii) Direct   DEC direct
    (iv) Register-indirect DEC @ Ri

(v) INC byte :

Function : Increment

Flags affected : None

Description : This instruction adds 1 to the register or memory location specified by the operand. This instruction supports four addressing modes.

    (i)   Accumulator   INC A
    (ii)   Register   INC Rn
    (iii) Direct   INC direct
    (iv) Register indirect   INC @ Ri = (i = 0 or 1

(vi) INC DPTR :

Function : Increment data pointer

Flags affected : None

Description : This instruction increments the 16-bit register DPTR (data pointer) by 1.

For example :
    MOV DPTR, # 1678H
    INC DPTR

after execution DPTR = 1679H

(vii) MUL AB :

Function : Multiply A and B

Flags affected : OV, CY

Description : This instruction multiplies an unsigned byte in A by an unsigned byte in register B. The result in placed in A and B where A has lower byte and B has upper byte.

For example :
    MOV A, # 25H
    MOV B, # 78H
    MUL AB
after execution;   ; A = 58H, B = 11H, CY = 0 and OV = 1

(viii) DIV AB

Function : Divide

Flags affected : CY and OV

Description : This instruction divides a byte accumulator by the byte in register B. After division, the quotient will be in register A and the remainder in register B. If you divide by 0, the values in register A and B are undefined and the OV flag is set to high to indicate an invalid result.

For example :
    MOV A, # 35
    MOV B, # 10
    DIV AB   ; A = 3 and B = 5

(ix) SUBB A, Source byte :

Function : Subtract with borrow

Flags affected : OV, AC, CY

Description : This instruction subtracts the source byte and the carry flag from the accumulator and puts the result in the accumulator. The subtraction performed by the internal hardware of the CPU are as follows :

(a) Take the 2's complement of the source byte
(b) Add this to register A
(c) Invert the carry

   For example :
   MOV A, # 45H
   CLR C
   SUBB A, # 23H

This instruction supports 4 addressing modes :

(a)	Immediate :	SUBB A, # data
(b)	Register :	SUBB A, Rn
(c)	Direct :	SUBB A, direct
(d)	Register - indirect	SUBB A, @ Rn

(x) SWAP A : [May/June 2012, 2013]

Function : Swap nibbles with the accumulator

Flags affected : None

Description : The swap instruction interchanges the lower nibble (D0 – D3) with the upper nibble (D4 – D7) inside register A.

For example :

    MOV A, # 59H   ; A = 59H

    SWAP A   ; A = 95H

Logical Instructions

(i) ANL (dest-byte), (source-byte)

Function : Logical AND for byte variables

Flags affected : None

Description : This instruction performs a logical AND on the operands, bit by bit, storing the result in the destination.

For example :

    MOV A # 39H   ; A = 39H

    ANL A, 09H   ; A = 39H ANDed with 09

This instruction supports total of six addressing modes :

(a)	Immediate	ANL A, # data
(b)	Register	ANL A, Rn
(c)	Direct	ANL A, direct
(d)	Register indirect	ANL A, @ R0
(e)	ANL direct, # data	ANL 32H, # 44H if [32H] = 67H AND 44H and 67H
(f)	ANL direct, A	MOV B, # 44H
		MOV A, # 67H
		ANL 0F0H, A

(ii) ORL (dest-byte), (source-byte)

Function : Logical OR for byte variable

Flags affected : None

Description : This instruction performs a logical OR on the byte operands, bit by bit and stores the result in the destination. This instruction supports six addressing modes. In four of them accumulator must be the destination :

(a)	Immediate	ORL A, # data
(b)	Register	ORL A, Rn
(c)	Direct	ORL A, direct
(d)	Register indirect	ORL A, @ Ro

(e) ORL direct, # data   ORL 32H, # 44H   if [32H] = 67H

                                    MOV A, 32H

     44H   0100 0100

     67H   0110 0111

            0110 0111   A = 67H

(f) ORL Direct, A

     MOV B, # 44H

     MOV A, # 67H

     ORL 0F0H, A

(iii) XRL (dest-byte), (source-byte)

Function : Logical exclusive - OR for byte variables.

Flags affected : None

Description : This performs a logical exclusive – OR on the operands, bit by bit, stores the result in the destruction. This instruction support total of six addressing modes.

(a) Immediate   XRL A, # data

(b) Register   XRL A, Rn

(c) Direct   XRL A, direct

(d) Register-indirect   XRL A, @ Rn

(e) XRL direct, # data

For example :

     XRL 32H, # 44H

     MOV A, 32H

     A will have 23H

(f) XRL direct, A

For example :

     MOV B, # 44H

     MOV A, # 67H

     XRL 0F0H, A

(iv) CLR A

Function : Clear accumulator

Flags affected : None

Description : This instruction clears register A. All bits of the accumulator are set to 0.

For example :

     CLR A

     MOV R0, A   ;   clear R0

     MOV R2, A   ;   clear R2

     MOV P1, A   ;   clear R1

(v) CPL A

Function : Complement accumulator

Flags affected : None

Description : This instruction complements the contents of register A. The result is the 1's complement of the accumulator.

For example :

    MOV A, # 55H

AGAIN: CPL A

    MOV P1, A

    SJMP AGAIN

(vi) RL A   [May/June 2012]

Function : Rotate left the accumulator.

Flags affected : None

Description : This instruction rotates the bits to the left. The bits rotated out of A are rotated back into A at the opposite end.

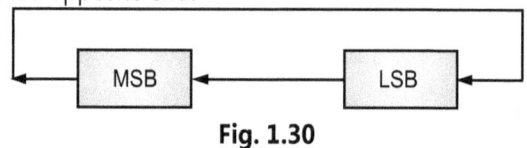

Fig. 1.30

For example :

MOV A, # 69H	; A = 0110 1001
RL A	; A = 1101 0010
RL A	A = 1010 0101

(vii) RLC A   [May/June 2012]

Function : Rotate A left through carry.

Flags affected : CY

Description : This instruction rotates the bits of the accumulator left. The bits rotated out of register A are rotated into CY and the CY bit is rotated into the opposite end of the accumulator.

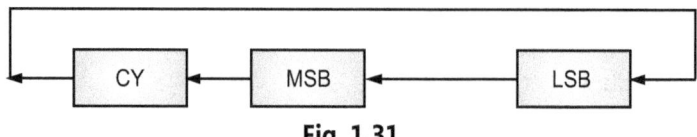

Fig. 1.31

For example :

CLR C	; CY = 0
MOV A, # 99H	; A = 1001 1001
RLC A	; A = 0011 0010 and CY = 1
RLC A	; A = 0110 0101 and CY = 0

(viii) RR A   [May/June 2012]

Function : Rotate A right

Flags affected : None

Description : This instruction rotates the bits of register A right. The bits rotated out of A are rotated back into A at the opposite end.

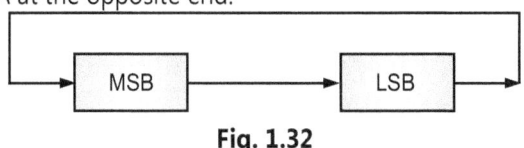

Fig. 1.32

For example :

```
MOV A, # 66H        ; A = 0110 0110
RR   A              ; A = 0011 0011
RR   A              ; A = 1001 1001
```

(ix) RRC A   [May/June 2012]

Function : Rotate A right through carry.

Flags affected : CY

Description : This instruction rotates the bits of the accumulator right. The bits rotated out of register A are rotated into CY and the CY bit is rotated into the opposite end of the accumulator.

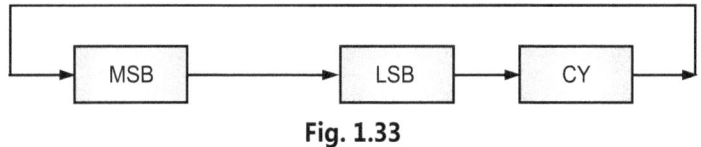

Fig. 1.33

For example :

```
SETB  C             ; CY = 1
MOV A, # 99H        ; A = 1001 1001
RRC A               ; A = 1100 1100 and CY = 1
RRC A               ; A = 1110 0110 and CY = 0
```

Bit Addressable Instructions :

(i) CLR bit :

Function : Clear bit

Description : This instruction clears a single bit. The bit can be carry flag or any bit-addressable location in 8051.

For example :

```
CLR C               ; CY = 0
CLR P2.4            ; Clear P2.4 = 0
CLR ACC.7           ; Clear D7 bit of accumulator ACC.7 = 0
```

(ii) SETB bit :

Function : Set bit

Description : This sets high the indicated bit. The bit can be carry or any directly addressable bit of a port or RAM location.

For example :

SETB P1.3	;	P1.3 = 1
SETB P2.6	;	P2.6 = 1
SETB ACC.6	;	ACC.6 = 1
SETB 05	;	Set high D5 of RAM location 20H
SETB C	;	Set CY = 1

(iii) CPL bit : [May/June 2013]

Function : Complement bit

Description : This instruction complements a single bit. The bit can be any bit addressable location in the 8051.

For example :

SETB P1.0	;	Set P1.0 high
CPL P1.0		Complement register bit

(iv) ANL C, Source-bit :

Function : Logical AND for bit variable.

Flags affected : CY

Description : In this instruction the carry flag is ANDed with a source bit and the result is placed in carry.

For example :

MOV C, P2.1

ANL C, P2.2

CLR A

(v) ORL C, Source bit :

Function : Logical OR for bit variables.

Flags affected : CY

Description : In this instruction the CY flag is ORed with a source bit and the result is placed in the carry flag. Therefore if the source bit 1, CY is set; otherwise CY flag remains uchanged.

For example :

MOV C, P2.1

ORL C, ACC.2

Program and Machine Control Instructions

(i) ACALL target address :
Function : Absolute call
Flags affected : None
Description : ACALL instruction calls subroutines with a target address, within 2k bytes from the current program counter (PC).

(ii) AJMP target address :
Function : Absolute jump
Flags affected : None
Description : This instruction transfers program execution to the target address unconditionally. The target address for this instruction must be within 2k bytes of program memory.

(iii) CJNE (dest-byte) (source-byte) (target) :   [May/June 2011]
Function : Compare and jump if not equal.
Flags affected : CY
Description : The magnitudes of the source byte and destination byte are compared. If they are not equal, it jumps, to the target address. To find out if it is greater or less after the comparison, check the CY flag. The CY flag indicates, which value is greater.

    Dest < Source   CY = 1
    Dest > Source   CY = 0

This instruction supports four addressing modes. In two of them, A is the destination.

(a) Immediate   CJNE A, # data, target
(b) Direct   CJNE A, direct, target
(c) Register   CJNE Rn, # data target
(d) Rgister-indirect   CJNE @ Ri, # data, target

(iv) DJNZ byte, target
Function : Decrement and jump if not zero.
Flags affected : None
Description : In this instruction a byte is decremented, and if the result is not zero it will jump to the target address. This instruction supports two formats :

(a) Register   DJNZ Rn, target where n = 0 to 7
(b) Direct   DJNZ direct, target

For example :
```
         CLR A
         MOV R2, # 20
back :   INC A
         MOV P1, A
         DJNZ R2, back
```

(v) JB bit, target and JNB bit, target :

Function : Jump if bit set. Jump if bit not set

Flags affected : None

Description : These instructions are used to monitor a given bit and jump to a target address if a given bit is high or low. In the case of JB, if the bit is high, it will jump, while for JNB if the bit is low it will jump. The given bit can be any of the bit addressable bits of RAM, ports, or registers of the 8051.

For example :

(1)   SETB P1.4   ; make P1.5 as input bit

HERE: JB P1.4, HERE   ; stay here as long as P1.4 = 1

         MOV P2, # 44H   ; since P1.4 = 0 send 44H to P2

(2)   JNB ACC.1, next   ; jump if D1 is 0

       INC A   ; D1 = 1 make it 1.

Next :

(vi) JBC bit, target :

Function : Jump if bit is set and clear bit

Flags affected : None

Description : If the desired bit is high it will jump to the target address; at the same time the bit is cleared to zero.

For example :

    JBC ACC.6, NEXT

    MOV P1, A

    NEXT :

This instruction will jump to label NEXT if D_6 bit of reg. A is high, at the same time D6 cleared to zero

(vii) JC Target :

Function : Jump if CY = 1

Flags affected : None

Description : This instruction checks the CY flag. If it is high, it will jump to the target address.

(viii) JNC target

Function : Jump if CY = 0

Flags affected : None

Description : This instruction examines the CY flag, and if it is zero it will jump to the target address.

(ix) JMP @ A + DPTR :
Function : Jump indirect
Flags affected : None
Description : This instruction is an unconditional jump to a target address. The target address is provided by the total sum of register A and the DPTR register, this is not a widely used instruction.

(x) JNZ target :
Function : Jump if accumulator is not zero.
Flags affected : None
Description : This instruction jumps if register A has a value other than zero.
For example :
```
        MOV R5, # 16
        MOV R3, # 00
        MOV R1, # 40H
BACK :  MOV A, @ R1
        JNZ NEXT
        INC R3
NEXT :  INC R1
        DJNZ R5, BACK
```

(xi) JZ target :
Function : Jump if A = zero
Flags affected : None
Description : This instruction examines the contents of the accumulator and jumps if it has value 0.
For example :
```
        MOV R0, # 50H
HERE :  MOV A, @ R0
        JZ NEXT
        MOV P1, A
        ACALL DELAY
        INC R0
        SJMP HERE
NEXT :
```

(xii) J Condition target :
Function : Conditional jump

Description : In this type of jump, control is transferred to a target address if certain conditions are met. The target address cannot be more than −128 to +127 bytes away from the current PC.

JC	jump if carry
JNC	jump if no carry
JZ	jump zero
JNZ	jump if no zero
JNB bit	jump if no bit
JB bit	jump bit
JBC bit	jump bit clear bit
DJNZ Rn, Label	Decrement and jump if not zero
CJNE A, # value	Compare A with value and jump if not equal

(xiii) LCALL 16-bit address and ACALL 11-bit address : [Nov./Dec. 2011]

Function : Transfers control to a subroutine.

Flags affected : None

Description : There are two types of CALL : ACALL and LCALL. In ACALL the target address is within 2k bytes of the current PC (program counter). When the target address is in the 64k bytes then LCALL is used.

ACALL is a two-byte instruction in which 5 bits is the opcode and the other 11 bits are the 11-bit address of the target subroutine. 2^{11} = 2k range. LCALL is a 3-byte instruction in which first byte is the opcode and other 2 bytes are the 16-bit address of the target subroutine.

(xiv) LJMP 16-bit address and SJMP 8-bit address :

Function : Transfers control unconditionally to a new address. In 8051 there are two unconditional jumps : LJMP (long jump) and SJMP (short jump).

(a) LJMP (long jump) : This is a 3-byte instruction. The first byte is the opcode and next two bytes are the target address. The difference between LCALL and LJMP is that the CALL instruction will return and continue execution onwards whereas JMP will not return.

(b) SJMP (short jump) : This is a 2-byte instruction. The first byte is the opcode and the second byte is the signed number displacement, which is added to the PC (program counter) to get the target address. Therefore, in the jump the target address must be within −128 to +127 bytes of the PC (program counter).

(xv) NOP :

Function : No operation.

Flags : None

Description : This performs no operation and execution. Continues with the next instruction. It is sometimes used for timing delays to waste clock cycles. This instruction only updates the PC to point to the next instruction following NOP.

Unit - I
Chapter 2

8051 PROGRAMMING IN C

2.1 WHY PROGRAM THE 8051 IN C ?

The size of the hex file produced by the compiler is the major problem in microcontroller programming because microcontrollers have limited on-chip ROM and the code space for the 8051 is limited to 64 K bytes.

Programming in assembly language is tedious and time consuming whereas C programming is less time consuming and much easier to write. Programming in C, has following advantages :
1. Programming in C is less time consuming and easy compared to assembly language programming.
2. It is easier to modify and update.
3. C code is portable to other microcontrollers with little or no modification.
4. C also provides some library functions.

When you write a program in C you need a compiler to convert it into machine code. The widely used compiler for 8051 and many other microcontrollers is **"Keil μ Vision"** Keil μ vision has a header file for every microcontroller. This header file contains variable declaration, macro definitions and definitions for special function registers (SFRs). The header file for 8051 is reg51h.

Bit Addressable I/O Programming :

A bit of any bit addressable SFR is defined as follows
   P1^0 for port 1 bit 0
   P0^6 for port 0 bit 6
   PSW^7 for carry flag in PSW register etc.

Also for interrupt there is a standard syntax defined.
   Void function name (void) interrupt number [using register bank].

2.2 DATA TYPES IN 8051 C

> Q. Explain different C data types used for programming 8051 microcontroller.
> [8 M] [May/June 2010, Nov./Dec. 2011]

The use of data types is important in case of 8051 C programming. Data types must be used depending on the range to make compact programs, therefore less memory space is required for program and data.

The most widely used and most useful C data types are listed below in the table for 8051 microcontroller.

Table 2.1 : Commonly used data types in 8051 C

Data Type	Size in Bits	Range or Usage
Unsigned character	8	0 to 255 (00 to FFH)
Signed character	8	– 128 to + 127
Unsigned int	16	0 to 65535 (0000H to FFFFH)
Signed int	16	– 32768 to + 32,767
S bit	1	Bit addressable locations of SFR
Bit	1	RAM bit addressable only
SFR	8-bit	RAM addresses 80-FFH only

Program 2.1

Write an 8051 C program to send values of –4 to +4 to port 2.

```c
# include <reg51.h>
void main ( )
{
  unsigned char i
  char mydisp[ ] = {+1, –1, +2, –2, +3, –3, +4, –4};
  for (i = 0; i < = 8; i++)
  P2 = mydisp [i];
}
```

Program 2.2

Write an 8051 C program to count 00H to FFH on port 1.

```c
# include <reg51.h>
void main ( )
{
  unsigned char a;
  for (a = 0; a < = 255; a++)
  {
    P1 = a;
  }
}
```

Program 2.3

Write an 8051 C program to toggle bit D_2 of the port 2 (P2.2) 30,000 times.

Solution :

```c
# include <reg51.h>
Sbit MYBIT = P2^2;
void main (void)
{
  unsigned int z;
  for (z = 0; z <= 30000; z++)
  {
    MYBIT = 0;
    MYBIT = 1;
  }
}
```

2.3 TIME DELAYS IN 8051 C

Q. Compare delay generation using : [6 M] [Nov./Dec. 2011]
  (i) Simple for loop.
  (ii) Using 8051 timer.

There are two methods to generate a time delay in 8051 C :

(1) Using a simple for loop (2) Using the 8051 timers.

While generating a time delay using a for loop, three factors which causes the change in accuracy of the delay :

1. Because of the 8051 design. As the number of machine cycles and the number of clock periods per machine cycle vary from one version to another version of the microcontroller.

2. The crystal frequency connected to the X1 – X2 input pins. The duration of the clock period for the machine cycle is a function of this crystal frequency.

3. Selection of compiler different compilers produce different code. In other words, each compilers produces different hex code.

Because of these reasons when programs are written for time delay in C, you should be use oscilloscope to measure the exact duration.

Program 2.4 [May/June 2011]

Write a 8051 C program to toggle the bits of port 2 continuously with a 250 ms delay.

Solution :

```
# include <reg51.h>
void msdelay (unsigned int);
void main (void)
{
  while (1)
  {
    P2 = 0X55;
    ms delay (250);
    P2 = 0XAA;
    msdelay (250);
  }
}
void msdelay (unsigned int itime)
{
  unsigned int i, j;
  for (i = 0; i < itime; i++)
  for (j = 0; j < 1275; j++);
}
```

Program 2.5

Write a 8051 C program to toggle all the bits of P0 and P2 continuously with a 250 ms delay.

Solution :

```
# include <reg51.h>
void MSDELAY (unsigned int);
void main (void)
{
  while (1)
  {
    P0 = 0X55;
    P2 = 0X55;
    MSDELAY (250);
    P0 = 0XAA;
    P2 = 0XAA;
```

```
    MSDELAY (250);
  }
}
void MSDELAY (unsigned int itime)
{
  unsigned int i, j;
  for (i = 0; i < time; i++)
  for (j = 0; j < 1275; j++)
}
```

2.4 I/O PROGRAMMING IN 8051 C

Bit size I/O

The ports P_0 – P_3 are byte accessible. We use the labels P_0 – P_3 as defined in the 8051/52 header file.

Program 2.6   [May/June 2012]

Write an 8051 C program that shows the count from 00 to FFH on the LEDs. LEDs are connected to bits P_0 and P_1.

Solution :

```
# include <reg51.h>
# define LED P1
void main (void)
{
  P0 = 00;              // clear P0
  LED = 0;              // clear P1
  for (i,j)             // repeat forever
  {
    P0++;               // increment P0
    LED++;              // increment P1
  }
}
```

Program 2.7   [May/June 2011]

Write an 8051 C program to get a byte of data from P_0, wait 1/2 second and then second it to P_2.

Solution :

```c
# include <reg51.h>
void MSDELAY (unsigned int);
void main (void)
{
  unsigned char mybyte;
  P0 = 0XFF        ;        // make P0 and input port
  while (1)
  {
    mybyte = P0    ;        // get a byte from P0
    MSDELAY (500);
    P2 = mybyte    ;        // send it to P2
  }
}
void MSDELAY (unsigned int itime)
{
  unsigned int i, j;
  for (i = 0; i < time; i++)
  for (j = 0; j < 1275; j++);
}
```

2.5 BIT ADDRESSABLE I/O PROGRAMMING

Q. Explain bit addressability for I/O ports of 8051. [8 M] [May/June 2012, 2013]

The ports $P_0 - P_3$ are bit addressable, we can access a single bit without disturbing the rest of the ports bits. We use S bit data type access a single bit of $P_0 - P_3$. The simple way to use the format Pa^b where a is the port 0, 1, 2 or 3 and b is the bit 0 – 7 of that port.

Program 2.8

Write an 8051 C program to monitor bit P1.7. If it is high, send 55H to P_0 otherwise send AAH to P_2.

Solution :

```c
# include <reg51.h>
Sbit mybit = P1^7;
void main (void)
```

```
{
    mybit = 1         // make mybit as input
    while (1)
    {
        if (mybit ==1)
        P0 = OX55;
        else
        P2 = OXAA;
    }
}
```

Program 2.9

A door sensor is connected to the P1.5 pin and a buzzer is connected to P1.1. Write an 8051 C program to monitor the door sensor and when it opens, sound the buzzer. You can sound the buzzer by sending a square wave of a few hundred Hz.

Solution :

```
# include <reg51.h>
void MSdelay (unsigned int);
Sbit Dsensor = P1^5;
Sbit Buzzer = P1^1;
void main (void)
{
    Dsensor = 1;              // make P1.7 an input
    while (Dsensor ==1)
    {
        buzzer = 0;
        MSdelay (500);
        buzzer = 1;
        MSdelay (500);
    }
}
void MSdelay (unsigned int itime)
{
    unsigned int i, j;
    for (i = 0; i < itime; i++)
    for (j = 0; j < 1275; j++);
}
```

2.6 ACCESSING SFR ADDRESSES 80H - FFH

We can access the SFR RAM space 80 - FFH using SFR data types. A single bit of any SFR can also be accessed if the bit address is specified. There is no need to put # include <reg51.h> file in the program.

Program 2.10

Write an 8051 C program to toggle all the bits of P0, P1 and P2 and P3 continuously with a 300 ms delay. Use the SFR keyword to declare the port addresses.

Solution :

```
SFR P0 = 0X80;        // declaring P0 using SFR data type
SFR P1 = 0X90;        // declaring P1 using SFR data type
SFR P2 = 0XA0;        // declaring P2 using SFR data type
SFR P3 = 0XB0;        // declaring P3 using SFR data type
void MSdelay (unsigned int);
void main (void)
{
  while (1)
  {
    P0 = 0X00;
    P1 = 0X00;
    P2 = 0X00;
    P3 = 0X00;
    MSdelay (300);
    P0 = 0XFF;
    P1 = 0XFF;
    P2 = 0XFF;
    P3 = 0XFF;
    MSdelay (250);
  }
}
void MSdelay (unsigned int itime)
{
  unsigned int i, j;
  for (i = 0; i < i time; i++)
  for (j = 0; j < 1250; j++);
}
```

Program 2.11

Write an 8051 C program to turn bit P1.0 on and off 30,000 times

Solution :

```c
Sbit mybit = 0X90;
void main (void)
{
  unsigned int x;
  for (x = 0; x < 30,000; x++)
  {
    mybit = 1;
    mybit = 0;
  }
}
```

Using bit data type for bit addressable RAM

The Sbit data type is used only for bit-addressable SFR registers. Sometimes, it is needed to store some data in a bit-addressable section of the data RAM space which is 20 – 2FH.

Program 2.12

Write an 8051 C program to get the status of bit P1.5, save it and send it to P2.1 continuously.

Solution :

```c
# include <reg51.h>
Sbit inbit = P1^5;
Sbit outbit = P2^1;
bit membit;                    // bit addressable memory
void main (void)
{
  while (1)
  {
    membit = inbit;            // get a bit from P1.5
    outbit = membit;           // and send it to P2.1
  }
}
```

2.7 LOGIC OPERATIONS IN 8051 C

The logical operators used in C are AND (&&) OR (| |) and NOT (!). Many programmers are unaware with the bit wise operators AND ($), OR (|), EX-OR (^), Inverter (~), shift right (>>) and shift left (<<). These bitwise operators are widely used in software engineering for embedded systems and control. Table shows bit wise logic operators for C.

Table 2.2 : Bit wise logic operators for C

A	B	AND A and B	OR A|B	EX-OR A ^ B	Inverter Y = ~ B
0	0	0	0	0	1
0	1	0	1	1	0
1	0	0	1	1	-
1	1	1	1	0	-

Program 2.13

Write an 8051 C program to toggle all the bits of P_0 and P_2 continuously with a 300 msec delay. Use the EX-OR operator.

Solution :

```
# include <reg51.h>
void msdelay (unsigned int);
void main (void)
{
  P0 = 0X00;
  P1 = 0X00;
  P2 = 0X00;
  while (1)
  {
    P0 = P0^0XFF;
    P1 = P1^0XFF;
    P2 = P2^0XFF;
    msdelay (300);
  }
}
void msdelay (unsigned int itime)
{
  unsigned int x, y;
  for (x = 0; x < itime; x++)
  for (y = 0; y < 1250; y++)
}
```

2.7.1 Bitwise Shift Operations in C

There are two bit-wise shift operators in C :
(1) Right shift (>>) and (2) Left shift (<<) their format in C is as follows :
Data >> number of bits to be shifted right
Data << no. of bits to be shifted left

Program 2.14

Write an 8051 C program to read the P1.0 and P1.1 bits and issue an ASCII character to P0 according to the following table.

Table 2.3

P1.1	P1.0	
0	0	Send X to P0
0	1	Send Y to P0
1	0	Send Z to P0
1	1	Send W to P0

Solution :

```
# include <reg51.h>
void main (void)
{
   unsigned char i;
   i = P1;              // read P1
   i = i & 0X3;         // make the unused bits
   switch (i)           // make decision
   {
     case (0);
     {
       P0 = 'X';        // issue ASCII 'X'
       break;
     }
     case (1);
     {
       P0 = 'Y';        // issue ASCII 'Y'
       break;
     }
     case (2);
     P0 = 'Z';          // issue ASCII Z
```

```
    break;
}
case (3);
P0 = 'W';            // issue ASCII W
    break;
}
```

2.8 DATA CONVERSION PROGRAMS IN C

The new microcontrollers have real time clock (RTC) that displays the time and data even when the power is switched OFF. RTC provides the time and data in packed BCD. To display then they must be converted to ASCII.

2.8.1 ASCII Numbers

On ASCII keyboards when the key 0 is pressed 0110000 (30H) is given to the computer. If the key 1 is pressed 0110001 (31H) is given and so on.

Table 2.4 : Lists the ASCII codes for digits 0 – 9

Key	ASCII (hex)	Binary	BCD (unpacked)
0	30	011 0000	0000 0000
1	31	011 0001	0000 0001
2	32	011 0010	0000 0010
3	33	011 0011	0000 0011
4	34	011 0100	0000 0100
5	35	011 0101	0000 0101
6	36	011 0110	0000 0110
7	37	011 0111	0000 0111
8	38	011 1000	0000 1000
9	39	011 1001	0000 1001

2.8.2 Packed BCD to ASCII Conversion

> **Q. Write short note on 'Conversion of Packed BCD to ASCII'**
>
> **[6 M] [Nov./Dec. 2012, 2011]**

The RTC provides the time of the day in hours; minutes; seconds and date in (year : month : day) continuously even if the power is switched OFF. This data is in packed BCD. To convert packed BCD to ASCII, it first converted to be in unpacked BCD. Then the unpacked BCD is added with 30H.

e.g.	**Packed BCD**	**Unpacked BCD**	**ASCII**
	0X19	0X01, 0X09	0X31, 0X39
	0001 1001	0000 0001, 0000 1001	0011 0001, 0011 1001

2.8.3 ASCII to Packed BCD Conversion

To convert ASCII to packed BCD; it is first converted to unpacked BCD and then combined to make packed BCD.

e.g.	Key	ASCII	Unpacked BCD	Packed BCD
	3	33	0000 0011	
	5	35	0000 0101	0011 0101 = 35H

After this conversion the packed BCD numbers are processed and the result will be in packed BCD format.

Program 2.15

Write an 8051 C program to convert packed BCD 0X29 to ASCII and display the bytes on P_1 and P_2.

Solution :

```
# include <reg51.h>
void main (void)
{
  unsigned char x, y, z;
  unsigned char mybyte = 0X29;
  X = mybyte & 0X0F;        //mask lower 4 bits
  P₁ = X|0X30;              // make it ASCII
  Y = mybyte & 0XF0;        // mask upper 4 bits
  Y = Y >> 4;               // shift to lower 4 bits
  P₂ = Y|0X30;              // make it ASCII
```

Program 2.16

Write an 8051 program to convert ASCII digits 3 and 8 to packed BCD and display it on Port 0.

Solution :

```
# include <reg51.h>
void main ( )
{
  unsigned char data 1 = 0X33;
  unsigned char data 2 = 0X38;
  P₀ = (data 2 & 0X0F) + (data 1 & 0X0F) (<<4);
  while (1)
}
```

2.8.4 Checksum Byte

Q. Write short notes on 'Checksum byte in ROM'   [6 M] [May/June 2013]

Every system must perform the checksum calculation to maintain the integrity of the ROM contents. The process of checksum is used to detect any corruption of the contents of the ROM. Example of ROM corruption is current surge, to ensure data integrity the process uses checksum bytes. The checksum bytes are the extra bytes that are tagged to the end of a series of bytes of data.

Step 1 : Add all bytes together and discard the carry.
Step 2 : Take the 2's complement of the total sum.
This is the checksum byte, which becomes the last byte of the series.

For example : The checksum byte of data 25H, 35H, 45H, 65H can be calculated as follows.

25H + 35H + 45H + 65H = $\boxed{1}$ 04H.

2's complement of 04H (0000 0100)
```
      1111 1011
    +        1
      ─────────
      1111 1100   (FCH) – checksum byte
```

Program 2.17   [May/June 2010]

Write a program to calculate the checksum byte of the data 25H, 62H, 3FH and 52H and display the result on port 1.

Solution :

```c
# include <reg51.h>
void main (void)
{
  unsigned char Data [ ] = {0X25, 0X62, 0X3F, 0X52};
  unsigned char Sum = 0;
  unsigned char x;
  unsigned char checksum byte;
  for (x = 0; x < 4; x++)
  {
    P2 = data [x];           // issue each type to P2
    Sum = Sum + data [x];    // add together
    P1 = Sum;                // is sum the sum to P1
  }
  Checksymbyte = ~ Sum + 1;  // make 2's component
  P1 = Checksumbyte;         // show the checksumbyte
}
```

2.8.5 Binary (hex) to Decimal and ASCII conversion in 8051 C

Printf function converts data from binary to decimal or vice-versa but it takes lot of memory space. This increases the size of the hex file. In 8051 microcontroller systems, it is recommended to use separate conversion function.

Binary to decimal conversion is mostly used in ADC (Analog-to-digital conversion) chips, DACs. In some RTCs data such as time and date are shown in binary. To show the binary data it needs to be converted it to decimal and then to ASCII. The hex format is a convenient way to represent binary data.

The binary data 00-FFH is converted into decimal to give 000 – 255.

> **Q. Write a 8051 C program to convert FAH (1111 1010) to decimal and display the decimal digits on port P0, P1 and P2.** [8 M] [Nov./Dec. 2011, May/June 2013]

Program 2.18

Write an 8051 C program to convert FFH to decimal and display the digits on port P_0, P_1 and P_2.

Solution :

```
# include <reg51.h>
void main (void)
{
    unsigned char x, binbyte, d1, d2, d3;
    binbyte = 0XFF;         // binary (hex) byte
    X = binbyte/10;         // divide by 10
    d1 = binbyte % 10;      // find remainder (LSD)
    d2 = x% 10;             // middle light
    d3 = x/10;              // most significant digit (MSD)
    P0 = d1;
    P1 = d2;
    P2 = d3;
}
```

2.9 ACCESSING CODE ROM SPACE IN 8051 C

In 8051 there are three spaces to store data :
1. 128 bytes of RAM which is mostly used register banks which ranges from 00 – 7FH.
2. 64 k bytes of ROM space with address 0000 – FFFFH used to store opcodes.
3. 64 k bytes of external memory used as both RAM and ROM to use the external memory MOVX instruction is used.

In assembly language programming, 128 bytes of RAM space is used by register bank and the stack and remaining space is used as a scratch pad RAM.

The 8051 compiler first allocates first 8 bytes of the RAM to bank 0 and then some RAM to the stack. Then it allocates the remaining variables declared by the C program.

In assembly language 08H is the default starting address of stack. In C the compiler moves the stack's starting address in the range 50 – 7FH. It allows to allocate contiguous RAM locations to array elements.

Fig. 2.1 shows RAM locations in 8051.

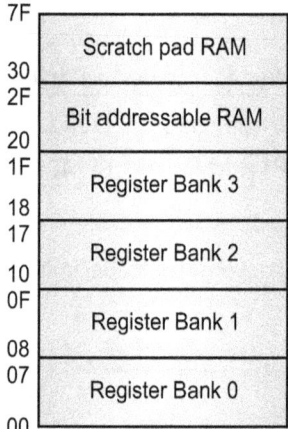

Fig. 2.1 : RAM locations in 8051

Program 2.19

Write a C program to send out the value 32H serially one bit at a time via P2.0. The LSB should go out first.

Solution :

```
#include <reg51.h>
Sbit out = P2^0;
Sbit serial = ACC^0;
void main (void)
{
  unsigned char datbyte = 0X32;
  unsigned char x;
  ACC = datbyte;
  For (x = 0; x < 8; x++)
  {
    ACC = datbyte;
    out = serial;
    ACC = ACC >> 1;
  }
  while (1)
}
```

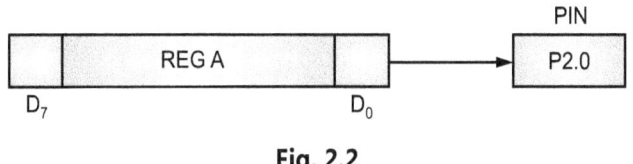

Fig. 2.2

2.10 DATA SERALIZATION

Q. Explain data serialization using 8051 C with suitable example. [May/June 2010]

It is the method of sending data one bit at a time through a single pin of microcontroller. There are two methods to transfer the data byte serially :

1. Using serial port.
2. Serializing data is to transfer data one bit a time and control the sequence of data and spaces in between them.

Program 2.20

Write a C program to send out the value 56H serial at a time via P2.0. The MSB should go out first.

Solution :

```
# include <reg51.h>
Sbit out = P2^0
Sbit serial = ACC^7;
void main ( )
{
   unsigned char datbyte = 0X56;
   unsigned char x;
   ACC = databyte;
   for (x = 0; x < 8; x++)
   {
      out = serial
      ACC = ACC << 1;
   }
   while (1)
}
```

Program 2.21

Write a C program to bring in a byte of data serially one bit at a time via P2.0. The MSB should come in first.

Solution :

```c
# include <reg51.h>
Sbit in = P2^0;
Sbit serial ACC^0;
void main (void)
{
  unsigned char dat = 0, x;
  for (x = 0; x < 8; x++)
  {
    Acc = dat;
    serial = in;
    dat = Acc;
    dat = dat << 1
  }
  while (1)
}
```

Program 2.22

Write a C program to bring in a byte of data serially one bit at a time via P1.0. The LSB should come in first.

Solution :

```c
# include <reg51.h>
Sbit serial = P1^0
Sbit ACC MSB = ACC^7
void main (void)
{
  unsigned char datbyte = 0X56;
  unsigned char i;
  for (i = 0; i < 8; i++)
  {
    ACC MSB = serial ;
    ACC = ACC >> 1;
  }
  P2 = ACC;
}
```

2.11 COUNTERS AND TIMERS

Counting of external events such as the frequency of a pulse train, or the generation of precise internal time delays are required for the many microcontroller application. These tasks can be accomplished using software techniques. This makes the processor busy so to reduce the burden on processor, two 16-bit up counters named as T_0 and T_1 are provided for the use of the programmer.

Each counter is programmed to count internal clock pulses which also acts as a timer or programmed to act as a counter by counting external pulses.

The counters are divided into two 8-bit registers namely timer low (TL0 and TL1) and high (TH0, TH1) bytes. All counter action is controlled by timer mode control register (TMOD) and timer/counter control register (TCON).

When timer is used as a counter to count a certain number of internal pulses or external events, a number is placed in one of the counter. The number is nothing but the maximum countless the desired count plus 1. The counter then increments the number to the maximum and then again comes to 0 by setting a timer flag.

When a counter is programmed to be a timer it will count the internal clock frequency of the 8051 oscillator divided by 12d. For example, if oscillator frequency is 6 MHz then the timer clock will have 500 kHz frequency.

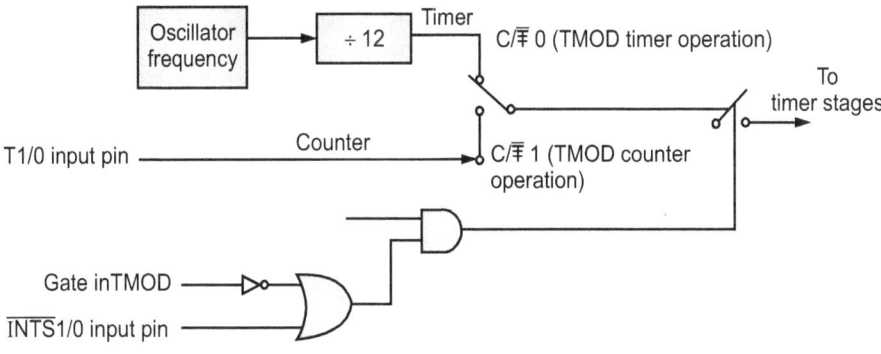

Fig. 2.3 : Timer/counter control logic

To act as a timer, the $C/\overline{T}$ bit in the TMOD register must be 0 and bit TRX in the TCON register must be 1 (timer run) and gate bit in the TMOD register must be 0 or external pin $\overline{INTX} = 1$.

2.11.1 TMOD Register

> **Q. Draw and explain the role of TMOD and TCON register of 8051, while programming 8051 microcontroller for embedded applications.**
>
> **[8 M] [May/June 2012]**

Fig. 2.4 shows Timer Mode Control (TMOD) special function register.

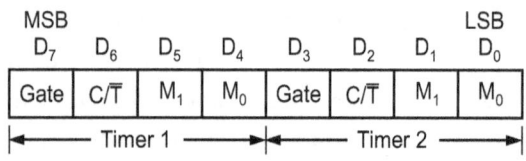

Fig. 2.4

Bit D_7 and D_3 : Gate

This is a OR gate to RUN/STOP time 1 or 0 with the help of program it is set to 1, to enable timer to run if bit TR0/1 in TCON register is set and signal on external interrupt $\overline{INT1/0}$ pin is high.

Bit D_6 and D_2 : $C/\overline{T}$

It is used to decide counter or timer operation, when it is set to 1 it is used as a counter by counting pulses from external input pins. When it is set 0, it acts as a timer by counting internal frequency.

Bits D_1 and D_5, M_1 and bits D_4 and D_0 : M_1 and M_0

It is used to select the timer mode of operation

Table 2.5 : TMOD is not bit-addressable

M_0	M_0	Mode
0	0	Mode 0
0	1	Mode 1
1	0	Mode 2
1	1	Mode 3

2.11.2 Timer Control (TCON) Special Function Register

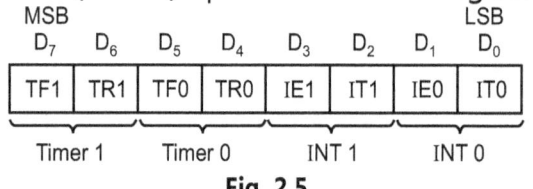

Fig. 2.5

Bit D_7 : Timer 1 overflow flag (TF1)

When it is set, timer 1 rolls from all 1's to all 0's and cleared by processor vectors to execute interrupt service routine located at 001BH program address.

Bit D_6 : Timer 1 run control bit (TR1)

This is set to enable the timer 1 to count and reset to halt the timer.

Bit D_5 : Timer 0 overflow flag (TF0)

When it is set timer 0 rolls from all 1's to all 0's and cleared by processor vectors to execute interrupt service routine located at 000BH program address.

Bit D₄ : Timer 0 run control bit (TR0)

This is set to enable timer 0 to count and reset to halt the timer.

Bit D₃ : External interrupt 1 Edge flag (IE1)

When a high to low edge signal is received on port 3, pin no. 3 ($\overline{INT1}$), it is set and cleared by processor vectors to execute interrupt service routine located at 0013H program address.

Bit D₂ : External interrupt 1 signal type control bit (IT1)

It is set by the program to enable external interrupt 1 during a falling edge of the signal and cleared by program to enable a low-level signal on external interrupt to generate an interrupt.

Bit D₁ : External Interrupt 0 Edge Flag (IE0)

When a high-to-low edge signal is received on port 3 pin 2, it is set to 1 and cleared to zero by processor vectors to interrupt service routine located at 0003H program address. It is not related to timer operation.

Bit D₀ : External interrupt 0 signal type control bit (IT0)

This is used to enable external interrupt zero by triggering at a falling edge of the signal when it is set to 1 and cleared to enable a low-level signal on external interrupt 0 to generate an interrupt.

This is a bit addressable.

2.12 TIMER OPERATION MODES

Q. Explain with suitable example mode 1 and mode 2 programming of 8051 timers.
[8 M] [May/June 2010]

Depending upon the mode selection control bits M_1 and M_0 in TMOD register the timer can operate in any one of the four modes :

1. Mode 0
2. Mode 1
3. Mode 2
4. Mode 3

2.12.1 Mode 0

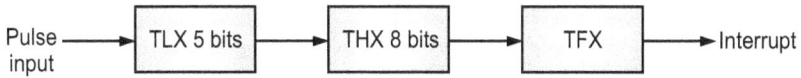

Fig. 2.6 : Timer/counter mode 0 : 13 bit counter

In this mode timer operates as a 13-bit register (TLX - 5 bits and THX - 8 bits). The pulse input is divided by 32d in TL so that TH counts the original oscillator frequency reduced by a total 384 d.

The timer is enabled by writing 00 in TMOD register. If the timer count exceeds 13 bits i.e. 1FFFH the next count will be zero. 0000H by generating an interrupt to inform to the programmer that one cycle is over. Also TF1 and TF0 timer overflow bit will be set. The timer interrupt is enabled using Interrupt Enable register (IE).

2.12.2 Mode 1

Operation in mode 1 is same as mode 0. The only difference is that mode 0 was a 13 bit time/counter register, but in mode 1 it is 16-bit timer/counter register.

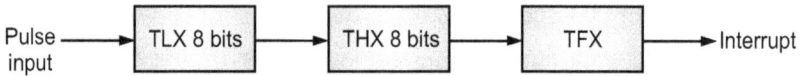

Fig. 2.7 : Time Mode 1 operation as 16 bit timer/counter

The mode is set by writing 01 in mode selection bits in TMOD register.

2.12.3 Mode 2

This mode is configured as the 8-bit timer/counter by using TLX only with auto-reload feature. THX is used to hold the value that is loaded into TLX every time TLX overflows from FFH to 00H, when TLX overflows, the timer flag is set.

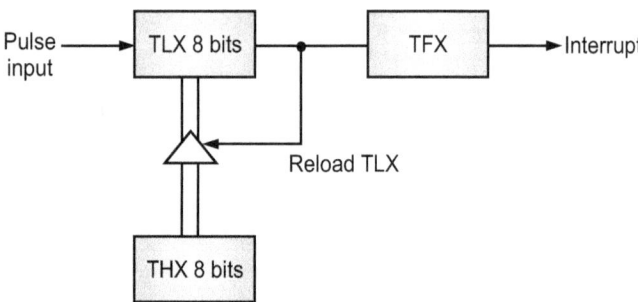

Fig. 2.8 : Timer mode 2 with auto-reload feature

Count is stored in THX. TLX will start count up from the number stored in THX, when TLX overflow interrupt is generated to indicate overflow and again initialized with the contents of THX.

2.12.4 Mode 3

In mode 3 timer 1 just holds the count whereas timer 0 registers TL0 and TH0 are configured as two separate 8-bit counters. TL0 is controlled by the gate arrangement as shown in Fig. 2.9 and sets timer flag TF0 whenever it overflows from FFH to 00H.

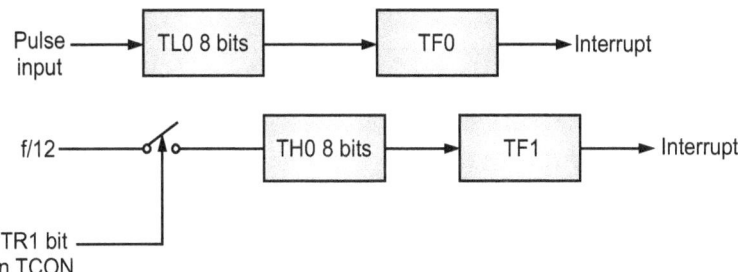

Fig. 2.9 : Timer mode 3 as two 8-bit timer/counter

The important point in this mode is no interrupt is generated by timer 1 while timer 0 uses the TF1 overflow flag. The important application of mode 3 is it is used for the baud rate generation for the serial port.

The difference between the counting and timing is that the source of the clock pulses to the counters. When it is used as a timer, the clock pulses are generated by dividing the oscillator frequency by 12. When it is used as a counter, pin T_0 (P3.4) supplies pulses to counter 0 and pin T_1 (P3.5) to counter 1. The $C/\overline{T}$ is used to control the timer/counter operation.

2.13 PROGRAMMING OF TIMERS AND COUNTERS USING ASSEMBLY LANGUAGE PROGRAMMING

Program 2.23

Write an assembly language program to generate a square wave of 2 kHz frequency if crystal frequency is 11.0592 MHz on pin 1.4.

Solution :

The time period of the square wave is $\frac{1}{2 \times 10^3} = 500$ μs.

Assume that the duty cycle of the square wave is 50%. Therefore, the square wave will be high for 250 μs and it will be low for 250 μs.

Crystal frequency is 11.0592 MHz means the counter will count up every $\frac{1}{11.0592 \times 10^6} = 1.085$ μs.

$$\frac{250 \text{ μs}}{1.085 \text{ μs}} = 230,$$

The values that should be loaded into TH and TL are

$$65536 - 230 = (65306)_{10} \approx \text{FF1AH}$$

∴ T_L = 1AH and T_H = FFH

Program

Comments	Instructions	Comments
	MOV TMOD, # 10H	Load TMOD register in time mode
Label 1 :	MOV TL1, # 1AH	Load TL
	MOV TH1, # 0FFH	Load TH
	SETB TR1	Start Timer 1
Label 2 :	JNB TF1, Label 2	Remain until overflow
	CLR TR1	Stop timer 1
	CPL P1.4	Clear port pin
	CLR TF1	Clear timer 1 flag
	SJMP Label 1	Reload timer

Program 2.24

Write an assembly language program for 8051 such that LED connected to port 1.5 will flash at a rate 0.5 sec., when line P2.1 goes high use timer 0 for generating delay.

Solution :

$$\text{Assume crystal frequency} = 12 \text{ MHz}$$

$$\therefore \quad \text{Timer clock frequency} = \frac{12 \text{ MHz}}{12} = 1 \text{ MHz}$$

$$\therefore \quad T = 1 \text{ μs}$$

Therefore, maximum delay = 65536×1 μs = 65.536 ms

To get a delay of 0.5 sec, program the timer for 10 times so that 0.5 sec delay is obtained i.e. 50 ms. To obtain a 50 ms delay 50,000 must be subtracted from 65536.

i.e. $65536 - 50000 = 15536$ or (3CB0)H

i.e. $T_L = $ B0H and $T_L = $ 3CH

Program for Delay Routine

Label	Instructions	Comments
Delay :	MOV R0, # 0AH	Initialize counter to 10
Label 1 :	MOV TL0, # B0H	Load TL
	MOV TH0, # 3CH	Load TH
	SETB TR0	Start timer 0
Label 2 :	JNB TF0 label 2	Remain until overflow
	CLR TR0	Stop timer 0
	CLR TF0	Clear timer 0 flag
	DJNZ R0, Label 1	Decrement and repeat if $R_0 \neq 0$
	RET	

	MOV TMOD, # 01	Timer 0 mode 1
	MOV P2, # 0FFH	Consider port 2 as input port
Label 3 :	JB P2.1, Label 3	Continue till P2.1 = 1
HERE :	CPL P1.5	Toggle P1.5
	ACALL DELAY	Call subroutine
	SJMP HERE	Repeat

Program 2.25

Write an assembly language program to switch ON or OFF a LED connected on P1.2 when external interrupt $\overline{INT0}$ is activated.

Program :

Label	Instructions	Comments
	ORG 0000H	Bypass interrupt vector table.
	LJMP main	
	ORG 0003H	Interrupt vector for interrupt 0
	SETB P1.2	Turn ON LED
Label 1 :	MOV R0, # 500	wait for sometime
	DJNZ R0, Label 1	
	RETI	Return to the main program
	ORG 0030H	
Main :	MOV IE, # 81H	Enable INT0
Label 2 :	SJMP label 2	
	END	end program

Program 2.26

Write an assembly language program to generate a square wave of 1 kHz and 75% duty cycle at pin P1.5. Assume microcontroller is operating at 6 MHz.

Solution : Time for one machine cycle = $\dfrac{12}{6 \text{ MHz}}$ = 2 µ sec.

Square wave of period = $\dfrac{1}{1 \text{ kHz}}$ = 1 m sec.

Hence, the delay required for ON period = $\dfrac{750 \text{ µs}}{2 \text{ µs}}$ = 375 and delay required for OFF period = $\dfrac{250 \text{ µs}}{2 \text{ µs}}$ = 125.

∴ Count = $(65536 - 375)_{10}$ = $(65161)_{10}$ = $(FE89)_{16}$

and $(65536 - 125)_{10}$ = $(65411)_{10}$ = $(FF83)_{16}$

Label	Instructions	Comments
	ORG 0000H	
	LJMP main	
	ORG 001BH	
	CPL P1.5	
	CLR TR1	
	MOV TL1, R1	
	MOV 00, R3	
	MOV R3, 01	
	MOV R1, 00	
	MOV TH1, R2	
	MOV 00, R4	
	MOV R4, 02	
	MOV R2, 00	
	SETB TR1	
	CLR TF1	
	RETI	
	ORG 0100H	
Main :	SETB P1.5	
	MOV IE, # 88H	
	MOV TMOD, # 10H	
	MOV R1, # 83H	
	MOV R2, # 0FFH	
	MOV R3, # 89H	
	MOV R4, # 0FEH	
	MOV TH1, R4	
	MOV TL1, R3	
	SETB TR1	
	SJMP TR1	
Here :	SJMP Here	
	END	

2.14 PROGRAMMING THE TIMERS/COUNTERS IN EMBEDDED C

Program 2.27

Write a C program to toggle all bits of port 1 continuously. Use timer 0 to generate delay of 10 sec. between each toggle.

Solution : Assume crystal frequency = 12 MHz

$$\therefore T = \frac{12}{12 \times 10^6} = 1\ \mu s$$

To obtain a 50 ms delay $\dfrac{50\ ms}{1\ \mu s}$ = 50,000 clocks are required

$\therefore$ Count = 65536 − 50000

= 15536 ≈ (3CB0)H

$\therefore$ TH1 = 3CH and TL1 = B0H

The delay loop is repeated 200 times to generate 10 sec. delay.

Program :

```
# include <reg 51.h>
void DELAY ( )
void main ( )
{
  while (1)
  {
    P1 = 0X00;
    DELAY ( );
    P1 = 0XFF;
    DELAY ( );
  }
}
void DELAY ( )
{
  unsigned char x;
  for (x = 0; x < 200; X++)
  {
    TMOD = 0X01;
    TL0 = 0XB0H;
    TH0 = 0X3CH;
    TR0 = 1
    while (TF0! = 1);
  }
}
```

Program 2.28

Write a C program for counting the pulses on P3.2 pin (T_1) and display the hex count on P_0(LSB) and P_1(MSB).

Program :

```c
# include <reg51.h>
Sbit in = P3^2;
void main ( )
{
  P0 = 0X00;
  P1 = 0X00;
  TMOD = 0X50;
  TL1 = 0X00;
  TH1 = 0X00;
  in = 1;
  TR1 = 1;
  while (1)
  {
    TF1 = 0;
    P0 = TL1;
    P1 = TH1;
  }
}
```

Program 2.29

Write an 8051C program to switch On or OFF a LED connected on P1.5 pin. Complement the LED whenever switch connected on P3.1 is pressed.

Program :

```c
# include <reg51.h>
Sbit mybit = P1^5;
void INTR( ) interrupt 0
{
  mybit = ~ mybit;
}
void main ( )
{
  IE = 0X81;
  while (1);
}
```

Chapter - 3

SERIAL COMMUNICATION AND INTERRUPT PROGRAMMING

> **Q. What is serial communication? Explain asynchronous serial communication with suitable diagram.** [May/June 2010]

3.1 BASICS OF SERIAL COMMUNICATION

The word communication is nothing but the data transfer between the two points. Data transfer in computer takes place in two ways : parallel and serial.

In serial Communication, data is sent one bit at a time, whereas in parallel communication the data is sent a byte or more at a time. Practically, transmission of bits simultaneously requires more number of wires but it is impractical to use more number of wires. Parallel data transfer cannot be used for the devices like cassette tapes, CRT terminal etc. In such situation serial communication is used.

Comparison between parallel data transfer and serial data transfer.

Table 3.1

Serial data transfer	Parallel data transfer
Only one bit is transmitted at a time.	Number of bits are transferred in parallel.
Data transfer is slow.	Data transfer is fast.
Suitable for long distance.	Suitable for short distance.
Only 2 wires required for transmission of data.	9 wires are required to transmit the 8-bit data.

Serial communication uses two methods : (1) asynchronous, (2) synchronous.

The synchronous method transfers a block of data at a time, whereas asynchronous method transfers a single byte at a time.

3.1.1 Types of Communication Systems

Depending on transmission, communication systems are classified as (1) simplex, (2) duplex.

Simplex is one way transmission system. Data in other direction cannot be transmitted. System A is transmitter and B is receiver only.

Duplex is further divided in two groups :

(1) Half duplex, (2) Full duplex.

In half duplex, data may travel in both direction but not at the same time.

When data travels in both direction simultaneously then it is full duplex mode of data transmission.

3.1.2 Serial Transmission Formats

The data can be transferred in two formats in serial communication.

(1) Synchronous   (2) Asynchronous

3.1.2.1 *Asynchronous Data Transfer*

It is mostly used for character oriented transmission. In asynchronous method, each character is placed between start and stop bits. This is called as framing. In data framing, the data such as ASCII characters are packed between a start bit and a stop bit. The start bit is always one bit, but the stop bit can be one or two bits. The start bit is always a 0 and the stop bit is 1. When there is no transfer, the signal is 1 which is called as 'mark'. The 0 is called as space.

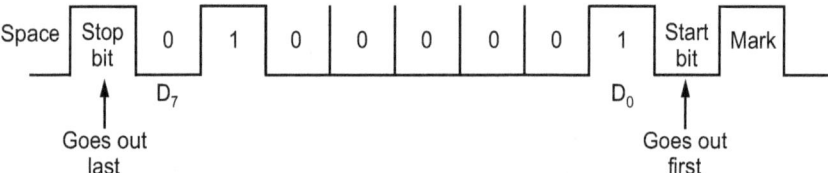

Fig. 3.1 : Asynchronous data formats

The table 3.2 gives the list of asynchronous data format standards.

Table 3.2

Specification	Typical Values
Data bits/character	5, 6, 7, or 8
Stop bits	1, 1 $\frac{1}{2}$ or, 2
Parity bits	Odd or even parity
Baud rates	75, 100, 150, 300, 600, 1200, 2400, 4800, 9600, 19200

3.1.2.2 *Synchronous Data Transfer*

The blocks of data bytes are transferred serially. Before sending data, special characters are transferred by transmitter to achieve synchronization between transmitter and receiver. This special character is called as **'sync character'**. To start the transmission the sync character bits are sent by transmitter followed by data bits, when the receiver is synchronized, it will accept data bits in same sequence.

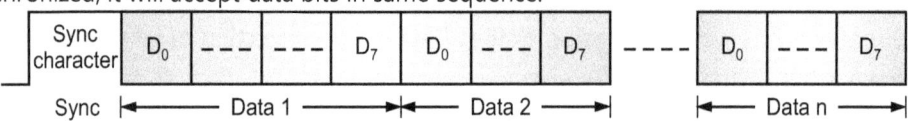

Fig. 3.2 : Synchronous data format

3.1.2.3 Comparison of Asynchronous and Synchronous Format

Table 3.3

Synchronous Data Transfer	Asynchronous Data Transfer
1. It is used to transfer a block of data at a time.	1. It is used one data bit at a time.
2. High data rate $\geq$ 20 kbps is available.	2. Suitable for $\leq$ 20 kbps data transfer rate.
3. Sync characters are required.	3. Sync characters are not required.
4. No start bit and stop bit is used.	4. Start bit and stop bit for each character is required.
5. Same clock is used for transmitter and receiver.	5. Two separate clocks can be used for transmitter and receiver.
6. Speed is high.	6. Speed is less.

Baud Rate

In serial communication, baud rate is defined as number of bits transmitted per second or it is the rate at which number of bits transmitted

$$\text{Baud} = \frac{\text{No. of bits}}{\text{Second}}$$

Typical Baud rates are 110, 150, 300, 600, 1200, 2400, 4800, 9600 and 19200.

3.2 REGISTERS OF 8051 USED FOR SERIAL COMMUNICATION

> **Q. Explain use of SBUF and SCON of 8051 for serial communication.**
> **[May/June 2012]**

In serial communication, to allow data transfer between the PC and an 8051 system without any error, the baud rate of the 8051 system should match the baud rate of the PC's COM port. Baud rate in 8051 is programmable. We can change the baud rate with the help of timer 1.

The 8051 divides the crystal frequency by 12 to get the machine cycle frequency. For example, XTAL = 11.0592 MHz and it is divided by 12 (11.0592 MHz/12 = 921.6 kHz). The 8051's serial communication UART circuitry divides the machine cycle frequency of 921.6 kHz by 32 one more time before it is used by timer 1 to set the baud rate. When timer 1 is used to set the baud rate it must be programmed in mode 2 i.e. 8-bit autoload. To get baud rates compatible with the PC, TH1 should be loaded with value as shown in Table.

Table 3.4 : Timer 1 TH1 register values for various Baud rates

Baud rate	TH1 (hex)	TH1 (decimal)
9600	FD	−3
4800	FA	−6
2400	F4	−12
1200	E8	−24

3.2.1 SBUF Register

It is an 8-bit register used for serial communication in 8051. SBUF register is used whenever a byte of data to be transferred via the TXD line. As well as it holds the byte of data when it receives the data with 8051's RXD line. SBUF can be accessed like any other registers in the 8051.

For example,　　MOV SBUF, # 'D'
　　　　　　　　　MOV SBUF, A

When the bytes are placed in SBUF, it is framed with the start and stop bits and transferred serially via the TXD pin. Similarly, when the bits are received serially via RXD, the 8051 deframes it by eliminating the stop and start bits and placing it in the SBUF.

3.2.2 SCON (Serial Control) Register

> **Q. What is the significance of SCON register of 8051? Explain all the bits of SCON register of 8051.**　　　　　　　　　　**[Nov./Dec. 2011, May/June 2011, 2013]**

The SCON register in an 8-bit register used to program the start bit, stop bit and data bits of data framing, among other things.

D_7	D_6	D_5	D_4	D_3	D_2	D_1	D_0
SM0	SM1	SM2	REN	TB8	RB8	TI	RI

Bits D_7, D_6 : SM0, SM1 (serial port mode specifier)

These two bits determine the framing of data by specifying the number of bits per character and the start and stop bits.

SM0	SM1	
0	0	Mode 0 used as shift register with baud rate (fosc/12)
0	1	Mode 1 used as 8-bit UART baud rate is variable
1	0	Mode 2 used as 9-bit UART baud rate fosc/64 or fosc/32
1	1	Mode 3 used as 9-bit UART baud rate is variable

Bit D_5 : SM2

This bit enables the multiprocessor communication capability of 8051 in mode 2 and 3. In mode 2 or 3, if SM2 = 1 then RI will not be activated if the received 9th data bit (RB8) is 0. In mode 1, if SM2 = 1 then RI will not be activated if a valid stop bit was not received. In mode 1 SM2 should be zero.

Bit D_4 : Receiver Enable (REN)

It is set/reset by software to enable/disable reception.

Bit D_3 : TB8 (Not widely used)

IT is the 9th data bit that will be transmitted in modes 2 and 3.

Bit D_2 : Not widely used (RB8)

It is the 9th data bit that was received in mode 2 and 3.

Bit D_1 : Transmit Interrupt flag (TI)

It is bit D_1 of the SCON register. When 8051 finishes the transfer of the 8-bit character, it raises the TI flag to indicate that it is ready to transfer another byte.

Bit D_0 : Receive Interrupt (RI)

It is the D_0 bit of the SCON register, when 8051 receives data serially via RXD, it raises the RI flag to indicate that it is ready to accept another data byte.

3.3 PROGRAMMING THE 8051 TO TRANSFER DATA SERIALLY

To transfer the data bytes serially, the following steps must be taken.

Step 1 : The TMOD register must be loaded with the value 20H to indicate the use of Timer 1 in mode 2 to set the baud rate.

For e.g. The machine cycle frequency of 8051 = $\frac{11.0592}{12}$ MHz = 921.6 kHz

The frequency provided by UART = $\frac{921.6}{32}$ kHz = 28,800 Hz

(a) To obtain baud rate 9600 = $\frac{28,800}{3}$ = 9600

TH1 = FFH – 3 = FDH

(b) To obtain baud rate 4800 $\frac{28,800}{6}$ = 4800

TH1 = FFH – 6 = FAH

Step 2 : The TH1 must be loaded with one of the values as shown in Table 3.4 to fix the baud rate for serial communication.

Step 3 : SCON register must be loaded with 50H to indicate Serial Mode 1.

Step 4 : TR1 must be set to 1 to start Timer 1.

Step 5 : Clear TI bit using "CLR TI" instruction.

Step 6 : The character byte which is to be transferred must be written into the SBUF register.

Step 7 : Check the TI bit to see whether the character has been transmitted completely or not.

Step 8 : To transfer next byte repeat the steps from 5 onwards.

Program 3.1

Write a program to transfer a letter Y serially at 9600 baud continuously and also to send a letter 'N' through port 0, which is connected to display device.

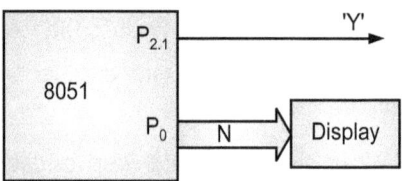

Fig. 3.3

Here one byte of data is transmitted serially through pin 22 (P2.1) and another is sent in parallel form through port 0.

Program :

Label	Instructions	Comments
	MOV TMOD, # 20H	
	MOV TH1, # FDH	; to set baud rate 9600
	MOV SCON, # 50H	; 8-bit, 1 stop, REN enabled
	SETB TR1	; start Timer 1
Again :	MOV SBUF, # 'Y'	; Transfer 'Y' serially
L1 :	JNB TI, L1	; Wait for transmission to be over
	CLR TI	; Clear TI for next transmission
	MOV P$_0$, # 'N'	
	SJMP Again	; repeat.

Program 3.2

Write an assembly language program to send message WELCOME TO COM port of PC at 4800 baud rate. Assume XTAL frequency = 11.0592 MHz.

Program :

Label	Instructions	Comments
	MOV TMOD, # 20H	Timer 1, mode 2
	MOV TH1, # FAH	4800 baud rate
	MOV SCON, # 50H	8 bit 1 stop REN enabled
	SETB TR1	

L1:	MOV A, # 'W'	
	ACALL SERIAL	
	MOV A, # 'E'	
	ACALL SERIAL	
	MOV A, # 'L'	
	ACALL SERIAL	
	MOV A, # 'C'	
	ACALL SERIAL	
	MOV A, # 'O	
	ACALL SERIAL	
	MOV A, # 'M'	
	ACALL SERIAL	
	MOV A, # 'E'	
	ACALL SERIAL	
	SJMP L1	Load SBUF
Serial :	MOV SBUF, A	Put the data in SBUF
L2:	JNB TI, L2	Wait for last bit to transfer
	CLR TI	Get ready for next character byte
	RET	

3.4 PROGRAMMING THE 8051 TO RECEIVER DATA SERIALLY

To receives character bytes serially, the following steps must be taken.

Step 1 : The TMOD should be loaded with the value 20H, to indicate the use of Timer 1 in mode 2, to fix the baud rate.

Step 2 : TH1 should be loaded with one of the values in table 3.4 to set the baud rate.

Step 3 : The SCON register should be loaded with the value 50H to indicate serial mode 1.

Step 4 : TR1 must set to 1 + 0 start timer 1.

Step 5 : RI must be cleared by the instruction 'CLR RI'.

Step 6 : The RI flag must be monitored to see if the entire character has been received or not.

Step 7 : When RI is raised, SBUF has the byte. Its contents are moved into a safe place.

Step 8 : To repeat go to step 5.

Program 3.3

Write a program to receive the data which has been sent in serial form and sent it out to port 0 in parallel form. Also save the data at RAM location 50H.

```
Solution :  MOV TMOD, # 20H      ; Timer 1 mode 2 auto reload
            MOV TH1, # FDH       ; Set 9600 baud rate
            MOV SCON, # 50H      ; 8-bit 1stop, REN enabled
            SETB TR1             ; Start timer 1
            CLR RI               ; RI is cleared for reception
   L1:      JNB RI, L1           ; Wait for character to come in
            MOV A, SBUF          ; Move received data to A
            MOV 50H, A           ; Store at RAM location 50H
            END
```

Program 3.4

Write an assembly program to take data from port 0 and 1, one after the other and transfer data serially continuously.

```
Solution :  ORG 0000H
            LJMP main
            ORG 1000H
Main :      MOV TMOD, # 20H      ; Timer 1 in mode 2
            MOV TH1, # 0FDH      ; Set 9600 Baud rate
            MOV SCON, # 50H      ; Mode 1 for serial communication
            MOV P0, # 0FFH       ; P0 as input port
            MOV P1, # 0FFH       ; P1 as input port
            SETB TR1             ; Run timer 1
Here :      MOV SBUF, P0         ; Send data from P0 to serial port
Wait :      JNB TI, Wait         ; Wait for transmission to complete
            CLR TI
            MOV SBUF, P1           Send data from P1 to serial port
Wait 1 :    JNB TI, wait 1
            CLR TI
            SJMP here
```

Program 3.5

Write an 8051 program to transfer 'WELCOME' Serially at 9600 baud rate continuously.

Label	Instructions	Comments
	MOV TMOD, # 20H	
	MOV TH1, # FDH	
	MOV SCON, # 50H	
	SETB TR1	
L1 :	MOV A, # 'W'	
	ACALL SERIAL	
	MOV A, # 'E'	
	ACALL SERIAL	
	MOV A, # 'L'	
	ACALL SERIAL	
	MOV A, # 'C'	
	ACALL SERIAL	
	MOV A, # 'O'	
	ACALL SERIAL	
	MOV A, # 'M'	
	ACALL SERIAL	
	ACALL SERIAL	
	MOV, # 'E'	
	ACALL SERIAL	
	SJMP L1	Load SBUF
L2 :	JNB TI, L2	Wait for last bit to transfer
	CLR TI	get ready for next byte
	RET	

3.5 DOUBLING THE BAUD RATE IN THE 8051

Baud rate of data transfer in 8051 can be increased in two ways :
1. Use of higher frequency crystal.
2. Change of SMOD bit in PCON register shown below.

D_7							D_0
SMOD	–	–	–	GF1	GF0	PD	IDL

Option 1 is not feasible in many conditions because the system uses fixed crystal frequency. There is a software way to double the baud rate by keeping crystal frequency fixed. This is done by using PCON register.

When the 8051 is powered up, SMOD bit (D7 bit) if the PCON register is zero.

Baud rate when SMOD = 0

When SMOD = 0, the 8051 divides 1/12 of the crystal frequency by 32 and uses that frequency to set the baud rate.

i.e. machine cycle frequency = $\frac{11.0592}{12}$ MHz = 921.6 kHz and $\frac{921.6 \text{ kHz}}{32}$ = 28,800 Hz.

Since SMOD = 0.

Baud rate for SMOD = 1

By keeping fixed crystal frequency, we can double the baud rate by making SMOD = 1.

When SMOD = 1, 1/12 of crystal frequency is divided by 16 instead of 32, which is used to set the baud rate. i.e. machine cycle frequency = $\frac{11.0592}{12}$ MHz = 921.6 kHz and $\frac{921.6 \text{ kHz}}{16}$ = 57,600 Hz since SMOD = 1.

Table 3.5 : Shows the comparison for SMOD = 0 and SMOD = 1

TH1 (decimal)	TH1 (hex)	SMOD = 0	SMOD = 1
- 3	FD	9600	19,200
- 6	FA	4800	9,600
- 12	F4	2400	4800
- 24	E8	1200	2400

Program 3.6

Port 0 of an 8051 is used to monitor a parameter in an industrial environment. If the parameter gives a reading above 5AH, a message 'HI' is to be sent serially. Otherwise a message 'OK' is to be sent. Write an assembly language program to send information 'HI' or 'OK' according to the parameter on P0 start from her.

Solution : Program :

```
        ORG 0090H
MSG 1:  DB  "HI"
        ORG 00A0H
MSG 2:  DB  "OK"
        END
        ORG 0000H
        MOV P0, # 0FFH
```

```
                MOV TMOD, # 20H
                MOV TH1, # FDH
                MOV SCON, # 50H
                SETB TR1
CHECK :         MOV A, P0                  ; Move P0 into A
                CJNE A, # 5AH, TEST        ; Check if it is equal to 5A if not go to test
                SJMP OK                    ; if equal to 5AH, go to OK
Test :          JNC HI                     ; if it is greater than 05AH, go to HI
OK :            MOV DPTR, # 00A0H          ; let DPTR point to message OK
                ACALL PARAMETER            ; call subroutine to access message ROM
                                             area
                SJMP check                 ; Monitor P0 continuously
HI :            MOV DPTR, # 0090H          ; let DPTR point to message HI
                ACALL PARAMETER            ; call subroutine to access message area
                SJMP CHECK                 ; monitor P0 continuously
PARAMETER:      CLR A
                MOVC A, @ A + DPTR
                ACALL SEND
                INC DPTR                   Subroutine to access program ROM area
                CLR A                      where messages are stored.
                MOVC A, @ A + DPTR
                ACALL SEND
                RET
SEND :          MOV SBUF, A
L1 :            JNB TI, L1                 Subroutine to send data serially.
                CLR TI
                RET
```

Program 3.7

A square wave is being generated at pin P1.5. This square wave is to be sent to a receiver connected in serial form to 8051. Write an assembly language program.

Solution : Timer 0 mode 2 is used to generate a square wave on pin 1.5. Whenever this pin goes high, a data FFH is transmitted serially and when this pin goes low, a data 00H is transmitted. This data can be converted in parallel form at the receiver side to regenerate the square wave there

```
            ORG 0000H
            MOV TMOD, # 22H       ;  Timer 0 and Timer 1 in mode 2
            MOV SCON, # 50H
            MOV TH1, # FDH
            MOV TH0, # 00H        ;  Count value for timer 0
            SETB TR1              ;  start timer 1
            MOV A, # 00H             move A, = 00
            CLR P1.5
HERE :      SETB TR0              ;  start timer 0
L1 :        JNB TF0, L1           ;  wait for timer 0 rollover
            CPL A                 ;  complement A
            CPL P1.5              ;  complement P1.5
            MOV SBUF, A           ;  move A to SBUF for transmission
            CLR TR0               ;  stop timer 0
            CLR TF0               ;  clear timer 0 flag
L2 :        JNB TI, L2            ;  check for TI flag
            CLR TI                ;  clear TI to enable next transmission
            SJMP HERE             ;  repeat again
            END
```

3.6 PROGRAMMING THE SECOND SERIAL PORT

The new generations of 8051 microcontroller comes with two serial ports. For example, DS89C420/30/40 and DS80C320.

The second serial port of the DS89C4X0 uses pins P1.2 and P1.3 for the RX and TX lines.

It uses MAX 232 for the RS232 connection to DB9. Fig. 3.4 shows the Max 232 connection to DS.89C4X0. The first and second serial port are named as serial # 0 and serial # 1 respectively.

The SCON has address 98H, SBUF has address 99H and PCON has 87H. The first serial port is supported by all assemblers and C compilers. The second serial port is not implemented by all versions of the 8051/52 microcontroller. Only a few versions of 8051/52. For example, DS89C4X0 come with the second serial port. Therefore, the second serial port uses some reserved SFR addresses for the SCON and SBUF registers.

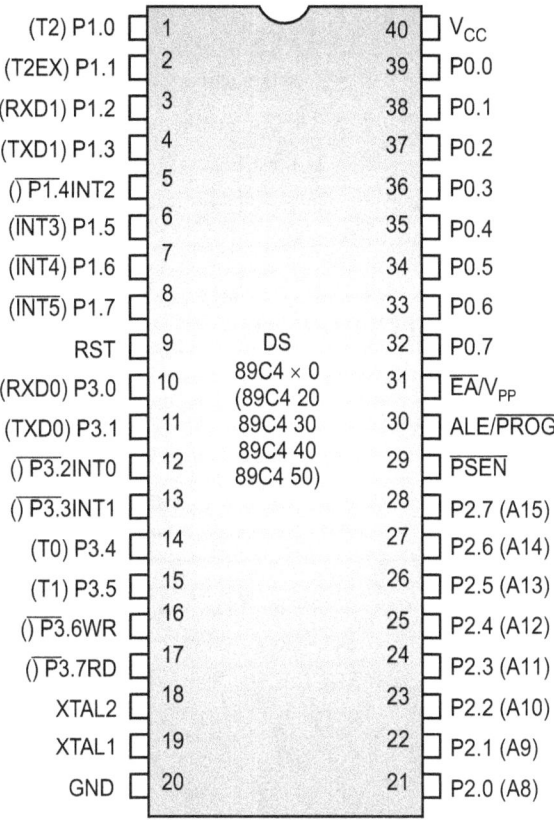

Fig. 3.4 : Pin diagram of DS89C4X0

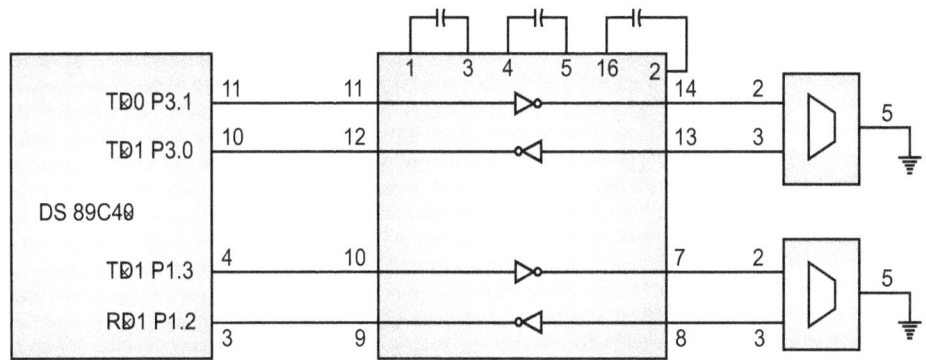

Fig. 3.5 : Max 232 connection to the DS89C4X0

Table 3.6 : Lists the SFR byte addresses for DS89C4X0 serial ports

SFR (byte address)	First serial port	Second serial port
SCON	SCON 0 = 98H	SCON 1 = C0H
SBUF	SBUF 0 = 99H	SBUF 1 = C1H
TL	TL1 = 8BH	TL1 = 8BH
TH	TH1 = 8DH	TH1 = 8DH
TCON	TCON 0 = 88H	TCON 0 = 88H
PCON	PCON = 87H	PCON = 87H

Programming the Second Serial Port using Timer 1 :

Each signal port has its own SCON and SBUF registers, both ports can use Timer 1 for setting the baud rate. On reset the chip DS89C4X0 uses Timer 1 for setting the baud rate of both serial ports. To avoid confusion in DS89C4X0 programs we use SCON 0 and SBUF 0 for the first and SCON 1 and SBUF 1 for the second serial ports.

SM0	SM1	SM2	REN	TB8	RB8	TI	RI

Bits	Serial # 0	Serial # 1
SM0	SCON 0.7 = 9FH	SCON 1.7 = C7H
SM1	SCON 0.6 = 9EH	SCON 1.6 = C6H
SM2	SCON 0.5 = 9DH	SCON 1.5 = C5H
REN	SCON 0.4 = 9CH	SCON 1.4 = C4H
TB8	SCON 0.3 = 9BH	SCON 1.3 = C3H
RB8	SCON 0.2 = 9AH	SCON 1.2 = C2H
TI	SCON 0.1 = 99H	SCON 1.1 = C1H
RI	SCON 0.0 = 98H	SCON 1.0 = C0H

Program 3.8

Write a program to continuously transfer letter A serially at 9600 baud. Use 8-bit data and 1 stop bit. Use timer 1.

Solution :

```
         SBUF1   EQU  0C1H        Second serial SBUF address
         SCON1   EQU  0C0H        Second serial SCON address
         TI1     BIT  0C1H        Second serial TI bit address
         RI1     BIT  0C0H        Second serial RI bit address
         ORG     000H             Starting position
Main :   MOV TMOD, # 20H          COM 2 uses timer 1 upon reset
         MOV TH1, # -3            9600 baud rate
         MOV SCON1, # 50H         COM 2 has its own SCON 1
         SETB TR1                 Start timer 1
```

L3 :	MOV A, # 'A'		Send character 'A'
	ACAL L1		
	SJMP L3		
L1 :	MOV SBUF1, A	;	COM2 has its own SBUF
L2 :	JNB TI1, L2		COM2 has its own TI flag
	CLR TI1		
	RET		
	END		

Program 3.9

Write a program to send text string WELCOME to serial # 1. Set the baud rate at 4800 8-bit data and 1 stop bit.

Solution : SCON1 EQU   0C0H
         SBUF1 EQU   0C1H
         TI1   BIT   0C1H
         ORG 0000H   ; Starting position
         MOV TMOD, # 20H
         MOV TH1, # –6   ; 4800 baud rate
         MOV SCON1, # 50H
         SETB TR1
         MOV DPTR, # MSG   ; display "WELCOME"
L3 :   CLR A
         MOVC A, @ A + DPTR   ; read value
         JZ L1   ; check for end of line
         ACALL L2   ; send to serial port
         INC DPTR   ; move to next value
         SJMP L3
L1 :   SJMP L1
L2 :   MOV SBUF1, A   ; place value in Buffer
HERE :   JNB TI1, HERE   ; wait until transmitted
         CLR TI1   ; clear
         RET
MSG :   DB "WELCOME", 0
         END

Program 3.10

Program the second serial port to receive bytes of data serially and put them on P1.

Solution:
```
        SBUF1  EQU   0C1H          ; second serial SBUF address
        SCON1  EQU   0C0H          ; second serial SCON address
        RI1    BIT   0C0H          ; second serial RI bit add
        ORG    0000H               ; starting location
        MOV    TMOD, # 20H         ; COM2 uses timer 1 upon reset
        MOV    TH1, # -3           ; 9600 baud rate
        MOV    SCON1, # 50H        ; COM2 has its own SCON1
        SETB   TR1                 ; start timer 1
L1:     JNB    RI1, L1             ; wait for data to come in
        MOV A, SBUF1                ; save data
        MOV P1, A                   ; display on P1
        CLR RI1
        SJMP L1
        END
```

Program 3.11

Assume that a switch is connected to pin P1.0. Write a program to monitor the switch and perform the following:

(a) If SW = 0 send the message "WELCOME" to the serial #0 port.
(b) If SW = 1 send the message "BYE" to the serial # 1 port.

Solution:
```
MSG1:   DB     "WELCOME", 0
MSG2:   DB     "BYE", 0
        SCON1  EQU   0C0H
        TI1    BIT   0C1H
        SW1    BIT   P1.0
        ORG    0000H
        MOV    TMOD, # 20H
        MOV    TH1, # -6            ; 4800 baud rate
        MOV    SCON, # 50H
        MOV    SCON1, # 50H
        SETB   TR1
        SETB   SW1                  ; make SW1 an input
```

L2 :	JB SW1, L1	; check SW1 status
	MOV DPTR, # MSG1	if SW1 = 0 display "WELCOME"
L3 :	CLR A	
	MOVC A, @ A + DPTR	; read value
	JZ L2	; check for end of line
	ACALL SENDCOM1	; send to serial port
	INC DPTR	; move to next value
	SJMP L3	
L1 :	MOV DPTR, # MSG2	; if SW1 = 1 display "BYE"
L4 :	CLR A	
	MOVC A, @ A + DPTR	; real value
	JZ L2	; check for end of line
	ACALL SENDCOM2	; send to serial port
	INC DPTR	; move to next value
	SJMP L4	
SENDCOM1 :		
	MOV SBUF, A	; place value in buffer
HERE :	JNB TI, HERE	; wait until transmitted
	CLR TI	; clear
	RET	
SENDCOM2 :		
	MOV SBUF1, A	; place value in buffer
HERE 1 :	JNB TI1, HERE 1	; wait until transmitted
	CLR TI1	; clear
	RET	

3.7 SERIAL PORT PROGRAMMING IN C

The SFR registers can be accessed directly in 8051C using the reg51.h file. To use the second serial port byte address of new SFR registers must be declared.

Program 3.12

Write a program in 8051C to transfer the message "HELLO" serially at 4800 baud, 8-bit data and 1 stop bit. Do this continuously.

Solution :

```c
# include <reg51.h>
void serTX (unsigned char);
void main (void)
{
  TMOD = 0X20;
  TH1 = 0XFA;
  SCON = 0X50;
  TR1 = 1
  while (1)
  {
    SerTX ('H');
    SerTX ('E');
    SerTX ('L');
    SerTX ('L');
    SerTX ('O');
  }
}
void SerTX (unsigned char x)
{
  SBUF = x;
  while (TI ==0);
  TI = 0;
}
```

Program 3.13

Write a program in 8051C to receive bytes of data serially and put them in P_2 set the baud rate at 9600, 8-bit data and 1 stop bit.

Solution :

```c
# include <reg51.h>
void main (void)
{
  unsigned char mybyte;
  TMOD = 0X20;
  TH1 = 0XFD;
  SCON = 0X50;
```

```
   TR1 = 1;
   while (1)
   {
      while (RI ==0);
      mybyte = SBUF;
      P2 = mybyte;
      RI = 0;
   }
}
```

Program 3.14

Write an 8051C program to send two different strings to the serial port. Assuming that SW is connected to pin P1.0, monitor its status and make a decision as follows :

      SW = 0   ;   Send "ANKITA"
      SW = 1   ;   Send "LOKHANDE"

Assume XTAL = 11.0592 MHz, baud rate of 4800, 8-bit data, 1 stop bit.

Solution :

```
# include <reg51.h>
Sbit MYSW = P1^0;
void main (void)
{
   unsigned char x;
   unsigned char S1[ ] = "ANKITA";
   unsigned char S2[ ] = "LOKHANDE";
   TMOD = 0X20;
   TH1 = 0XFA;
   SCON = 0X50;
   TR1 = 1;
   if {MYSW ==0)
   {
      for (x = 0; x < 6, x++)
      {
         SBUF = S1 [x];
         while (TI == 0);
         TI = 0;
      }
```

```c
    }
    else
    {
        for (x = 0; x < 8; x++)
        {
            SBUF = S2 [x];
            while (TI == 0);
            TI = 0;
        }
    }
}
```

Program 3.15

Write an 8051C program to send the two messages "WELCOME" and "GOODBYE" to the serial port. Assuming that SW is connected to pin P1.0 monitor its status and set the baud rate as follows :

    SW = 0 9600 baud rate

    SW = 1 56K baud rate

Assume that XTAL = 11.0592 MHz for both cases.

Solution :

```c
# include <reg51.h>
Sbit MYSW = P1^0;
void main (void)
{
    unsigned char x;
    unsigned char MSG1 [ ] = "WELCOME";
    unsigned char MSG2 [ ] = "GOODBYE";
    TMOD = 0X20;
    TH1 = 0XFD;
    SCON = 0X50;
    TR1 = 1;
    if (MYSW == 0)
    {
        for (x = 0; x < 8; x++)
        {
            SBUF = MSG1 [x];
```

```
      while (TI == 0);
      TI = 0;
    }
  }
  else
  {
    PCON = PCON|0X80;
    for (x = 0; x < 8; x++)
    {
      SBUF = MSG2 [x];
      while (TI == 0);
      TI = 0;
    }
  }
}
```

Program 3.16

Write a C program to transfer letter 'A' serially at 4800 baud continuously. Use the second serial port with 8-bit data and 1 stop bit. We can only use Timer 1 to set the baud rate.

Solution :

```
# include <reg51.h>
Sfr SBUF1 = 0XC1;
Sfr SCON1 = 0XC0;
Sbit TI1 = 0XC1;
void main (void)
{
  TMOD = 0X20;
  TH1 = 0XFA;
  SCON1 = 0X50;
  TR1 = 1;
  while (1)
  {
    SBUF1 = 'A'
    while (TI1 == 0);
    TI1 = 0;
  }
}
```

Program 3.17

Write a program to generate two square waves - one of 5 KHz frequency at pin 1.3 and another of frequency 25 KHz at pin P2.3. Assume XTAL = 22 MHz.

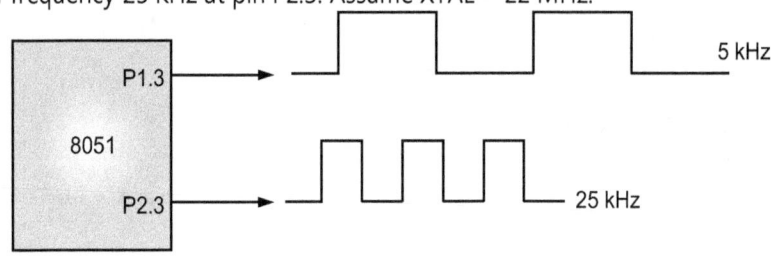

Fig. 3.6

Solution :

```
        ORG  0000H
        LJMP MAIN
// ISR for Timer 0
        ORG 000B              ; interrupt vector for Timer 0
        CPL P1.3
        RETI
// ISR for Timer 1
        ORG 001BH             ; interrupt vector for Timer 1
        CPL P2.3
        RETI
// Main program for initialization
        ORG 0030H
MAIN :  MOV TMOD, # 22H
        MOV IE, # 8AH
        MOV TH0, # 048H
        MOV TH1, # 0B6H
        SETB TR0
        SETB TR1
WAIT :  SJMP WAIT
        END
```

Program 3.18

Write a program to toggle pin P1.4 every second.

Solution : To obtain delay of 1 second, we need to use a register, in addition to a timer. Here register R_0 is used along with timer 1.

```
    ORG 0000H
    LJMP MAIN
// ISR for timer 1 to generate square wave
    ORG 001BH
    DJNZ R0, START
    CPL P1.4                    toggle P1.4 every second
    MOV R0, # 28                reload register value
    MOV TL1, # 00H              reload counter value
    MOV TH1, # 00H              reload counter value
START: RETI
// main program for initilization
    ORG 0030H
    MOV TMOD, 10H               Timer 1, mode 1
    MOV IE, # 88H               enable time 1 interrupt
    MOV R0, # 28                count for 1 second delay
    MOV TL1, # 00H              count value for TL1
    MOV TH1, # 00H              count value for TH1
    SETB TR1
L1 :  SJMP L1
```

In the main program the TL1 and TH1 are initialized but they have to be reloaded in the ISR. The register R0 is monitored in the ISR, because each time the timer flag is set, an interrupt is generated. This interrupt has to occur 28 times to get a delay of 1 second.

3.8 PROGRAMMING EXTERNAL HARDWARE INTERRUPT

> **Q. Compare edge triggered interrupts with level triggered interrupts. Illustrate how 8051 differentiates in these two.** [May/June 2012]

The 8051 has two external hardware interrupts designated as INT0 and INT1. These are used as external hardware interrupts at the pin 12 (P3.2) and pin 13 (P3.3) of the 8051. When these pins are activated, the 8051 gets interrupted and jumps to the location of interrupt vector table to execute interrupt service routine. For INT0 and INT1, 0003H and 0013H locations are reserved in interrupt vector table respectively. They can be enabled or disabled using IE register.

There are two types of activation for the external hardware interrupts :
(1) Level triggered,   (2) Edge triggered

In level triggered mode, if the INT0 and INT1 pins are high and a low level signal is applied to them then interrupt occurs. The microcontroller executes its current instruction and serves the interrupt service routine by jumping to the location in the interrupt vector table before execution of RETI instruction the low-level signal must be removed from the pin.

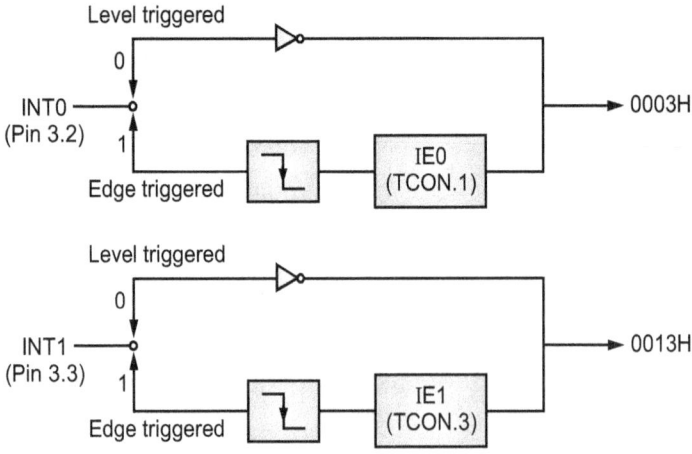

Fig. 3.7 : Activation of INT0 and INT1

The 8051 makes INT0 and INT1 low level triggered interrupts upon reset. To make INT0 and INT1 edge triggered, the bits of the TCON register must be programmed. IT0 and IT1 bits of the TCON register determines the level or edge-triggered mode of the hardware interrupts upon reset, these two bit are 0's meaning level-triggered interrupts. With the help of "SETB TCON.0" and "SETB TCON.2" the external hardware interrupt becomes edge triggered.

D_7	D_6	D_5	D_4	D_3	D_2	D_1	D_0
TF_1	TR_1	TF_0	TR_0	IE_1	IT_1	IE_0	IT_0

Fig. 3.8 : TCON register

Program 3.19

Write a program to generate a square wave that is half the frequency of signal applied at INT0 pin on port 1.

Solution :

```
        ORG 0000H
        LJMP MAIN
        ORG 0003H           address of interrupt 0
        CPL P1
        RETI
```

MAIN :	SETB TCON.0	activate $\overline{INT0}$ interrupt
	MOV IE, # 81H	enable hardware interrupt $\overline{INT0}$
L1 :	SJMP L1	
	END	

Program 3.20

Write an assembly language program to switch ON and OFF a LED connected on P1.5 when external interrupt $\overline{INT0}$ is activated.

Solution :

```
         ORG 0000H
         LJMP MAIN
         ORG 0003H
         SETB P1.5
L1 :     MOV R0, # 300H
         DJNZ R0, L1
         RETI
         ORG 0030H
MAIN :   MOV IE, # 81H        ; Enable INT0
L2 :     SJMP L2
         END
```

Program 3.21

Two switches are connected to pins P3.2 and P3.3, when a switch is pressed, the corresponding line goes low. Write a program to

(a) Light all LEDs connected to port 0, if the first switch is pressed.
(b) Light all LEDs connected to port 2, if the second switch is pressed.

Pin 3.2 is pin for interrupt 0 and pin 3.3 is pin for interrupt 1.

Solution :

	ORG 0000H	By pass interrupt vector table
	LJMP MAIN	
	ORG 0003H	Interrupt vector address for interrupt to
L1 :	MOV P0, # 0FFH	Turn ON LEDs of port 0
	MOV R0, # 500	
	DJNZ R0, L1	Keep all LEDs on for a short time
	RETI	
	ORG 0013H	Interrupt vector address for interrupt 1

L2 :	MOV P2, # 0FFH	turn on all LEDs of port 2
	MOV R0, # 500	
	DJNZ R0, L2	
	RETI	
	ORG 0030H	
MAIN:	MOV IE, # 85H	Enable $\overline{INT0}$ and $\overline{INT1}$
L3 :	SJMP L3	
	END	

3.9 PROGRAMMING THE SERIAL COMMUNICATION INTERRUPTS

Two flag bits RI and TI are used for serial port interrupt. The serial interrupt is mainly used for receiving data and is never used for sending data serially.

In 8051 only one interrupt is set aside for serial communication. This interrupt is used to both send and receive data. If the interrupt bit in the IE register is enabled, when RI or TI is raised the 8051 gets interrupted enabled, when RI or TI is raised the 8051 gets interrupted and jumps to memory location 0023H to execute ISR. To provide a single interrupt, TI and RI are ORed together.

Program 3.22

Write a program in which the 8051 reads data from P1 and writes it to P2 continuously while giving a copy of it to the serial COM port to be transferred serially. Assume XTAL = 11.0592 MHz. Set the baud rate 4800.

Solution :	ORG 0000H	
	LJMP MAIN	
	ORG 0023H	
	LJMP SERIAL	jump to serial interrupt ISR
	ORG 0030H	
MAIN :	MOV P1, # FFH	make P1 an input port
	MOV TMOD, # 20H	timer 1 mode 2
	MOV TH1, # 0FAH	4800 baud rate
	MOV SCON, # 50H	8-bit, 1 stop, REN enabled
	MOV IE, # 10010000B	enabled serial interrupt
	SETB TR1	start timer 1

BACK :	MOV A, P1	read data from port 1
	MOV SBUF, A	give a copy to SBUF
	MOV P2, A	send it to P2
	SJMP BACK	stay in loop indefinitely
	// Serial port ISR	
	ORG 0100H	
Serial :	JB TI, L1	jump if TI is high
	MOV A, SBUF	
	CLR RI	clear RI
	RETI	return from ISR
L1 :	CLR TI	clear TI
	RETI	
	END	

Program 3.23

Write a program in which 10 bytes of data stored in RAM locations starting from 45H are transferred serially. At the end of data transfer, the value of R0 is displayed on P1.

Solution :	ORG 0000H	
	LJMP MAIN	
	ORG 0023H	
	LJMP L1	
	ORG 0030H	
MAIN :	MOV TMOD, # 20H	
	MOV TH1, # 0FDH	set baud rate
	MOV SCON, # 50H	8-bit, 1 stop, REN enabled
	MOV IE, # 90H	serial port interrupt enable
	SETB TR1	start timer 1
	MOV R0, # 10	counter for no. of bytes
	MOV R1, # 45H	RI is the pointer to the RAM
BACK :	MOV A, @ R1	move data from RAM to A
	MOV SBUF, A	data to be transmitted is loaded into SBUF
	DJNZ R0, BACK	repeat till all data is sent
HERE :	SJMP HERE	
	// Serial port ISR	

L1 :	JNB TI, L2	if TI is not high, it implies reception
	MOV A, R0	If TI is high, move value of R0 into A
	MOV P1, A	transfer it to P1
	CLR TI	clear TI for next transmission
	RETI	
L2 :	MOV A, SBUF	if reception, move received data to SBUF
	CLR RI	clear RI to enable next reception
	RETI	
	END	

Program 3.24

Write a program to :

(a) Generate a square wave at P1.5 using timer 0 in mode 1, interrupt mode.

(b) Take data from port P2 and send it serially and continuously.

(c) When INT0 is activated, port P0 is made 0 for a short time, to switch off the LEDs connected to it. The LEDs will also remain OFF if the switch connected to INT0 pin (P3.2) is kept pressed.

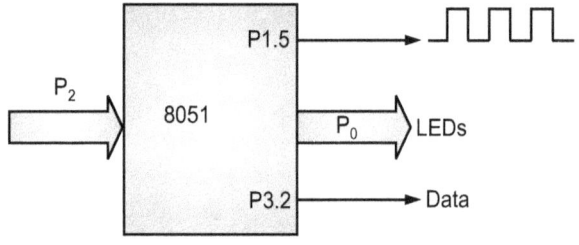

Fig. 3.9

Solution : ORG 0000H
        LJMP MAIN
// Timer 0 ISR
        ORG 000BH
        CPL P1.5
        MOV TH0, # 00H
        MOV TL0, # 0F0H
        RETI
// INT0 interrupt vector
        ORG 0003H
        SJMP LED

```
// Serial port interrupt vector
        ORG 0023H
        LJMP SERIAL
// main program for initialization
        ORG 0030H
        MOV P2, # 0FFH
        MOV TMOD, # 21H
        MOV TH1, # 0FDH
        MOV TH0, # 00H
        MOV TL0, # 0F0H
        MOV SCON, # 50H
        MOV IE, # 93H
        SETB TR1
        SETB TR0
BACK :  MOV A, P2
        MOV SBUF, A
        SJMP BACK
// serial port ISR
SERIAL : JNB TI, L1
        CLR TI
        RETI
L1 :    MOV A, SBUF
        CLR RI
        RETI
// ISR for INT0
LED :   MOV P0, # 00H
        MOV R0, # 0FFH
HERE :  DJNZ R0, HERE
        MOV P0, # 0FFH
        RETI
        END
```

3.10 INTERRUPT PROGRAMMING IN C

The C compiler uses interrupt number to identify the interrupt. Each interrupt is assigned a unique number as shown in Table 3.7.

Table 3.7

Interrupt	Name	Numbers used by 8051C
External Interrupt 0	$\overline{INT0}$	0
Timer interrupt 0	TF0	1
External interrupt 1	$\overline{INT1}$	2
Timer interrupt 1	TF1	3
Serial communication	RI + TI	4
Timer 2 (8052 only)	TF2	5

Program 3.25

Write a C program that continuously gets a single bit of data from P2.6 and sends it to P2.4 in the main, while simultaneously (i) Creating a square wave of 2 microsecond on pin P2.5 and (ii) Sending letter A to the serial port. Use Timer 0 to create the square wave. Assume XTAL = 11.0592 MHz. Use 4800 baud rate, we will use Timer 2 in mode 2 (auto reload)

Solution :

```
# include <reg51.h>
Sbit inbit = P2^6
Sbit outbit = P2^4
Sbit wave = P2^5
void timer 0 (void) interrupt 1
{
   wave = ~ wave;
}
void serial 0 (void) interrupt 4
{
  if (TI == 1)
  {
     SBUF = 'A';
     TI = 0;
  }
  else
```

```
    {
       RI = 0;
    }
}
void main ()
{
   inbit = 1;
   TH1 = -6;
   TMOD = 0X22;
   SCON = 0X50;
   TR0 = 1;
   TR1 = 1;
   IE = 0X92;
   while (1)
   {
      outbit = inbit;
   }
}
```

Program 3.26

Write a C program that continuously receives a single bit of data from P1.5 and sends it to P2.2 while simultaneously creating a square wave of 4500 μs on pin P2.4. Use timer 0 to create the square wave. Assume that XTAL = 11.0592 MHz.

Solution : Timer 0 in mode 2 Half period = 200 μs

$$\therefore \frac{200}{1.085 \text{ μs}} = 184$$

TH0 = 256 − 184 = 72 i.e. 48H

Program :

```
# include <reg51.h>
Sbit inbit = P1^5
Sbit outbit = P2^2
Sbit wave = P2^4
void timer 0 (void) interrupt 1
```

```
{
    wave = ~ wave;
}
void main (void)
{
    inbit = 1;
    TMOD = 0X02;
    TH0 = 0X72;
    IE = 0X82;
    while (1)
    {
        outbit = inbit;
    }
}
```

Program 3.27

Write a C program using interrupts to do the following :

(a) Receive data serially and send it to P0.

(b) Read port P1 transmit data serially and give a copy to P2.

(c) Make timer 0 generate square wave of 5 kHz on P0.1.

Assume XTAL = 11.0592 MHz. Set baud rate 4800.

Solution :

```
# include <reg51.h>
Sbit signal = P0^2
void timer 0( ) interrupt 1
{
    signal = ~ signal;
}
void serial 0 ( ) interrupt 4
{
    if (TI == 1)
    {
        TI = 0;
    }
```

```
    else
    {
        P0 = SBUF;
        RI = 0;
    }
}
void main ( )
unsigned char i;
P1 = 0XFF;
TMOD = 0X22;
TH1 = 0XF0;
SCON = 0X50;
TH0 = 0XA4;
IE = 0X92;
TR1 = 1;
TR0 = 1
while (1)
{
    i = P1;
    SBUF = i;
    P2 = i;
}
```

Program 3.28

Write a C program using interrupts to do the following :

(a) Generate a 10,000 Hz frequency on P1.4 using to 8-bit autoreload.

(b) Use timer 1 as event counter to count up a 1 Hz pulse and display it on port 0. The pulse is connected to EXI.

Assume that XTAL = 11.0592 MHz. Set baud rate at 9600.

Solution : Count calculation $\dfrac{1}{10{,}000}$ = 100 µs

$$\text{Half cycle period} = \dfrac{100\ \mu s}{2} = 50\ \mu s$$

$$= \dfrac{50\ \mu s}{1.085\ \mu s} = 46$$

Program :

```c
# include <reg51.h>
Sbit signal = P1^5
unsigned char count;
void timer 0 ( ) interrupt 1
{
  signal = ~ signal;
}
void timer 1 ( ) interrupt 3
{
  count ++;
  P0 = count;
}
void main ( )
{
  count = 0;
  TMOD = 0X42;
  TH0 = 0X-46;
  IE = 0X86;
  TR0 = 1;
  while (1)
}
```

Chapter - 4

INTERFACING OF 8051

4.1 LCD INTERFACING

Q. Illustrate functions, ISRs and tasks [8 M] [May/June 2011]

LCD can be used to display any character. In recent years the LCD is widely used by replacing LEDs.

LCD has following advantages :

1. It has the ability to display numbers, characters and graphics.
2. Use of refreshing controller into the LCD relieves the CPU.
3. Easiness of programming for characters and graphics.
4. Low cost.

A typical 16 × 2 LCD is shown in Fig. 4.1.

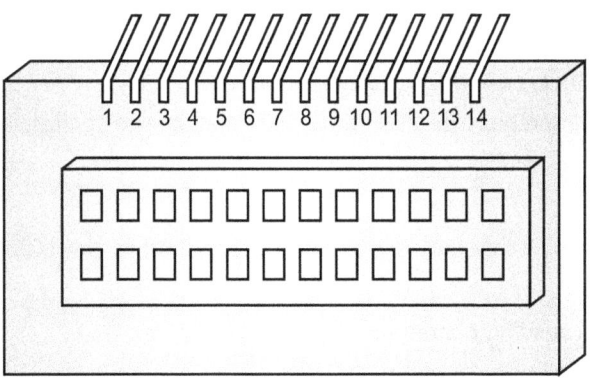

Fig. 4.1 : Structure of 16 × 2 LCD

4.1.1 LCD Pin Descriptions

The typical 16 × 2 LCD has 14 pins and the functions of the pins of LCD are listed in Table 4.1.

Table 4.1

Pin	Symbol	Input/Output	Description
1	V_{SS}	–	Ground
2	V_{CC}	–	+ 5V power supply
3	V_{EE}	–	Power supply to control contrast
4	RS	I	RS = 0 to select command register RS = 1 to select data register
5	R/W	I	R/W = 0 for write, R/W = 1 for read
6	E	I/O	Enable
7	DB0	I/O	The 8 bit data bus
8	DB1	I/O	The 8 bit data bus
9	DB2	I/O	The 8 bit data bus
10	DB3	I/O	The 8 bit data bus
11	DB4	I/O	The 8 bit data bus
12	DB5	I/O	The 8 bit data bus
13	DB6	I/O	The 8 bit data bus
14	DB7	I/O	The 8 bit data bus

RS; Register Select

There are two registers inside the LCD. The RS pin is used to select one of the registers.

If RS = 0, the instruction command code register is selected to allow the user to send a command. For example, clear display, cursor at home etc.

If RS = 1, the data register is selected to allow the user to send data to be displayed on the LCD.

R/W read/write :

This pin is used to allow the user to write information to the LCD or read information from it.

When R/W = 1 reading operation

When R/W = 0 writing operation

E, enable :

This pin is used to latch the data from the data pins. When data is supplied to data pins, a high-to-low pulse must be applied to this pin in order to latch the data present at the data pins. This pulse is of minimum 450 ns wide.

D₀ – D₇ :

The 8-bit data pins are used to send information to the LCD. When RS = 1, we can display letters and numbers by sending ASCII codes to these pins. When RS = 0, these pins are used to check busy flag bit to see if the LCD is ready to receive information. When R/W = 1, RS = 0 the busy flag is D_7 and can be read D_7 = 1.

When D_7 = 0, LCD is ready to receive new information.

4.1.2 LCD Command Codes

The commands which can be given to the LCD are listed in the Table 4.2.

Table 4.2

Code CHEX	Command to LCD Instruction Register
1	Clear display screen
2	Return home
4	Decrement cursor (Shift cursor to left)
6	Increment cursor (shift cursor to right)
5	Shift display right
7	Shift display left
8	Display OFF, cursor OFF
A	Display OFF, cursor ON
C	Display ON, cursor OFF
E	Display ON, cursor blinking
F	Display ON, cursor blinking
10	Shift cursor position to left
14	Shift cursor position to right
18	Shift the entire display to the left
1C	Shift the entire display to the right
80	Force cursor to beginning of 1st line
C0	Force cursor to beginning of 2nd line
38	2 lines and 5 × 7 matrix.

To send any of the above command to the LCD RS should be 0. To send data, RS = 1 then send a high-to-low pulse to the E pin to enable the internal latch of the LCD.

Table 4.3 : The list of LCD instructions

Instruction	RS	R/W	DB$_7$	DB$_6$	DB$_5$	DB$_4$	DB$_3$	DB$_2$	DB$_1$	DB$_0$	Description	Execution time (max)
Clear display	0	0	0	0	0	0	0	0	0	1	Clear entire display and sets DD RAM address 0 in address counter	1.64 ms
Return home	0	0	0	0	0	0	0	0	1	-	Set DD RAM address 0 as address counter. Also returns display being shifted to original position. DD RAM contents remain unchanged	1.64 ms
Entry mode set	0	0	0	0	0	0	0	1	1/D	S	Sets cursor move direction and specifies shift of display. These operations are performed during data write and read	40 µs
Display ON/ OFF control	0	0	0	0	0	0	1	D	C	B	Sets on/off of entire display (D), cursor ON/OFF (C) and blink of cursor position character (B)	40 µs
Cursor or display shift	0	0	0	0	0	1	S/C	R/L	-	-	Moves cursor and shifts display without changing DD RAM contents	40 µs
Function set	0	0	0	0	1	DL	N	F	-	-	Sets interface data length (DL) number of display lines (L) and character font (F)	40 µs

... *(Contd.)*

Instruction	RS	R/W	DB$_7$	DB$_6$	DB$_5$	DB$_4$	DB$_3$	DB$_2$	DB$_1$	DB$_0$	Description	Execution time (max)
Set CG RAM address	0	0	0	1		AGC					Set CG RAM address, CG RAM data is sent and received after this setting	40 μs
Set DD RAM address	0	0	1			ADD					Set DD RAM address. DD RAM data is sent and received after this setting.	40 μs
Read BUSY flag and address	0	1	BF			AC					Read Busy flag (BF) indicating internal operation is being performed and reads address counter contents	40 μs
Write Data CG OR DD RAM	1	0				Write data					Writes data into DD or CG RAM	
Read data CG or DD RAM	1	1				Read data					Read data from DD or CGRAM	40 μs

* **DD RAM – Display Data RAM**
* **CG RAM – Character Generator RAM**

4.1.3 LCD Connections

Fig. 4.2 shows the interfacing of 20 character X2 line LCD module with 8051. The data lines are connected to port 1 of 8051. The control lines RS, R/W are driven by port 2 pins P2.0, P2.1 and P2.2. The voltage at VEE pin is adjusted by potentiometer to adjust the contrast of the LCD.

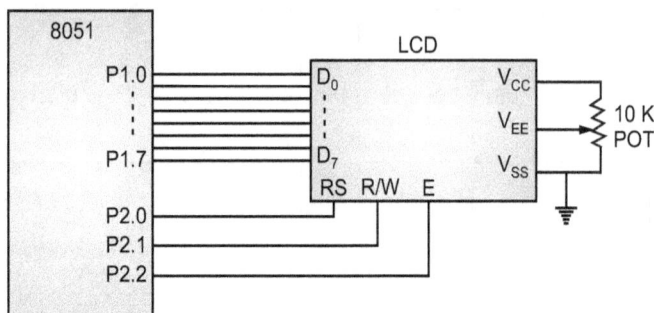

Fig. 4.2 : LCD connections

4.1.4 LCD Addressing

In LCD, data can be put at any location. The following shows address locations and how they are accessed.

Table 4.4 : LCD Addressing

	DB_7	DB_6	DB_5	DB_4	DB_3	DB_2	DB_1	DB_0
Line 1 (min)	1	0	0	0	0	0	0	0
Line 1 (max)	1	0	1	0	0	1	1	1
Line 2 (min)	1	1	0	0	0	0	0	0
Line 2 (max)	1	1	1	0	0	1	1	1

Table 4.5 : Shows cursor addresses for LCD

16 × 2 LCD	80 81 82 83 84 85 86 through 8F
	C0 C1 C2 C3 C4 C5 C6 through CF
20 × 1 LCD	80 81 82 83 through 93
20 × 2 LCD	80 81 82 83 through 93
	C0 C1 C2 C3 through D3
20 × 4 LCD	80 81 82 83 through 93
	C0 C1 C2 C3 through 93
	94 95 96 97 through A_7
	D_4 D_5 D_6 D_7 through E_7
40 × 2 LCD	80 81 82 83 through A_7
	C0 C1 C2 C3 through E_7

Program 4.1

Interface 2 line, 16 character LCD display to 8051 using only one port. Write assembly language program to display message 'WELCOME' on line 2 of LCD.

Solution : Fig. 4.3 shows the interfacing of a 16 character X 2 line LCD module with the microcontroller 8051. The data lines are connected to port 1 of 8051. The control lines RS, R/W and E are driven by P2.0, P2.1 and P2.2. The voltage at V_{EE} pin in adjusted by potentiometer to adjust contrast of LCD.

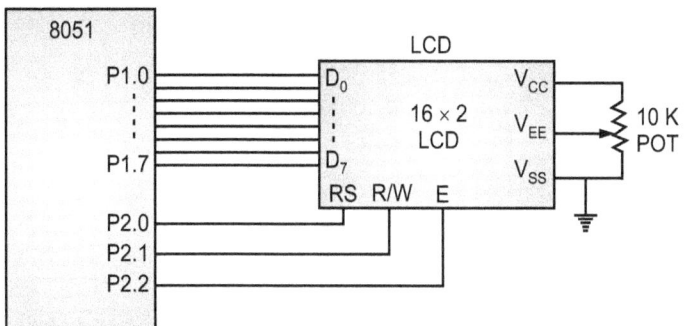

Fig. 4.3 : Interfacing 16 × LCD to 8051

Program:

Instruction	Comments
MOV 81H, # 30H	Initialize stack pointer
MOV A, # 3CH	Command code for 5 × 10 dots, DL = 8 bits N = 2 lines
LCALL COMMND	
MOV A, # 0EH	Command for setting display cursor ON
LCALL COMMND	
MOV A, # 01H	Command for clearing display
LCALL COMMND	
MOV A, # 06H	Shift cursor right
LCALL COMMND	
MOV A, # C0H	Cursor line 2, position 0
LCALL COMMND	
MOV A, # 'W'	Display letter 'W'
LCALL DISP	
MOV A, # 'E'	Display letter 'E'
LCALL DISP	
MOV A, # 'L'	Display letter 'L'
LCALL DISP	
MOV A, # 'C"	Display letter 'C'
LCALL DISP	
MOV A, # 'O'	Display letter 'O'
LCALL DISP	
MOV A, # 'M'	Display letter 'M'
LCALL DISP	
MOV A, # 'E'	Display letter 'E'
LCALL DISP	
L1 : SJMP L1	

COMMND Routine :

LCALL READY	Check if LCD is ready
MOV P1, A	Issue command code
CLR P2.0	Make RS = 0 to issue command
CLR P2.1	Make R/W = 0 to enable writing
SET B P2.2	Make E = 1
CLR P2.2	Make E = 0
RET	

DISP Routine :

LCALL READY	Check if LCD is ready
MOV P1, A	give data
SET B P2.0	RS = 1 to get data
CLR P2.1	R/W = 0 to enable writing
SET B P2.2	E = 1
CLR P2.2	E = 0
RET	

READY Routine :

	CLR P2.2	Disable display
	CLR P2.0	RS = 0 to access command register
	MOV P1, # 0FFH	Configure P1 as input port
	SET B P2.1	R/W = 1 to enable writing
L2:	SET B P2.2	E = 1
	JB P1.7, L2	Check D_7 bit if 1 LCD is busy wait till it become 0
	CLR P2.2	E = 0
	RET	

> **Program 4.2**

Draw and explain interfacing diagram for 20 × 2 LCD module. Write a program to display 'HELLO' message on LCD module.

Solution : Fig. 4.4 shows interfacing of 20 × 2 LCD module with LCD.

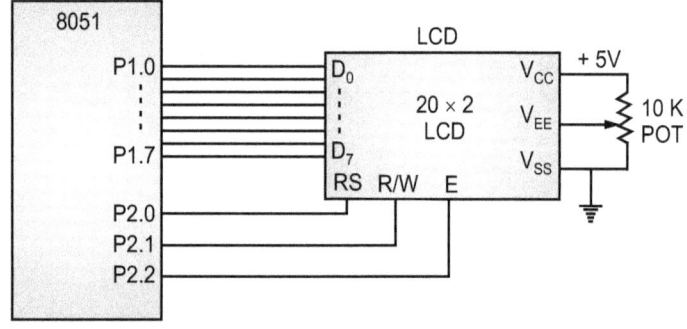

Fig. 4.4

Program	Instruction	Comments
	MOV A, # 38H	
	ACALL COMWRT	
	MOV A, # 0EH	
	ACALL COMWRT	
	MOV A, # 01H	
	ACALL COMWRT	
	MOV A, # 06H	
	ACALL COMWRT	
	MOV A, # 80H	
	ACALL COMWRT	
	MOV A, # 'H'	
	ACALL DISP	
	MOV A, # 'E'	
	ACALL DISP	
	MOV A, # 'L'	
	ACALL DISP	
	MOV A, # 'L'	
	ACALL DISP	
	MOV A, # 'O'	
	ACALL DISP	
HERE:	SJMP HERE	

//**COMWRT** : Command Routine
COMWRT: ACALL READY
        MOV P1, A
        CLR P2.0
        CLR P2.1
        SET B P2.2
        CALL DELAY
        CLR P2.2
        RET

//**DISP:** Display Subroutine
  DISP: ACALL READY
        MOV P1, A
        SET B P2.0
        CLR P2.1
        SET B P2.2

```
            CALL DELAY
            CLR P2.2
            RET
//READY: Ready Subroutine
  READY:    SET B P1.7
            CLR P2.0
            ETB P2.1
// Read command register and busy flag check
    BACK:   CLR P2.2              E = 0 for low to high pulse
            ACALL DELAY           Wait for sometime
            SET B P2.2            E = 1 for low to high pulse
            JB P1.7 BACK          Stay till busy flag = 0
            RET
// DELAY: Delay Subroutine
            MOV R3, # 10
    L1:     MOV R4, # 500
    L2:     DJNZ R4, L2
            DJNZ R3, L1
            RET
            END
```

Program 4.3

Interface 16 × 2, 8 bit LCD to 8051 and display message 'HELLO' on first line and "WELCOME" on second line.

Solution : Fig. 4.5 shows the interfacing of a 16 character X 2 line LCD module with the microcontroller 8051. The data lines are connected to port 1 of 8051. The control lines RS, R/W and E are driven by P2.0, P2.1 and P2.2. The voltage at V_{EE} pin is adjusted by potentiometer to adjust contrast of LCD.

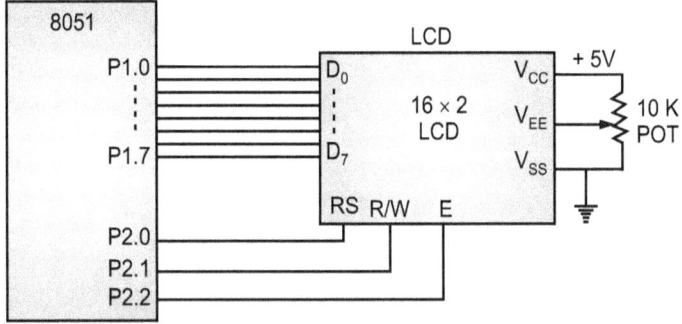

Fig. 4.5 : Interfacing of 16 × 2 LCD to 8051

Program:

	MOV 81H, # 30H	Initialize stack pointer
	MOV A, # 3CH	Command code for 5 × 10 dots DL = 8 bits, N = 2 lines
	LCALL COMMAND	
	MOV A, # 0EH	Command for setting display cursor ON
	LCALL COMMAND	
	MOV A, # 01H	Command for clearing display
	LCALL COMMAND	
	MOV A, # 06H	Command for moving cursor to the right
	LCALL COMMAND	
	MOV A, # 80H	Cursor line 1, position 0
	LCALL COMMAND	
	MOV A, # 'H'	
	LCALL DISP	
	MOV A, # 'E'	
	LCALL DISP	
	MOV A, # 'L'	
	LCALL DISP	
	MOV A, # 'L'	
	LCALL DISP	
	MOV A, # 'O'	
	LCALL DISP	
	MOV A, # C0H	Cursor line 2, position 0
	LCALL COMMAND	
	MOV A, # 'W'	
	LCALL DISP	
	MOV A, # 'E'	
	LCALL DISP	
	MOV A, # 'L'	
	LCALL DISP	
	MOV A, # 'C'	
	LCALL DISP	
	MOV A, # 'O'	
	LCALL DISP	

```
            MOV A, # 'M'
            LCALL DISP
            MOV A, # 'E'
            LCALL DISP
HERE:   SJMP HERE
```

// Command Routine

```
            LCALL READY         Check if LCD is ready
            MOV P1, A           Issue command code
            CLR P2.0            Make RS = 0 to issue command
            CLR P2.1            R/W = 0 to enable writing
            SET B P2.2          E = 0
            CLR P2.2            E = 1
            RET                 Return
```

// Display Routine

```
            LCALL READY         Check if LCD is ready
            MOV P1, A           Give data
            SET B P2.0          RS = 1 to get data
            CLR P2.1            R/W = 0 to enable writing
            SET B P2.2          E = 1
            CLR P2.2            E = 0
            RET
```

// Ready Routine

```
            CLR P2.2            Disable display
            CLR P2.0            RS = 0 inorder to access command register
            MOV P1, # 0FFH      Configure P1 as input port
            SET B P2.1          R/W = 1 to enable writing
L1:         SET B P2.2          E = 1
            JBP1.7, L1          Check D₇ bit, if 1 LCD is busy wait till it become 0
            CLR P2.2            Make E = 0 to disable display
            RET
```

Programming in C :
Program 4.4
Write an 8051 C program to send letters 'M', 'D' and 'E' to the LCD using delays.

Solution :

```c
# include <reg51.h>
Sfr data = 0X90;                    //P1 = LCD data pins
Sbit rs = P2^0;
Sbit RW = P2^1;
Sbit E = P2^2;
void main ( )
{
   lcdcmd (0X38);
   MSDelay (250);
   lcdcmd (0X0E);
   MSDelay (250);
   lcdcmd (0X01);
   MSDelay (250);
   lcdcmd (0X06);
   MSDelay (250);
   lcdcmd (0X86);                   // line 1, position 6
   MSDelay (250);
   lcddata ('M');
   MSDelay (250);
   lcddata ('D');
   MSDelay (250);
   lcddata ('E');
}
void lcdcmd (unsigned char value)
{
   ldata = value;                   // put the value on the pins
   rs = 0;
   RW = 0;
   E = 1;
   MSDelay (1);                     // strobe the enable pin
   E = 0;
   return;
}
```

```c
void lcddata (unsigned char value)
{
    ldata = value;              // put the value on the pins
    rs = 1;
    RW = 0;
    E = 1;
    MSDelay (1);                // strobe the enable pin
    E = 0;
    return;
}
void MSDelay (unsigned int itime)
{
    unsigned int i, j;
    for (i = 0; i < itime; i++)
    for (j = 0; j < 1275; j++)
}
```

Program 4.5

Write an 8051 C program to send letters 'P' 'Q' and 'R' to the LCD using the busy flag method.

Solution :

```c
# include <reg51.h>
Sfr ldata = 0X90;
Sbit rs = P2^0;
Sbit rw = P2^1;
Sbit en = P2^2;
Sbit busy = P1^7
void main ( )
{
    lcdcmd (0X38);
    lcdcmd (0X0E);
    lcdcmd (0X01);
    lcdcmd (0X06);
    lcdcmd (0X86);
    lcddata ('P');
    lcddata ('Q');
```

```c
  lcddata ('R');
}
void lcdcmd (unsigned char value)
{
  lcdready ( );
  ldata = value;
  rs = 0;
  rw = 0;
  en = 1;
  MSDelay (1);
  en = 0
  return;
}
void lcddata (unsigned char value)
{
  lcdready ( );
  ldata = value;
  rs = 1;
  rw = 0;
  en = 1;
  MSDelay (1);
  en = 0;
  return;
}
void lcdready ( )
{
  busy = 1;
  rs = 0;
  rw = 1;
  while (busy == 1)
  {
    en = 0;
    MSDelay (1);
    en = 1;
  }
  return;
```

```
}
void MSDelay (unsigned int itime)
{
  unsigned int i, j;
  for (i = 0; i < itime; i++)
  for (j = 0; j < 1275; j++);
}
```

Q. Explain with suitable diagram interfacing of KB0 with 8051 microcontroller.
[8 M] [May/June & Nov./Dec. 2011]

4.2 KEYBOARD INTERFACING

Keyboards and LCDs are the most widely used input/output devices of the 8051.

Whenever a key is pressed corresponding code is transmitted. The input keyboard is composed of a set of push button switches. Whenever the switch is pressed, it makes an electrical contact. In push button key, the metal contact bounces few times, therefore the voltage across the switch fluctuates and generates a spike in the signal. Hence, it is necessary to debounce the mechanical switches. This is called key debouncing.

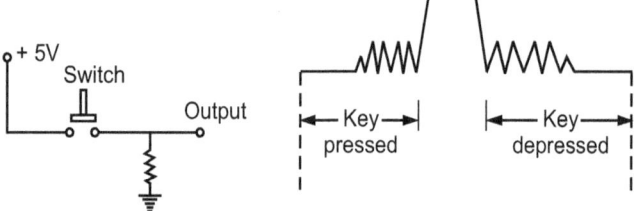

Fig. 4.6 : Bouncing of a key switch

The key debouncing can be done through hardware and software.

4.2.1 Hardware Key Debouncing

The circuit can be implemented using S-R latch.

Fig. 4.7 shows the circuit for hardware key debouncing.

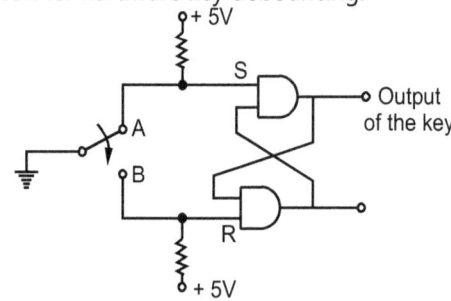

Fig. 4.7 : Hardware key debouncing

When switch is connected to A, then the output of the flip-flop go high, when switch is connected to B, the output of the flip-flop changes form high to low. The wiper of the switch bounces many times on contact B, but the output does not fluctuate between low and high. When the wiper is not connected to any of A or B, then the output of the latch remains constant.

4.2.2. Software key Debouncing

In software debouncing the microcontroller waits for some time before it accepts the key as an input. After some time the key is pressed and the key is accepted by microcontroller. The flowchart for software key debouncing is as shown in Fig. 4.8.

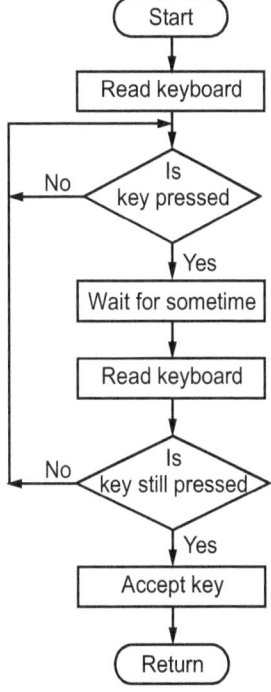

Fig. 4.8 : Flow chart for software key debouncing

4.2.3 Interfacing the Keyboard to the 8051

Mechanical switches are arranged in two forms :

(i) Non-matrix form.

(ii) Matrix form.

The keyboard is interfaced to the 8051 by using input ports.

(i) Non-matrix Keyboard : In non-matrix keyboard, the closing of the key is identified by reading the port data. In this form number of I/O lines is equal to number of keys. Fig. 4.9 shows the interfacing of 8 non-matrix type keyboard.

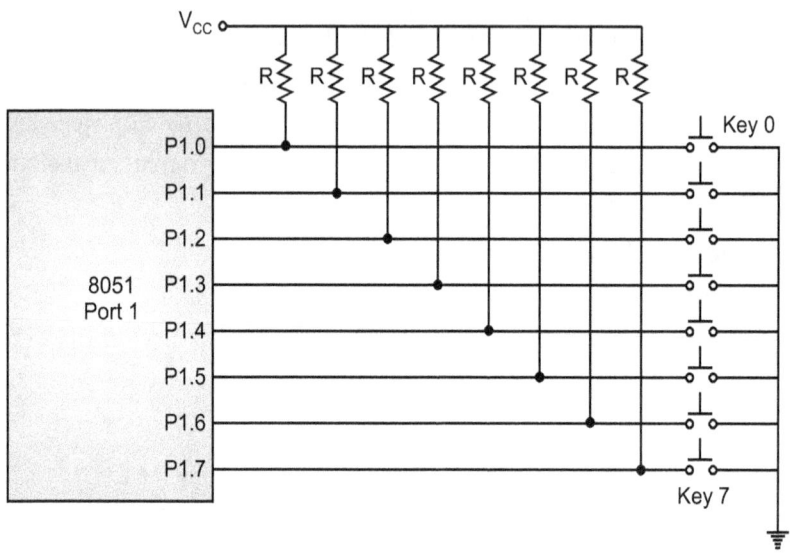

Fig. 4.9 : Non-matrix type keyboard

To identify the key pressed the following functions must be performed.
1. identify the key closure.
2. debounce the key.
3. transform the key closure into hexadecimal.

(ii) Matrix keyboard :

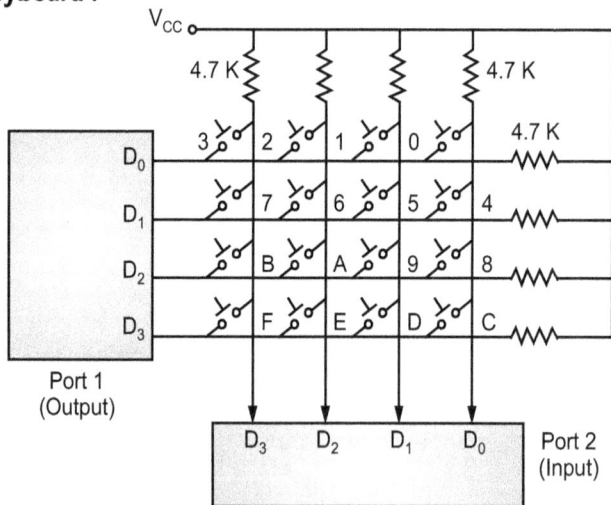

Fig. 4.10 : Matrix keyboard connections

Here the keys are arranged in matrix form of 4 rows and 4 columns, whenever the key is pressed it makes the connection between row and column. If 4 rows and four columns are used then to complete the matrix, it requires eight lines. Number of connections are reduced using this type of keyboard.

Fig. 4.11 shows the interfacing of matrix keyboard with the ports. Here rows are connected to an output port and the columns are connected to an input port. If no key is pressed, the input port will read 1 for all columns because they are all connected to V_{CC}. If all the rows are grounded and a key is pressed, one of the columns will have 0 because the key pressed provides the path to the ground. Therefore, the microcontroller will continuously scan the keyboard to detect and identify the key pressed.

To detect a key pressed, microcontroller grounds all rows, then it reads the columns. If the data read from any of the column is 1111, then no key has been pressed and the process continuous until a key press is detected. When the column bits has a zero then we can say that a key is pressed. After detection of key pressed, the microprocessor will start the process of identifying a key. After identification of the row it will identify the column.

Program 4.6

Interface a 4 × 4 matrix keyboard to the microcontroller 8051.

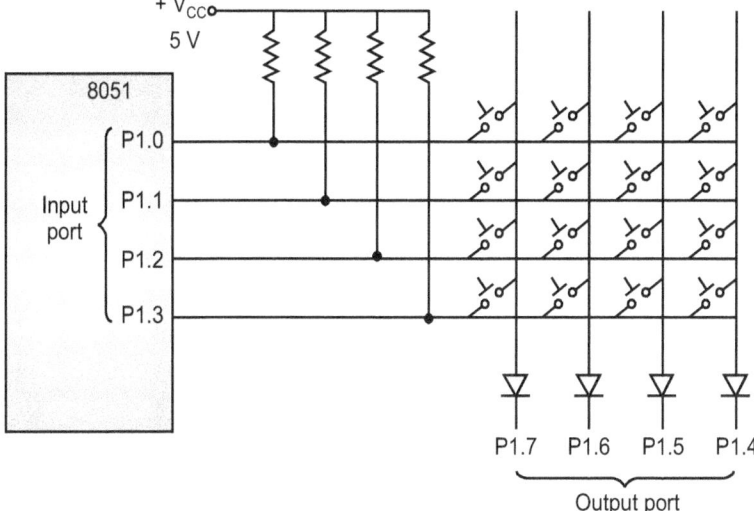

Fig. 4.11 : 4 × 4 matrix keyboard connections to port 1 of 8051

Algorithm :
1. Make P1.0, P1.1, P1.2 and P1.3 as input port and write 1 on these pins.
2. Check if all the keys are released. Write 0 on the pins P1.4, P1.5, P1.6 and P1.7.
3. Check all the input ports are at logic 1 if not, then wait.
4. Call debounce.
5. Wait for key closing.
6. Ground all the output port pins and then check if one of the return lines shows a logic 0.
7. Check the key pressed, if yes continuous other go to step 5.
8. Call debounce.

9. Check if key is really pressed, if not go to step 5.
10. Find the key code and display the key pressed.
11. Go to step 1.

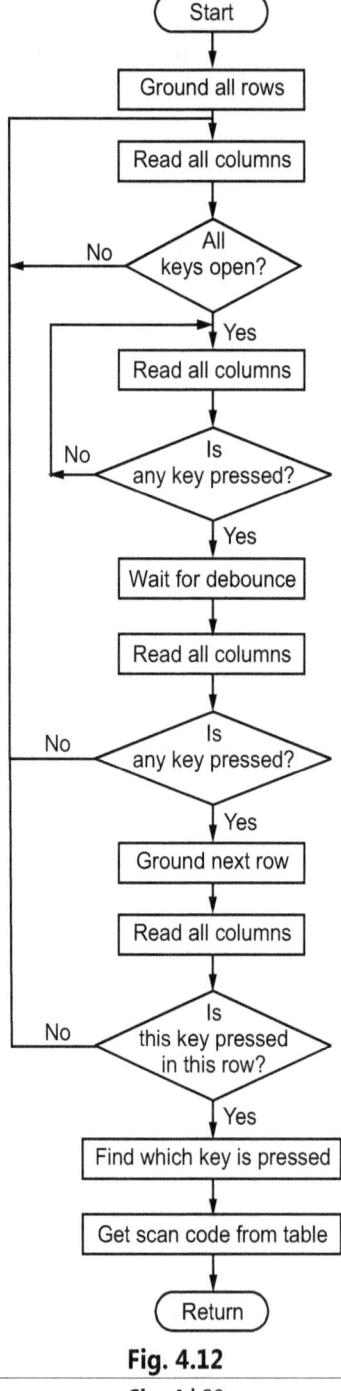

Fig. 4.12

Program: Org look-up-address db
30h, 31h, 32h, 33h, 34h, 35h,
36h, 37h, 38h, 39h, 41h, 42h,
43h, 44h, 45h, 46h
Org prog_address

START: MOV P1, # 0FH
MOV DPTR, # look-up-address

L1: MOV A, P1
ANL A, # 0FH
CJNE A, # 0FH, L1
LCALL DELAY

L3: MOV A, P1
ANL A, # 0FH
CJNE A, # 0FH, L2
LJMP L3

L2: LCALL DELAY
MOV A, P1
ANL A, # 0FH
CJNE A, # 0FH, L4
LJMP L3

L4: MOV R1, # 01H
MOV R0, # 0EFH
MOV R3, # 04H

L5: MOV P1, R0
MOV A, P1
JNB ACC.0, DISPLAY
INC DPTR
JNB ACC.1 DISPLAY
INC DPTR
JNB ACC.2 DISPLAY
INC DPTR
JNCB ACC.3 DISPLAY
INC DPTR
MOV A, R0
MOV R1, A
MOV R0, A
DJNZ R3, L5
LJMP START

Program 4.7

Interface 4 × 4 matrix keyboard to 8051 using port P1 and P2. Also write a assembly language program to ready key.

Fig. 4.13 shows 4 × 4 matrix keyboard connected to port P1 and P2 of 8051. Here P1.0, P1.1, P1.2 of P1.3 are connected to rows, P2.0, P2.1, P2.2 and P2.3 are connected to columns.

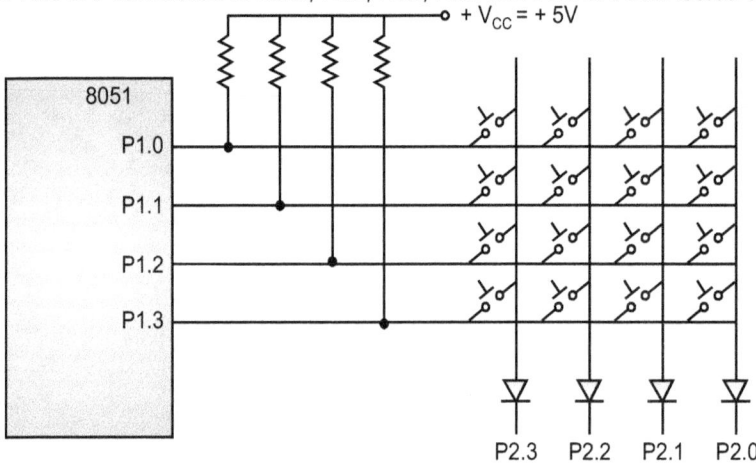

Fig. 4.13

Program:	MOV P2, # 0FFH	make P2 an input port
L1:	MOV P1, # 00H	ground all rows at once
	MOV A, P2	read all columns, ensure all keys open
	ANL A, 00001111B	mask unused bits
	CJNE A, # 00001111B, L1	check till all keys released
L3:	ACALL DELAY	call 20 ms delay
	MOV A, P2	see if any key is pressed
	ANL A, # 00001111B	mask unused bits
	CJNE A, # 00001111B, L2	key pressed, await closure
	SJMP L3	check if any key is pressed
L2:	ACALL DELAY	wait 20 ms debounce time
	MOV A, P2	check key closure
	ANL A, # 00001111B	mask unused bits
	CJNE A, # 00001111B, L4	key pressed, find row
	SJMP L3	if none, keep polling
L4:	MOV P1, # 11111110B	ground row 0
	MOV A, P2	read all columns
	ANL A, # 00001111B	mask unused bits

	CJNE A, # 00001111B, Row_0	key row 0, find the columns
	MOV P1, # 11111101B	ground row 1
	MOV A, P2	read all columns
	ANL A, # 00001111B	mask unused bits
	CJNE A, # 00001111B, Row_1	key row 1, find the columns
	MOV P1, # 11111011B	ground row 2
	MOV A, P2	read all columns
	ANL A, # 00001111B	mask unused bits
	CJNE A, # 00001111B Row_2	key row 2, find the columns
	MOV P1, # 11110111B	ground row 3
	MOV A, P2	read all columns
	ANL A, # 00001111B	mask unused bits
	CJNE A, # 00001111B Row_3	key row 3, find the column
	LJMP L3	if none, false input, repeat
ROW_0:	MOV DPTR, # KCODE 0	set DPTR = Start of row 0
	SJMP FIND	find column key belongs to
ROW_1:	MOV DPTR, # KCODE 1	set DPTR = start of row 1
	SJMP FIND	find column key belongs to
ROW_2:	MOV DPTR, # KCODE 2	set DPTR = start of row 2
	SJMP FIND	find column key belong to
ROW_3	MOV DPTR, # CODE 3	set DPTR = start of row 3
FIND:	RRC A	see if any CY bit is low
	JNC MATCH	if zero, get the ASCII code
	INC DPTR	point to next column address
	SJMP FIND	keep searching
MATCH:	CLR A	set A = 0
	MOVC A, @ A + DPTR	get ASCII code from table
	MOV P0, A	display pressed key
	LJMP L1	
	ORG 300H	
KCODE 0:	DB '0', '1', '2', '3',	Row 0
KCODE 1:	DB '4', '5', '6', '7',	Row 1
KCODE 2:	DB '8', '9', 'A', 'B',	Row 2
KCODE 3:	DB 'C', 'D', 'E', 'F',	Row 3

Program 4.8

Two switches are connected to pins P0.1 and P0.2. They are also vectored to interrupt location 0003H i.e. INT0. Write a program to test which key is pressed or to verify if both keys are pressed.

Solution : The two switches are connected to the $\overline{INT0}$ pin through an AND gate. When the switch is pressed the corresponding port line goes low. Whenever switch 1 (SW1) is pressed 01 is displayed on port 2, when switch 2 (SW2) is pressed 02 is displayed and when both switches are simultaneously pressed, of H is displayed.

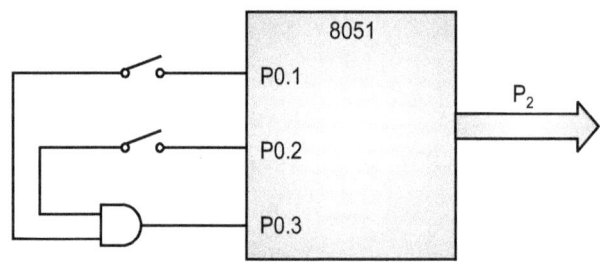

Fig. 4.14

Program:	ORG 0000H	
	LJMP MAIN	
	ORG 0030H	
MAIN:	SET B TCON 0	make $\overline{INT0}$ and edge triggered interrupt
	MOV IE # 81H	enable interrupt $\overline{INT0}$
HERE:	SJMP HERE	wait for interrupt
	ORG 0003H	
	LJMP TEST	jump to new location
	ORG 0080H	
TEST:	SET B P0.1	make P0.1 an input port
	SET B P0.2	make P0.2 an input port
	SET B C	set carry
TEST 1:	MOV C, P0.1	use carry flag to test the status of P0.1
	JNC SW1	if C = 0; it means SW1 is pressed
	MOV C, P0.2	use carry flag to test the status of P0.2
	JNC SW2	if C = 0 it means SW1 is pressed
	MOV P2, # 0FFH	if both switches are not pressed P2 = FFH
	RETI	

SW1:	MOV C, P0.2	since SW1 is found pressed, Test SW2
	JNC BOTH	since both are pressed, jump to both
	MOV P2, # 01H	only SW1 is pressed make P2 = 0
	SJMP TEST 1	continuous monitoring the switches
SW2:	MOV P2 # 02H	this is reached when SW2 is pressed
	SJMP TEST 1	continuously monitoring the switches
BOTH:	MOV P2, # 0FH	this is the case of both switches pressed
	SJMP TEST 1	
	END	

Program 4.9

Write a C program to read the keypad and send the result to the first serial port. Configure the serial port for 9600 baud, 8-bit and 1 stop bit.

Solution : Here rows are connected to P1.0, P1.1, P1.2 and P1.3 columns are connected to P2.0, P2.1, P2.2, P2.3.

Program :

```
# include <reg51.h>
# define CO2 P2
# define Row P1
void MSDelay (unsigned int value)
void SerTX (unsigned char);
unsigned char keypad [4] [4] = {'0', '1', '2', '3', '4', '5', '6', '7', '8', '9', 'A', 'B' 'C', 'D', 'E',
                                'F'};
void main ( )
{
    unsigned char colloc rowloc;
    TMOD = 0X20;              // timer 1 mode 2
    TH1 = -3;                 // 9600 baud rate
    SCON = 0X50;              // 8 bit, 1 stop
    TR1 = 1;                  // start timer 1
                              // keyboard routine. This sends the ASCII
                              // code for the pressed key to the serial port
    CoL = 0XFF;               // make P2 an input port
    while (1)                 // repeat forever
    {
        do
```

```c
{
    Row = 0X00;              // ground all rows at once
    Colloc = COL;            // read the columns
    Colloc & = 0X0F;         // mask used bits
}
while (Colloc! = 0X0F);      // check until all keys released
do
{
    MSDelay (20);            // call delay
    Colloc = COL;            // see if any key is pressed
    Colloc & = 0X0F;         // mask unused bits
}
while (Colloc == 0X0F);      // keep checking for key press
MSDelay (20);                // call delay for debounce
Colloc = COL;                // read columns
Colloc & = 0X0F;             // mask unused bits
}
while (Colloc == 0X0F);      // wait for key press
while (1)
{
    Row = 0XFE;              // ground row 0
    Colloc = COL;            // read columns
    Colloc & = 0X0F;         // mask unused bit
    if (Colloc ! = 0X0F)     // column detected
    {
        rowloc = 0;          // save row location
        break;               // exit while loop
    }
    Row = 0XFD;              // ground row 1
    Colloc = COL;            // read columns
    Colloc & = 0X0F;         // mask unused bits
    if (Colloc ! = 0X0F)     // column detected
    {
        rowloc = 1;          // save row location
        break;               // exit while loop
    }
    Row = 0XFB;              // ground row 2
    Colloc = COL;            // read columns
```

```c
        Colloc &= 0X0F;              // mask unused bits
        if (Colloc! = 0X0F)          // column detected
        {
            rowloc = 2;              // save row location
            break;                   // exit while loop
        }
        Row = 0XF7;                  // ground row 3
        Colloc = COL;                // read columns
        Colloc &= 0X0F;              // mask unused bits
        rowloc = 3;                  // save row location
        break;                       // exit while loop
    }
    // check column and send result to the serial port
    if (Colloc == 0X0E)
    SerTX (keypad [rowloc] [0])
    else if (Colloc == 0X0D)
    SerTX (keypad [rowloc [1]);
    else if (Colloc == 0X0B)
    SerTX (keypad [rowloc] [2]);
    else
    SerTX (Keypad [rowloc] [3]);
    }
}
void SerTX (unsigned char x)
{
    SBUF = x;                        // place value in buffer
    while (TI == 0);                 // wait until transmitted
    TI = 0;                          // clear flag
}
void MSDelay (unsigned int value)
{
    unsigned int x, y;
    for (x = 0; x < 1275; x++)
    for (y = 0; y < value; y++);
}
```

4.3 ADC 0804 AND 0808/09 INTERFACING

Q. *With suitable diagram explain interfacing and programming of ADC0808 with 8051 microcontroller.* [8 M] [May/June 2011]

Q. *Explain interfacing of ADC 0804 with 8051 microcontroller. Also give timing diagram of ADC 0804.* [8 M] [May/June 2010]

Analog to digital converter are widely used for data acquisition. Analog to digital converters are used to translate the analog signals to digital numbers so that the microcontroller can read and process them. The ADC chips are either parallel or serial. In parallel ADC, the more pins are dedicated to bringing out the binary data whereas in serial ADC only one pin used for data out.

4.3.1 ADC 0804 Chip

The ADC 0804 is a 8-bit parallel ADC in the family of ADC 0800 series from national semiconductor :

- It operates on +5 volts
- It has a resolution of 8 bits
- Conversion time varies depending upon the clocking signals applied to the CLK IN pin.

Fig. 4.15 shows the pin diagram of ADC 0804.

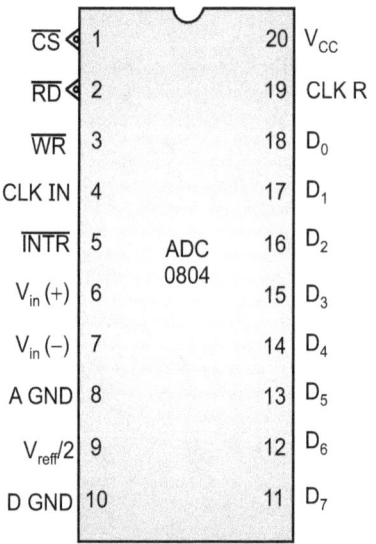

Fig. 4.15

$\overline{CS}$: It is an active low signal used to activate the ADC 0804 chip.

$\overline{RD}$: This is an active low input signal. ADC converts analog input into its binary equivalent and holds it in an internal register. $\overline{RD}$ is used to get the converted data out of the ADC 0804 chip.

When CS = 0, high to low pulse is applied to $\overline{RD}$ pin and the 8-bit digital output is shown on $D_0 - D_7$ data pins. It is also called as Output Enable (OE) pin.

$\overline{WR}$: This is an active low signal used to inform the ADC 0804 to start the conversion process. When $\overline{CS}$ = 0 a low to high transition starts the conversion process. The amount of time it takes to convert varies depending upon the CLK IN and CLK R values. When data conversion is complete, ADC 0804 forces the INTR pin low.

CLK IN and CLK R : When external clock is used for timing, then CLK IN is used as input pin. It also has an internal CLOCK generator. To use the internal clock generator, the CLK IN and CLK R pins are connected to a capacitor and a register. The clock frequency is determined as

$$f = \frac{1}{1.1\ RC}$$

The typical values are R = 10 kΩ and C = 150 pF.

The typical value of frequency is f = 606 kHz and conversion time is 110 μs.

$\overline{INTR}$: This is an active low output pin. Generally this pin is high and goes low when the data is available. After INTR goes low, CS = 0 and sends a high to low pulse to the $\overline{RD}$ pin to get data out of ADC 0804 chip.

V_{in} (+) and V_{in} (−) : These are the differential analog inputs where $V_{in} = V_{in}$ (+) − V_{in} (−). Often V_{in} (−) pin is connected to ground and V_{in} (+) pin is used as the analog input to be converted to digital.

V_{cc} : This is the +5 V power supply, also used as a reference voltage when $V_{ref/2}$ pin is open.

$V_{ref/2}$: This is an input pin used as a reference voltage, if this pin is open, the analog input voltage is in the range of 0 to 5 volts. There are many applications where the analog input applied to V_{in} needs to be other than the 0 to +5 V range. $V_{ref/2}$ is used to implement analog input voltages other than 0 to 5V. Table 4.6 shows the V_{in} range for various $V_{ref/2}$ inputs.

Table 4.6 : $V_{ref/2}$ Relation to V_{in} Range (ADC 0804)

$V_{ref/2}$ (V)	V_{in} (V)	Step size (mv)
Not connected	0 to 5	5/256 = 19.53
2.0	0 to 4	4/255 = 15.62
1.5	0 to 3	3/256 = 11.71
1.28	0 to 2.56	2.56/256 = 10

$D_0 - D_7$: These are the digital data output pins because ADC 0804 is a parallel ADC chip. These are tri-state buffered and the converted data is accessed only when CS = 0 and $\overline{RD}$ is forced to low. Output voltage is calculated as follows.

$$D_{out} = \frac{V_{in}}{Step\ size}$$

where, D_{out} = Digital data output
V_{in} = Analog input voltage
Stepsize = $(2 \times V_{ref/2})/256$

4.3.2 Analog Ground and Digital Ground

This pin provides ground for both analog signal and digital signal. Analog ground is used to connect to the ground of the analog V_{in} and digital ground is used to connect to the ground of the V_{CC} pin. Two ground pins are used to isolate the analog V_{in} signal from transient voltages caused by digital switching of the output $D_0 - D_7$.

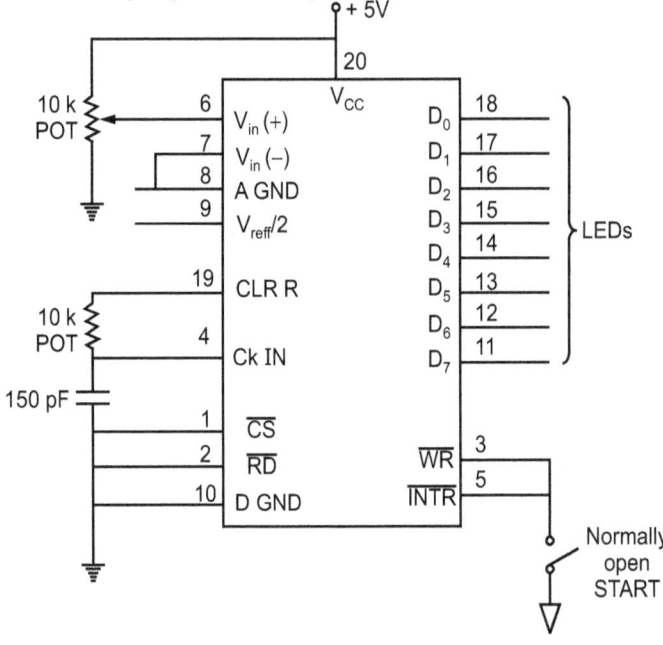

Fig. 4.16 : ADC 0804 chip

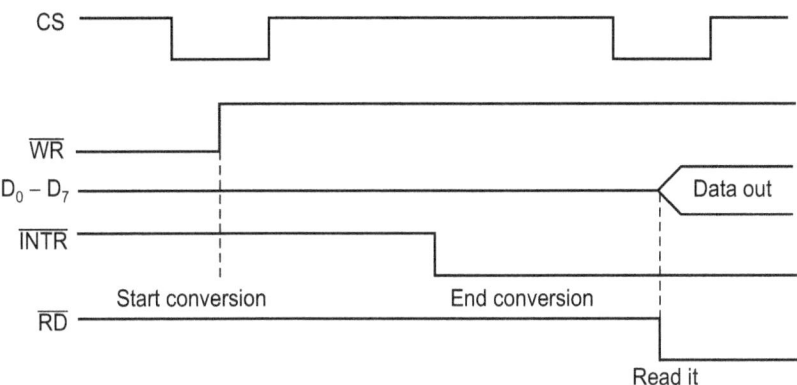

Fig. 4.17 : Read and write timing for ADC 0804

4.3.3 Programming ADC 0804

Program 4.10

Write an assembly language program to convert analog signal to digital signal and display the data using ADC 0804.

Solution : Fig. 4.18 shows connections of ADC 0804 to 8051 with self-clocking.

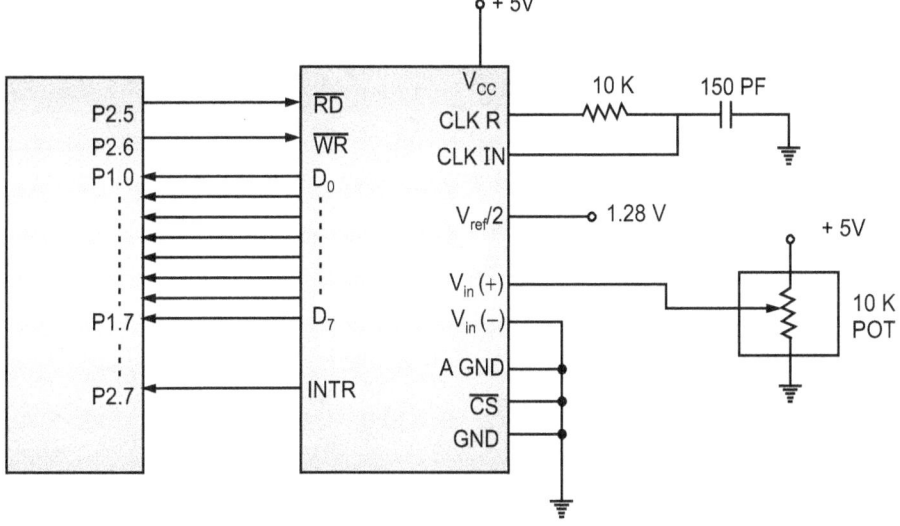

Fig. 4.18 : 8051 connections to ADC 0804 with self-clocking

Program :

```
        RD      BIT     P2.5
        WR      BIT     P2.6
        INTR    BIT     P2.7
        MYDATA  EQU     P1
        MOV P1, # 0FFH
        SET B   INTR
```

```
BACK:      CLR     WR
           SET B   WR
HERE:      JB      INTR, HERE
           CLR     RD
           MOV     A, MYDATA
           ACALL   CONVERSION
           ACALL   DATA_DISPLAY
           SET B   RD
           SJMP    BACK
```

// Converting Binary (hex) to ASCII

CONVERSION
```
           ORG OH
           ACALL BIN_DEC_CONVERT
           ACALL DEC_ASCII_CONVERT
           SJMP $
```

BIN_DEC_CONVERT :
```
           MOV R0, # RAM_ADDR
           MOV A, P1
           MOV B, # 10
           DIV AB
           MOV @ R0, B
           INC R0
           MOV B, # 10
           DIV AB
           MOV @ R0, B
           INC R0
           MOV @ R0, A
           RET
```

// Conversion of DEC digits to displayable ASCII digits

DEC_ASCII_CONVERT :
```
           MOV R0, # RAM_ADDR
           MOV R1, # ASCI_RESULT
           MOV R2, # 3
BACK:      MOV A, @ R0
           ORL A, # 30H
           MOV @ R1, A
```

```
            INC R0
            INC R1
            DJNZ R2, BACK
            RET
RAM_ADDR     EQU  40H
ASCII_RESULT EQU  50H
COUNT        EQU  3
// Subroutine for displaying the data
```
DATA_DISPLAY :
```
            ACALL READY
            MOV P1, A
            SET B P2.0
            CLR P2.1
            SET B P2.2
            ACALL DELAY
            CLR P2.2
            RET
```
READY: `SET B P1.7`
```
            CLR P2.0
            SET B P2.1
```

Programming ADC 0804 in C :

```
# include <reg51.h>
Sbit RD = P2^5;
Sbit WR = P2^6;
Sbit INTR = P2^7;
Sfr MYDATA = P1;
void main ( )
{
    unsigned char value;
    MYDATA = 0XFF;          // make P1 and input
    INTR = 1;               // make INTR and input
    RD = 1;                 // set RD high
    WR = 1;                 // set WR high
    while (1)
```

```
{
    WR = 0;                          // send WR pulse
    WR = 1;                          // L to H (start conversion)
    while (INTR == 1);               // wait for EOC
    RD = 0;                          // send RD pulse
    value = MYDATA                   // read value
    Convert AND DISPLAY (value);
    RD = 1;
}
}
```

4.3.4 ADC 0808/0809

- ADC 0808/0805 is from national semiconductor with 8 inputs and 8 data outputs.
- Eight analog inputs are multiplexed and selected using three address pins A, B and C.

4.3.4.1 Features of ADC 0808/0809

- 8 analog channels with multiplexer.
- 0 to 5V operating voltage range
- TTL compatible output
- Less conversion time (100 µs)
- High accuracy
- High speed
- 8-bit resolution
- Low power consumption

Table 4.7 : Channel selection of analog inputs

Selected Analog Channel	C	B	A
IN0	0	0	0
IN1	0	0	1
IN2	0	1	0
IN3	0	1	1
IN4	1	0	0
IN5	1	0	1
IN6	1	1	0
IN7	1	1	1

4.3.4.2 Pin Diagram of ADC 0808/0809

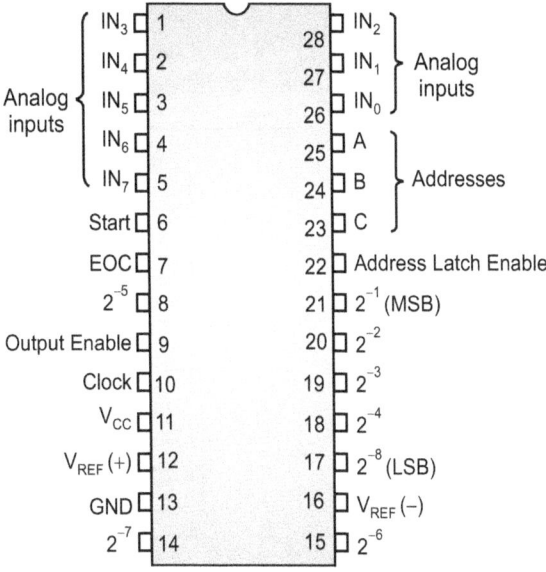

Fig. 4.19 : Pin configuration of IC ADC 0808/0809

Pin Description :

1. **Analog Inputs** (IN0 to IN7)

These are the 8 analog inputs. One of these eight inputs are selected depending on the address selection bits.

2. **Address pins A, B, C :**

These pins are used to select one of the eight analog inputs. For example, if C, B, A = 100 then IN4 is selected and the analog signal at this pin is converted into equivalent digital form.

3. **Reference Voltage** [V_{ref} (+) and V_{ref} (−)]

V_{ref} (+) and V_{ref} (−) set the reference voltage. If V_{ref} (−) = GND and V_{ref} (+) = 5V, the step size is 5V/256 = 19.53 mv. Therefore, to get a 10 mv step size we need to set V_{ref} (+) = 2.56 V and V_{ref} (−) = GND.

4. **ALE and Output Enable :**

The address latch enable is used to latch the addresses A, B and C to select IN0 − IN7. The output enable pin when activated it will make the digital output available on the output pins.

5. **SOC and EOC :**

Start of conversion or SC is same as the WR pin in other ADC chips. The end of conversion is indicated by EOC.

6. Digital Outputs (2^{-1} to 2^{-8})

The digital output is available to these pins. 2^{-1} represents the MSB and 2^{-8} represents the LSB of digital output.

Fig. 4.20 shows the functional block diagram of ADC 0808/0809.

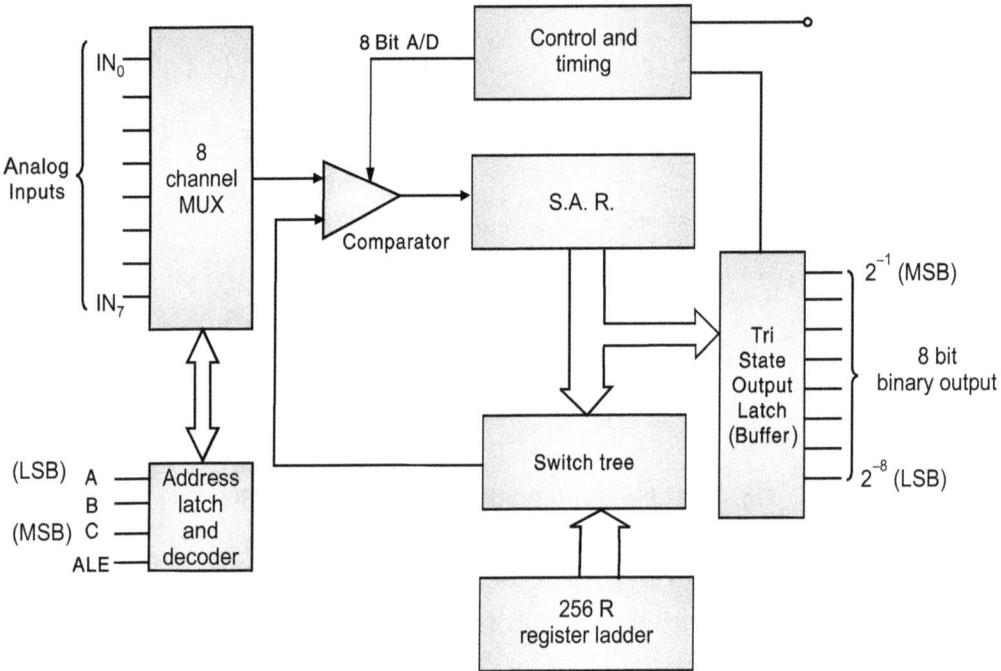

Fig. 4.20

4.3.4.3 Steps to Program the ADC 0808/0809

The following steps are used to get data from an ADC 0808/0809 :

1. Select analog channel by using bit to A, B and C.
2. Activate the ALE pin by using L-to-H pulse.
3. Activate SC (Start Conversion) by an L to -H pulse.
4. Monitor EoC (end of conversion) to see the completion of conversion H-to-L pulse indicates that the data is converted and is available. If EoC is not used, to read the converted data a time delay is required. The delay size depends on the speed of the external clock connected to the clk pin. EoC is same as INTR pin in other ADC chips.
5. Activate OE (output enable) to read data out of the ADC chip. An L to H pulse to the OE pin will give the digital data.

ADC 0808/0809 is not self-clocking. Clock must be provided form an external source to the CLK pin.

The speed of conversion depends upon the frequency of the clock connected to the CLK pin.

Fig. 4.21 shows the timing diagram for ADC 0809.

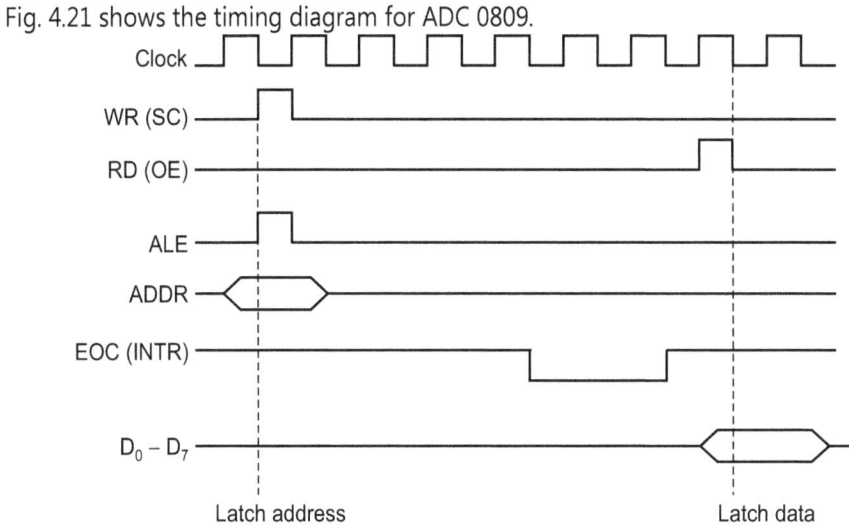

Fig. 4.21 : Timing diagram for ADC 0809

4.3.4.4 Interfacing ADC 0809 to 8051

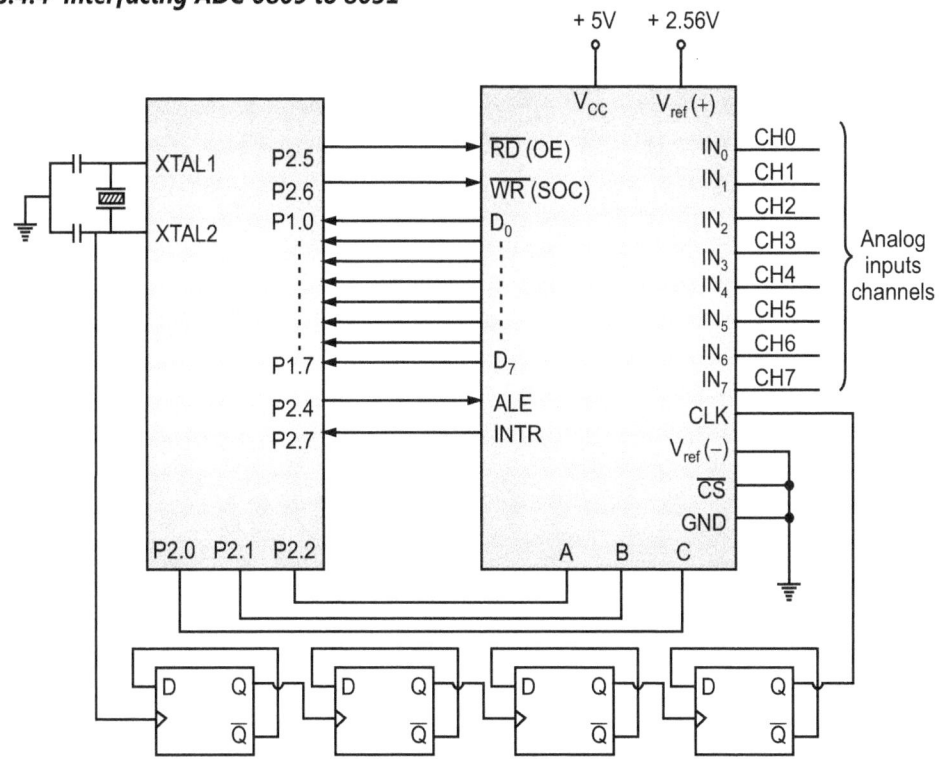

Fig. 4.22 : 8051 connections to ADC 0809

Program 4.11

Interface 8-bit, 8 channel ADC to 8051. Write assembly language program to convert CH0, CH3 and CH7 and store the result in external memory location starting from C000H. Repeat procedure for every 1 sec.

Solution : Fig. 4.22 shows the 8051 connections to ADC 0809

Program :

	CLR P2.6	make SOC low
	CLR P2.4	make ALE low
	MOV P0, # FFH	configure port 0 as input
	MOV P1, # FFH	configure port 1 as input
L1:	MOV DPTR, # C000H	– Initialize memory pointer
	MOV A, # 00H	– Set address for channel 0
	ACALL A_D	call ADL routine
	MOV X @ DPTR, A	– Increment memory pointer
	MOV A, # 03H	– Set address for channel 3
	ACALL A_D	call ADC routine
	MOV X @ DPTR, A	– Save digital value
	INC DPTR	increment DPTR
	MOV A, # 07H	set address for channel 7
	ACALL A_D	call ADL routine
	MOV X @ DPTR, A	save digital value
	ACALL DELAY	wait for 1 sec
	SJMP L1	Repeat

// Analog to Digital Conversion Routine

A_D:	MOV P2, A	– Get the channel and number set its address
	SET P2.4	send ALE
	NOP	
	CLR P2.4	
	SET P2.6	send SOC
	NOP	
	CLR P2.6	
HERE:	JB P2.7, HERE	wait for EOC
HERE 1:	JNB P2.7, HERE 1	
	MOV A, P1	get digital data
	RET	

// Delay Routine

DELAY:	MOV TMOD, # 01	Timer 1, mode 1
	MOV R0, # 1H	counter with 20
L2:	MOV TL0, # B0H	
	MOV TH0, # 3CH	
	SET B TR0	
L3:	JNB TF0, L3	check timer 0 flag until it rolls over
	CLR TR0	clear timer 0
	CLR TF0	clear timer 0 flag
	DJNZ R0, L2	
	RET	

4.3.4 Programming ADC 0808/0809 in C

Program 4.12

Write a C program to prefer A/D conversion on ADC 0808 and send digital value on LEDs connected to port 0. The select lines of ADC 0808 are connected to port 3 pins 0 to 2.

```c
# include <reg51.h>
Sbit ALE = P1^4;
Sbit OE = P1^5;
Sbit SOC = P1^6;
Sbit EOC = P1^7
void main ( )
{
  unsigned char a, i;
  P2 = 0XFF;                    // P2 = an input
  EOC = 1;
  ALE = 0;
  OE = 0;
  SOC = 0;
  while (1)
  {
    P3 = 0X03;                  // Select channel
    for (a = 0; a < 50; a++)    // Software delay
    ALE = 1;
    for (a = 0; a < 50; a++)    // Delay
    SOC = 1;                    // Start of conversion
    For (a = 0; a < 50; a++)    // Delay
```

```
ALE = 0;
SOC = 0;
while (EOC == 1);              // Wait for conversion
while (EOC == 0);              // Conversion complete
OE = 1;
For (a = 0; a < 50; a++)
i = P2;                        // Get the data
OE = 0;
P0 = i;                        // Display on port 0
}
}
```

4.4 INTERFACING DAC 0808

Q. DAC interfacing.   **[8 M] [May/June & Nov./Dec. 2011]**

The digital to analog converter (DAC) is a device widely used to convert digital pulses into analog signals. There are two types of digital to analog converter (DAC) : (1) Binary weighted register DAC. (2) R/2R ladder DAC.

The more popularly used IC for DAC is MC 1408 (DAC 0808).

4.4.1 DAC 0808

It is a 8-bit monolithic DAC manufactured by the national semiconductor. The digital inputs are converted to current (I_{out}). The total current provided by the (I_{out}) pin is directly proportional to the binary numbers at the D_0 – D_7 inputs and the reference current (I_{ref}) as follows.

$$I_{out} = I_{ref}\left(\frac{D_7}{2} + \frac{D_6}{4} + \frac{D_5}{8} + \frac{D_4}{16} + \frac{D_3}{32} + \frac{D_2}{64} + \frac{D_1}{128} + \frac{D_0}{256}\right)$$

where D_0 is the LSB

           D_7 is the MSB for the inputs.

4.4.2 Features of DAC 0808

- Power supply voltage range = ± 4.5 mw at ± 5V.
- Low power consumption = 33 mw at ± 5V.
- High speed multiplying input slew rate = 8 mA/µ sec.
- Fast settling time = 150 n/sec typically.
- Interfaces directly with TTL, DTL and CMOS logic levels.

4.4.3 Pin diagram of DAC 0808

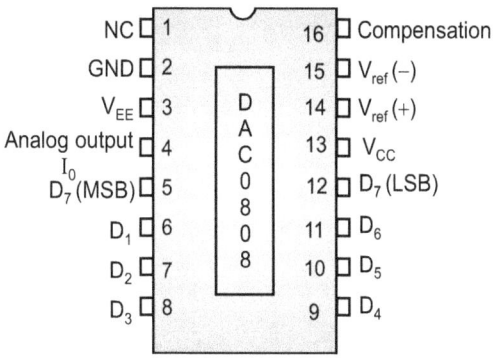

Fig. 4.23 : Pin diagram of 0808 DAC

The internal schematic for DAC 0808 is as shown in Fig. 4.24. It consists of R/2R ladder network along with current switches and reference current amplifier. D_0 – D_7 are the digital inputs where D_0 is the MSB and D_7 is the LSB. Output is available in the form of current therefore external current to voltage converter is used if the analog output is required in the form of voltage.

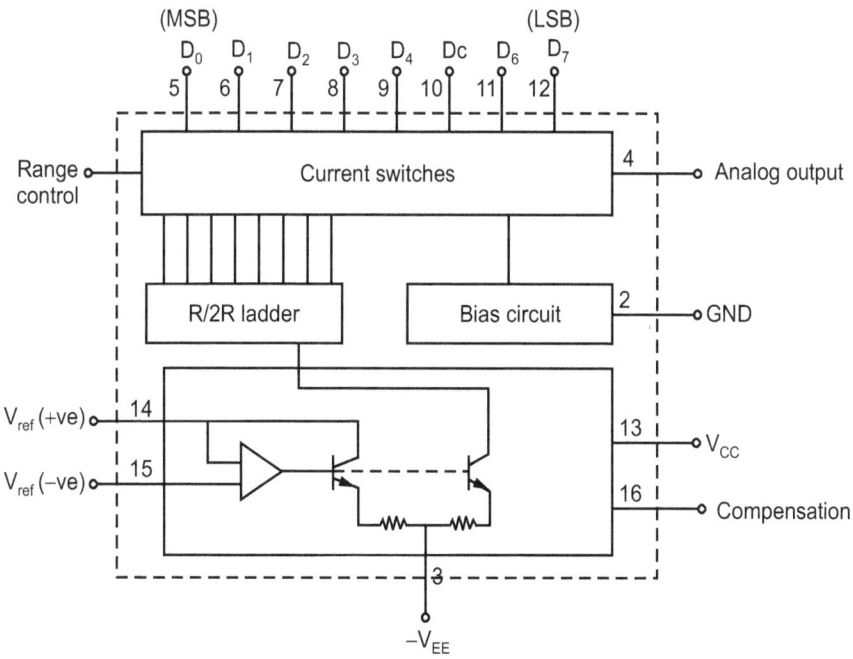

Fig. 4.24 : Internal schematic of DAC 0808

4.4.4 Interfacing of DAC 0808 to 8051

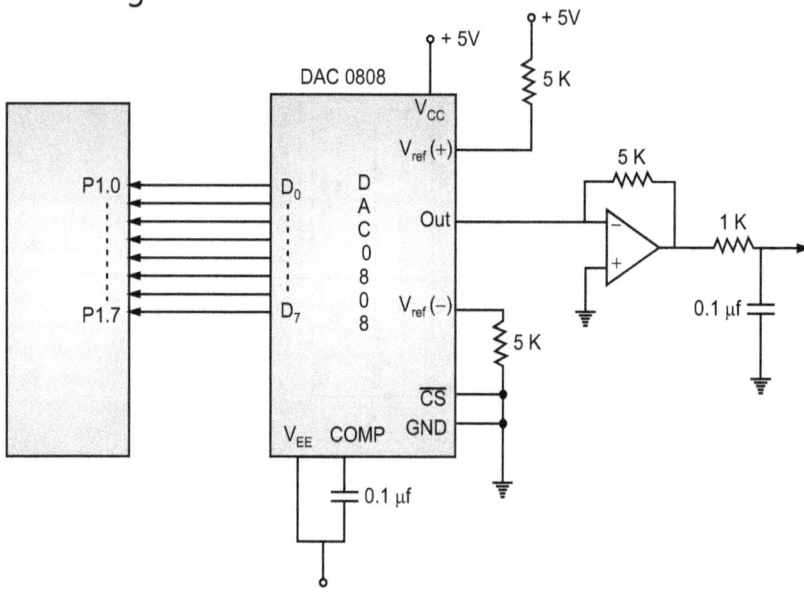

Fig. 4.25 : 8051 connection to DAC 0808

Program 4.13

Design a 8051 based system to interface DAC. Write the C and an assembly language programs to generate.

(1) Triangular wave, (2) Sinusoidal wave, (3) Trapezoidal wave.

Solution : Fig. 4.26 shows interfacing of DAC 0808 to 8051.

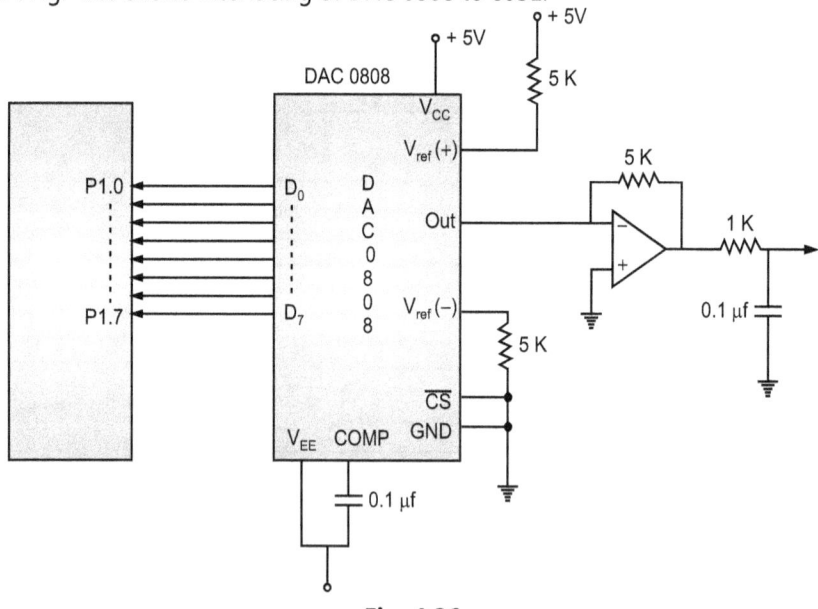

Fig. 4.26

(i) **Triangular wave :** Assembly/Program language

```
        ORG 0000H
        LJMP L1
        ORG 0100H
L1:     MOV A, # 00H          Initialize port 1
Here:   MOV P1, A
        INC A
        CJNE A, # 0FFH, HERE  // increment the port 1 till it reaches
                                 maximum (FFH)
S1!     MOV P1, A
        DEC A
        CJNE A, # 00H, S1     // once it reaches to maximum decrement the
                                 data in P1 till it reaches minimum (00H)
        SJMP HERE
        END
```

C Program :

```c
# include <reg51.h>
void main (void)
{
  P1 = 0X00;
  while (1)
  {
    while (P1 == 0XFF)
    P1 ++;
    while (P1 == 0X00)
    P1 --;
  }
}
```

(ii) **Sinusoidal wave generation :**

To generate a sine wave, we need a table in which the magnitude of the sine of angles between 0 to 360 degrees are given. The values of the sine function vary from −1 to +1.0 for 0 − to 360 − degree angles. Table 4.8 shows the angles, the sine values, the voltage magnitudes and the integer values representing the voltage magnitude for each angle.

Table 4.8

Angle θ (degrees)	sin θ	V_{out} 5V + (5 × sin θ)	Values sent to DAC voltage magnitude × 25.6
0	0	5	128
30	0.5	7.5	192
60	0.866	9.33	238
90	1.0	10	255
120	0.866	9.33	238
150	0.5	7.5	192
180	0	5	128
210	− 0.5	2.5	64
240	− 0.866	0.669	17
270	− 1.0	0	0
300	− 0.866	0.669	17
330	− 0.5	2.5	64
360	0	5	128

Assembly Language Program :

```
            ORG 0000H
            LJMP MAIN
            ORG 0100H
MAIN :      MOV R0, # 30H
            MOV @ R0, # 128
            INC R0
            MOV @ R0, # 192
            INC R0
            MOV @ R0, # 238
            INC R0
            MOV @ R0, # 255
            INC R0
            MOV @ R0, # 238
            INC R0
            MOV @ R0, # 192
            INC R0
```

```
            MOV @ R0, # 128
            INC R0
            MOV @ R0, # 64
            INC R0
            MOV @ R0, # 17
            INC R0
            MOV @ R0, # 0
            INC R0
            MOV @ R0, # 17
            INC R0
            MOV @ R0, # 64
            INC R0
            MOV R0, # 30H
HERE :      MOV P1, @ R0
            INC R0
            CJNE R0; # 3CH, HERE
            MOV R0, # 30H
            SJMP HERE
            END
```

C Program for Sinusoidal

```c
# include <reg51.h>
char array [ ] = {128, 192, 238, 255, 238, 192, 128, 64, 17, 0, 17, 64, 128};
unsigned char a = 0
void main (void)
{
  while (1)
  {
    P1 = array [a];    // Issue the data one by one from the array
    a++;
    if (a == 13)       //If last data is issued, repeat the procedure from beginning
  }
}
```

(iii) Trapezoidal wave
Assembly language program :

```
            ORG 0000H
            LJMP MAIN
            ORG 0100H
MAIN :      MOV A, # 00H
HERE :      MOV R7, # 0FFH
   NXT      DJNZ R7, NXT
AGAIN :     MOV P1, A
            INC A
            CJNE A, # 0FFH, AGAIN
            MOV R7, # 0FFH
   S1 :     DJNZ R7, 00S1
   L1 :     MOV P1, A
            DEC A
            CJNE A, # 00H, L1
            SJMP HERE
            END
```

Fig. 4.27

C Program :

```c
# include <reg51.h>
void main (void)
{
  P1 = 0X00;
  while (1)
  {
    while (P1 == 0XFF)
    P1 ++;
    for (x = 0; x < 500; x++)      // small software delay for flat to P
    while (P1 = 0X00)
    P1 --;
    for (x = 0; x < 500; x++);
  }
}
```

Program 4.14

Write an assembly language program to generate a square wave of 1 kHz with 50% duty cycle.

Solution : Assembly language program

HERE :	MOV A, # 00H	
	MOV P1, A	output low
	ACALL DELAY	
	MOV A, # 0FFH	output high
	MOV P1, A	
	ACALL DELAY	
	SJMP HERE	
	MOV R0, # 0FFH	
AGAIN :	DJNZ R0, AGAIN	
	RET	
	END	

C Program

```
# include <reg51.h>
main ( )
{
  unsigned int x;
  while (1)
  P1 = 00;                      output low
  for (x = 0; x < 1578; x++)
  P1 = 0XFF;                    output high
  for (x = 0; x < 1578, x++)
}
```

Program 4.15

Write an assembly language program to generate staircase waveform.

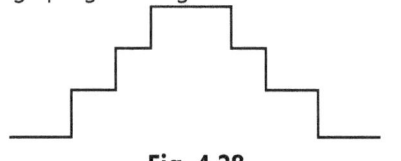

Fig. 4.28

Program :

```
        ORG 0100H
Table dB 01H, 02H, 03H, 04H, 03H, 02H, 01H
   S1 :  MOV DPTR # Table
          MOV R2, # 07H
   UP :   CLR A
          MOV C A, @ A + DPTR
          MOV P1, A
          INC DPTR
          DJNZ R2, UP
          SJMP S1
```

C Program :

```
# include <reg51.h>
Sfr datain = P1;
void main ( )
{
   unsigned char value [6] = {01, 02, 03, 04, 03, 02, 01}
   unsigned char b;
   while (1)
   {
     for (b = 0; b < 7; b++)
     {
        data in = value [b];
     }
   }
}
```

Program 4.16

Write an assembly language program to generate a sawtooth waveform for 8051.

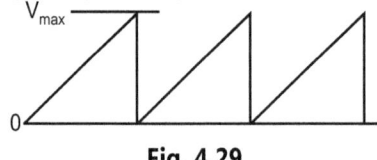

Fig. 4.29

Assembly Language Program :

```
         MOV A, # 00H
BACK:    MOV P1, A
         INC A
         SJMP BACK
```

C Program

```
# include <reg51.h>
void main ()
{
  Unsigned char[x]
  while 1
  {
    for (x = 0; x < 0; x++)
    P1 = x
  }
}
```

4.5 INTERFACING AND ACCESSING EXTERNAL DATA MEMORY

Semiconductor memories are called as the primary memory because they are directly connected to the CPU and the CPU first asks to the semiconductor memories for the information of code and data. The widely used semiconductor memories are ROM and RAM.

4.5.1 Important Characteristics for the Semiconductor Memories

1. Memory capacity
2. Memory organization
3. Memory speed.

1. Memory capacity : The number of bits that a semiconductor memory chip can store is called chip capacity. It may be in K bits, M bits and so on.

2. Memory organization : Memory chips are organized into a number of locations and each location may store 1 bit, 4 bits, 8 bits or even 16 bits depending upon the internal design. The number of bits stored in a location is equal to the number of data pins on the chip and the number of locations depends on the number of address pins. The number of locaions within a memory IC always equals 2 to the power of the number of address pins.

(i) A memory chip contains 2^K locations, where K is the number of address pins.
(ii) Each location contains M bits, where M is the number of data pins on the chip.
(iii) The entire chip will contain $2^K \times M$ bits.

3. Memory speed : Speed is the time required to access the data from the memory. The speed of the memory is commonly known as **access time**. The access time of memory chips varies from a few nanoseconds to hundreds of nanoseconds, depending on the IC technology.

4.5.2 ROM : (Read Only Memory)

ROM is a type of memory whose contents are not lost when the power is turned off. It is also called as **non-volatile** memory. Various types of ROM are available, such as PROM, EPROM, EEPROM, Flash ROM and mask ROM.

4.5.3 PROM (Programmable ROM)

PROM is a user programmable memory for every bit there exists a fuse. PROM is programmed by blowing fuses PROM is also called as OTP (one-time programmable). If the information burned into PROM is wrong, then PROM must be discarded permanently. It is also as burning ROM. It requires special equipment called as ROM burner or ROM programmer.

4.5.4 EPROM (Erasable Programmable ROM) and UV - EPROM

In EPROM, one can program the memory chip and erase it thousands of time. This is required during developing of the prototype of a microprocessor based project. Most popular ERPOM is called as UV-EPROM. UV stands for ultraviolet. UV-EPROM takes more time for erasing it is contents. UV-EPROM chips have a window through which the programmer can shine ultraviolet radiation to erase its contents.

4.5.5 EPROM (Electrically Erasable Programmable ROM)

EEPROM has more advantages compared to EPROM.
- In EPROM all contents of ROM are erased whereas in EEPROM selected bytes are erased.
- For EPROM to erase the contents, one has to remove the chip from the socket whereas EEPROM does not require the physical removal of the chip from its sockets.
- In EEPROM external eraser and programming device is not required whereas UV-EPROM requires external erasable and programming device.
- Cost per bit for EEPROM is much higher than UV-EPROM

4.5.6 Flash Memory EPROM

In early 1990s, flash EPROM has become a popular user-programmable memory chip.
- It takes less than a second to erase the entire contents.
- Erasable method is electrical therefore sometimes it is called as flash EEPROM.
- Difference between flash EPROM and EEPROM is in flash EPROM, the entire device is erased and in EEPROM selected byte is erased.
- It is used to upgrade the Bios ROM of the PC.

4.5.7 Mask ROM

In Mask ROM the contents are programmed by the IC manufacturer. It is not a user programmable ROM. Mask ROM is used when the large memory is required. Mask ROM is cheaper than other kinds of ROM but if an error occurs in the data, entire batch must be thrown away.

4.5.8 RAM (Random Access Memory)

Ram is called volatile memory since cutting of the power to the IC results in the loss of data. Sometimes it is called as read/write memory. There are three types of RAM :
1. Static RAM (SRAM)
2. NV-RAM (Non-volatile RAM)
3. Dynamic RAM (DRAM)

4.5.9 SRAM (Static RAM)

Static RAM is made of flip-flops therefore it does not require refreshing in order to keep data. The main drawback of SRAM is if the flip-flop is used it requires at least 6 transistors to build to store 1 bit. Therefore, the cost of the static RAM is very high.

4.5.10 NV-RAM (Non-volatile RAM)

Like other RAMs, it allows the CPU to read and write to it, but when the power is turned off it's contents are not lost. It combines the best of RAM and ROM. To retain its contents, every NV-RAM chip is internally made of the following components :
1. It uses extremely power efficient SRAM cells built out of CMOS.
2. It uses an internal lithium battery as a backup energy source.
3. It uses an intelligent control circuitry, to monitor the V_{CC} pin constantly to detect loss of the external power supply. The internal lithium battery is used to retain the content only when the external power source is off. Non-volatile RAM is a very expensive type of RAM.

4.5.11 Checksum byte ROM

To maintain the integrity of the ROM contents, every system must perform the checksum calculations. The checksum will detect if any data of the ROM is corrupted. ROM data may be corrupted because of the surge current either when the system is turned ON or during operation. The checksum process uses checksum bytes. It is tagged to the end of a series of bytes of data. To calculate checksum bytes following steps may be taken :
1. Add the bytes together and drop the carries.
2. Take the 2's complement of the total sum, and that is the checksum byte; which is the last byte of the series.

Add all the bytes, including checksum byte, the result must be zero. If it is not zero, then one or more bytes of data have been changed.

4.5.12 DRAM (Dynamic RAM)

Intel corporation introduced the first dynamic RAM in 1970. Its capacity was 1024 bits and it is used a capacitor of transistors needed to build the cell. The main disadvantage of DRAM is it needs refreshing due to leakage in the capacitor. The advantage of DRAM is its low cost per bit and low power consumption per bit.

Data cannot be accessed during refreshing. Therefore when there is a requirement of small amount of memory SRAM is used and when there is a requirement of large memory DRAM is used.

4.5.13 Interfacing Memory to 8051

The CPU provides the address of the data desired, but it is the job of the decoding circuitry to locate the selected memory block. To connect a memory chip to the CPU, following points must be noted :

1. The data bus of the CPU is connected directly to the data pins of the memory chip.
2. Control signals RD and WR from the CPU are connected to the OE (output enable) and WE (write enable) pin of the memory chip, respectively.
3. In the case of the address buses, while the lower bits of the addresses from the CPU go directly to the memory chip address pins, the upper ones are used to activate the CS pin of the memory chip. It is the CS pin that along with RD/WR allows the flow of data in or out of the memory chip. No data can be written into or read from the memory chip unless CS is activated.

4.5.14 Interfacing 8051 to External Program ROM

Fig. 4.30 shows the interfacing of 8 KB external program ROM with 8051. If $\overline{EA}$ pin is connected to V_{CC} it indicates that a program code is stored in the on-chip ROM. If the $\overline{EA}$ pin is connected to GND then it is an off chip ROM. (External ROM).

$\overline{PSEN}$ is connected to $\overline{OE}$ pin of ROM. For 8 KB, the number of address lines required is $2^{13} \cong 8\ KB = 13$

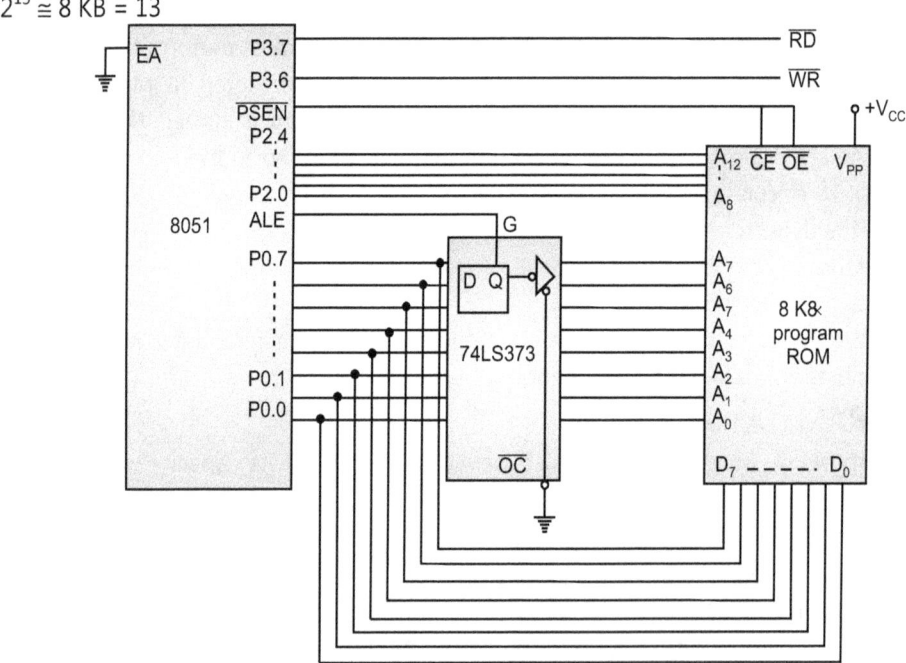

Fig. 4.30 : Interfacing of external program ROM to 8051

4.5.15 Interfacing External DATA ROM to 8051

8051 has 128 bytes of address space in which 64 k bytes are reserved for program code and another 64 k bytes are reserved for data. Data memory space is accessed using DPTR register where as program code can be accessed using program counter. For external memory access MOVX instruction is used where X stands for external.

To access the external ROM, $\overline{RD}$ pin is used. The ROM which contains program codes can be fetched using $\overline{PSEN}$ signal and $\overline{RD}$ is used to fetch the data.

4.5.16 Interfacing External Data RAM to 8051

Fig. 4.31 shows the interfacing of external data RAM to 8051. Here $\overline{RD}$ pin is connected to $\overline{OE}$ (output enable) and $\overline{WR}$ pin is connected to $\overline{WE}$ (write enable)

Fig. 4.31 shows the connection of external Data ROM with 8051.

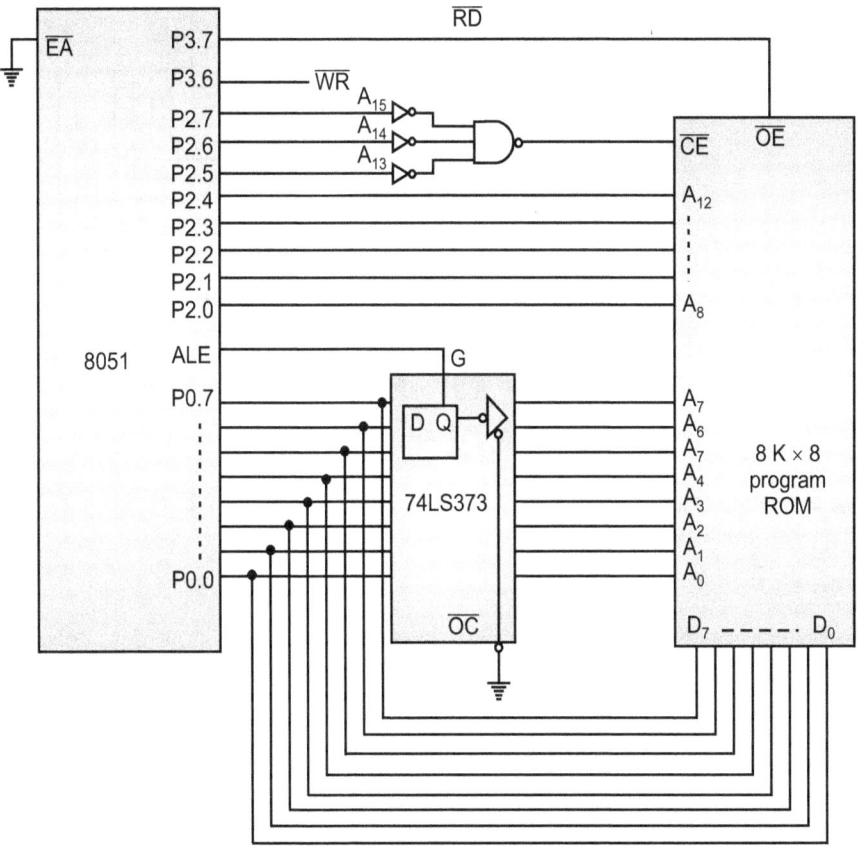

Fig. 4.31 : 8051 Connections to External Data ROM

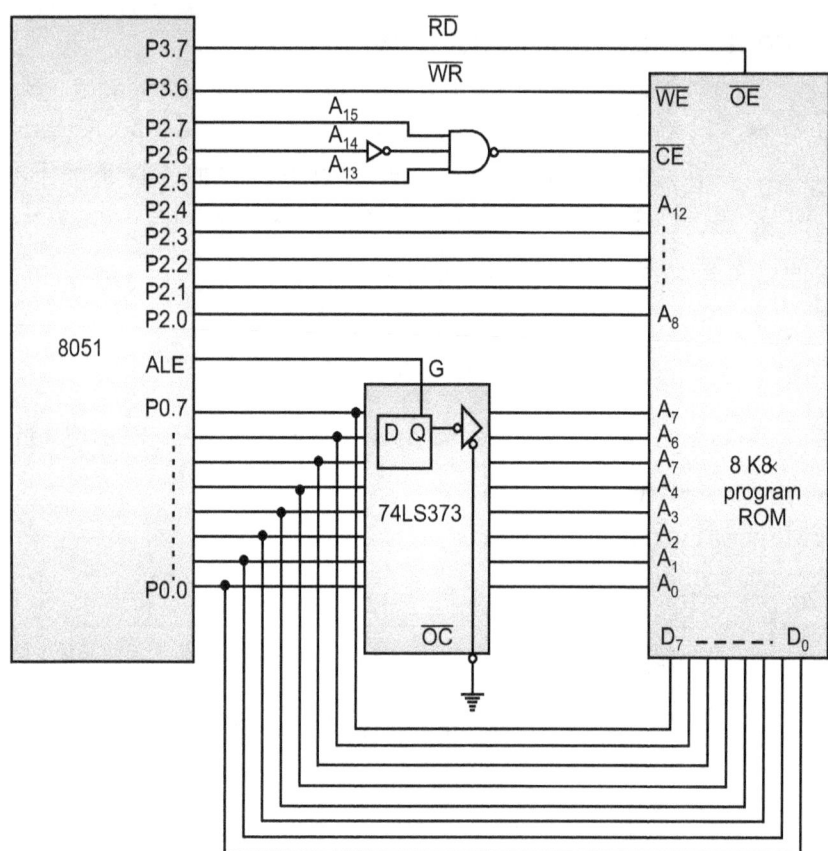

Fig. 4.32 : 8051 Connections to External Data RAM

4.5.17 Interfacing to Large External Memory

In some applications, we need a large amount of memory to store data. The 8051 supports only 64 k bytes of external data memory because DPTR is of 16 bit. Therefore to support large external memory $A_0 - A_{15}$ of the 8051 directly connected to external memory's $A_0 - A_{15}$ pins and some of the port 1 pins are used to access 64 k byte block inside a single 256 k × 8 memory chip.

Program 4.17

In a certain application, we need 256 k bytes of NVRAM to store data collected by an 8051 microcontroller. Show the interfacing of a single 256 k × 8 NV-RAM chip to 8051. Also show how various blocks of this single chip are accessed.

Solution : The 256 k × 8 NV-RAM has 18 address pins ($A_0 - A_{17}$) and 8 data lines. In Fig. 4.33 $A_0 - A_{15}$ are connected directly to the memory chip and A_{16} and A_{17} are controlled by P1.0 and P1.1 respectively. The chip select signal of external RAM is connected to P1.2 of the 8051. 256 k bytes of memory are divided into four block and each block is accessed according to table 4.9.

Table 4.9

Chip Select	A_{17}	A_{16}	
P1.2	P1.1	P1.0	Block address space
0	0	0	00000H to 0FFFFH
0	0	1	10000H to 1FFFFH
0	1	0	20000H to 2FFFFH
0	1	1	30000H to 3FFFFH
1	X	X	External RAM disabled

For example to access the 20000H to 2FFFFH address space, we need the following :

```
CLR   P1.2            ; enable external RAM
MOV   DPTR, # 0       ; start of 64 k memory block
CLR   P1.0            ; A16 = 0
SETB  P1.1            ; A17 = 1 for 20000H block
MOVA, SBUF            ; get data from serial port
MOVX  @ DPTR, A       ; save data in block 20000H address
INC   DPTR            ; next location
```

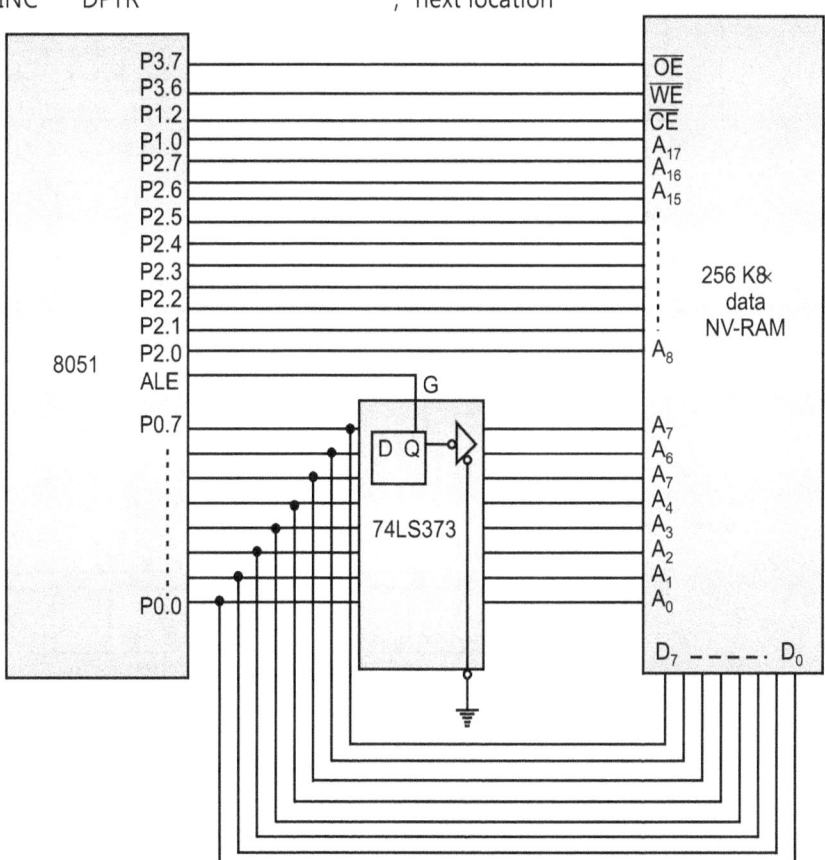

Fig. 4.33 : 8051 accessing 256k × 8 external NV-RAM

Program 4.18

Interface 8 kb of RAM and 4 kb of EPROM with 8051. The starting address of ROM is 8000H.

Solution : Let use 4 k × 8 devices, 12 address lines are required on the EPROM and RAM chips.

A_{12} to A_{15} are used to generate the chip select signal for the memory devices using 74138 decoder.

Device	Decoded by 74138					Decoded on EPROM RAM IC										Address
	A_{15}	A_{14}	A_{13}	A_{12}	A_{11}	A_{10}	A_9	A_8	A_7	A_6	A_5	A_4	A_3	A_2	A_1	A_0	
EPROM	1	0	0	0	0	0	0	0	0	0	0	0	0	0	0	0	8000H
	1	0	0	0	1	1	1	1	1	1	1	1	1	1	1	1	to 8FFFH
RAM 1	1	0	0	1	0	0	0	0	0	0	0	0	0	0	0	0	9000H
	1	0	0	1	1	1	1	1	1	1	1	1	1	1	1	1	to 9FFFH
RAM 2	1	0	1	0	0	0	0	0	0	0	0	0	0	0	0	0	A000H
	1	0	1	0	1	1	1	1	1	1	1	1	1	1	1	1	to AFFFH

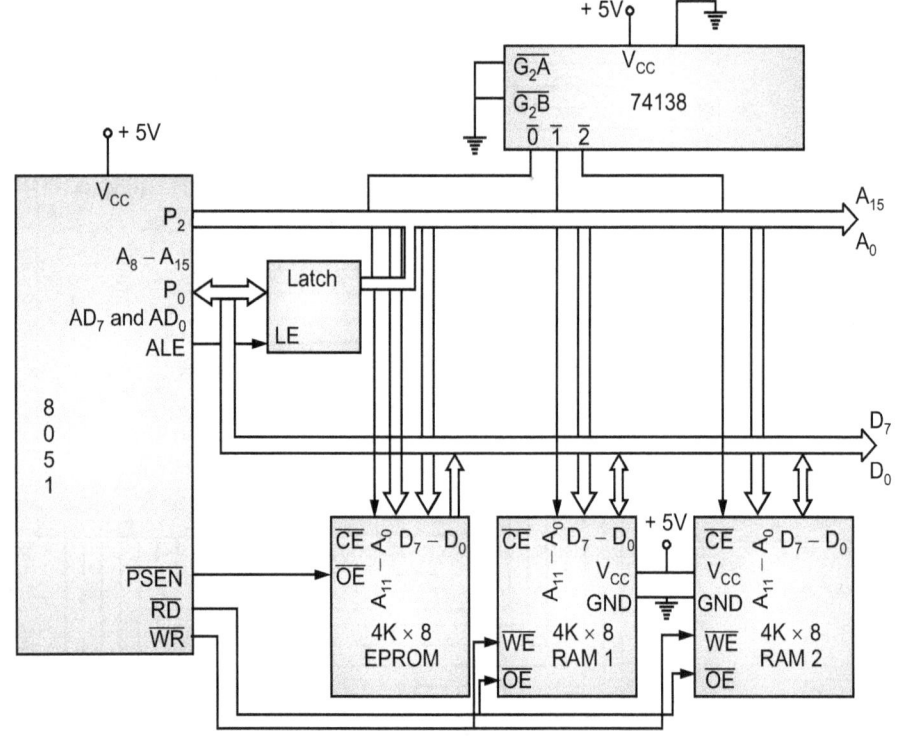

Fig. 4.34

4.5.18 Accessing External Data Memory in 8051 C

Program 4.19

Write a C program (a) to store ASCII letters 'A' to 'E' in external RAM addresses starting at 0 then (b) get the same data from the external RAM and send it to P1 one byte at a time.

Solution :

```
# include <reg51.h>
# include <absacc.h>              // notice the header file for XBYTE
void main (void)
{
  unsigned char x;
  XBYTE [0] = 'A';                // write ASCII 'A' to external RAM location
  XBYTE [1] = 'B';
  XBYTE [2] = 'C';
  XBYTE [3] = 'D';
  XBYTE [4] = 'E';
  for (x = 0; x < 5; x++)
  P1 = XBYTE [x];
}
```

Program 4.20

An external ROM uses the 8051 data space to store the look-up table (starting at 200H) for DAC data. Write a C program to read 50 bytes of table data and send it to P1.

Solution :

```
# include <reg51.h>
# include <absacc.h>
void main (void)
{
  unsigned char count;
  for (count = 0; count < 50; count ++)
  P1 = XBYTE [0X200 + count];
}
```

Program 4.21

Write a C program to move the message 'WELCOME' into external RAM and read the same data in external RAM and send it to the serial port. Assume that the external RAM with addresses 0000-2FFFH for a given 8051 based system.

Solution :

```
# include <reg51.h>
# include <absacc.h>
unsigned char msg [7] = "WELCOME";
void main (void)
{
  unsigned char x;
  TMOD = 0X20;                // use timer 1, 8-bit auto reload
  TH1 = 0XFD;
  SCON = 0X50;
  TR1 = 1;
  For (x = 0; x < 7; x++)
    XBYTE [0X000 + x] = msg [x];
  For (x = 0, x < 7; x++)
  {
    SBUF = XBYTE [0X000 + x];
    while (TI == 0);
    TI = 0;
  }
}
```

4.5.19 Accessing 1 K Byte SRAM

The DS89C4X0 chip family has 1 K byte of SRAM which is accessed by using MOV X instruction. This 1 K byte of SRAM can be very useful in many applications. For example, C compilers that need to store data variable. On power - ON reset, access to 1 KB SRAM is denied. To access, 1 KB SRAM some bits in the SFR register must be enabled called as PMR (Power Management Register). The location of PMR is at C4H. The PMR bits related to 1 KB SRAM is shown in Fig. 4.35.

D_7							D_0
1	0	0	0	0	0	DME1	DME0

Fig. 4.35

DME1	DME0	Data Memory Address Range	Memory Access
0	0	0000 – FFFFH	External data memory
X	1	0000 – 03FFH	Internal SRAM data memory
1	0	Reserved	Reserved

Power Management Register (PMR) is an SFR in the DS89C4X0 family and is located at address C4H.

Program 4.22

Write a C program to enable the access to the 1 KB SRAM of the DS89C4X0 and put the ASCII letters 'A', 'B' and 'C' in SRAM. Also read the same data from SRAM and send each one to ports P0, P1 and P2.

Solution :

```
# include <reg51.h>
# include <abscacc.h>          // check the header file for XBYTE
Sfr PMRREG = 0XC4;
void main (void)
{
    unsigned char x;
    PMRREG = 0X81;
    XBYTE [0] = 'A';            // write ASCII 'A' to external RAM location 0
    XBYTE [1] = 'B';            // write ASCII 'B' to external RAM location 1
    XBYTE [2] = 'C';            // write ASCII 'C' to external RAM location 2
    For (x = 0; x < 3; x++)
    {
        P0 = XBYTE [x];         // read ext RAM data and send it to P0
        P1 = XBYTE [x];         // read ext RAM data and send it to P1
        P2 = XBYTE [x];         // read ext RAM data and send it to P2
    }
}
```

Program 4.23

Write a C program to enable access to a 1 KB RAM of the DS89C4X0 and move a block of data from the code space of the DS89C4X0 chip into 1 KB SRAM. Also read the same data from SRAM and send it to the serial port of the 8051 one byte at a time.

Solution :

```
# include <reg51.h>
# include (absacc.h>
Sfr PMRREG = 0XC4;
void main (void)
{
    code unsigned char msg [ ] = "WELCOME";
```

```c
    unsigned char i;
    PMRREG = PMRREG|0X1;
    TMOD = 0X20;
    TH1 = 0XFD;
    SCON = 0X50;
    TR1 = 1;
    For (i = 0; i < 7; i++)
    {
        XBYTE [0X0 + i] = MSG [i]
    }
    For (i = 0; i < 7; i++)
    {
        SBUF = XBYTE [0X0 + i];
        while (TI == 0)'
        TI = 0;
    }
    while (1);
}
```

4.5.20 Accessing 1 K-Byte SRAM is Assembly

Program 4.24

Write a program to enable access to the 1 KB SRAM of the DS89C4X0 and multiply two bytes stored in consecutive locations in the SRAM. Also store the result in the next two locations in the SRAM and also output the result bytes to port 0 and port 1.

Solution:

```
        DATA EQU 0000H
        ORG 0000H
        MOV A, 0CHH             // read PMR register
        SET B ACC 0             // make DME0 = 1
        MOV 0C4H, A             // enable 1 KB SRAM
        MOV DPTR, # data
        MOV X A, @ DPTR
        MOV B, A
        INC DPTR
        MOV X A, @ DPTR
        MVL AB
        INC DPTR
```

```
MOV X @ DPTR, A
MOV P0, A
INC DPTR
MOV A, B
MOV X @ DPTR, A
MOV P1, A
END
```

Program 4.25

Write a program to enable access to the 1 KB SRAM of the DS89C4X0 and add two 16-bit numbers. One number is stored in the external SRAM in two consecutive locations 0400H onwards, with the LSB in the lower address. The other 16-bit number is stored in internal RAM locations 45H and 46H. The result is stored in the next locations in internal RAM.

Solution:

```
DATA EQU 0400H          // Address of LSB of first number
ORG 0000H
MOV A, 0C4H             // read PMR register
SET B ACC.0             // make DME0 = 1
MOV A, 0C4H             // read PMR register
SETB ACC.0              // make DME0 = 1
MOV 0C4H, A             // enable 1 KB SRAM
CLR C                   // clear C
MOV DPTR, # DATA        // let DPTR point to LSB of 16 bit word
MOV X A, @ DPTR         // move LSB to A
ADD A, 45H              // add it to the byte in RAM location 45H
MOV 47H, A              // move sum to RAM location 47H
INC DPTR                // increment DPTR to point to upper byte
MOV X A, @ DPTR         // move upper byte to A
ADDC A, 46H             // add it to byte in RAM location 46H
MOV 48H, A              // move sum to RAM location 48H
CLR A                   // clear A
ADDC A, # 00            // A = A + 0 + C
MOV 49H, A              // move A into RAM location 48H
```

Program 4.26

Write a program in assembly to enable access to the 1 KB SRAM of the DS89C4X0 and move a block of data from code space of the DS89C4X0 chip into 1 KB SRAM. Also read the same data from RAM and send it to the serial port of the 8051 one byte at a time.

Solution:

```
            DATA-ADD R  EQU  400H      ; code data
            COUNT       EQU  7         ; message size
            RAM_ADDR    EQU  40H       ; 8051 internal RAM address
            ORG 0000H
            ACALL COPY_1               ; copy from code ROM to internal RAM
            MOV A, 0C4H                ; read PMR
            SET B ACC.0                ; enable PMR bit for 1 K SRAM
            MOV 0C4H, A                ; write it to PMR of DS89C4X0
            ACALL COPY_2               ; copy from internal RAM to 1 KB SRAM
            MOV TMOD, # 20H            ; set up serial port
            MOV TH1, # –3              ; set 9600 baud rate
            MOV SCON, # 50H
            SET B TR1
            ACALL COPY_COM             ; copy from 1 KB SRAM to serial port
            SJMP $                     // stay here
COPY_1:     MOV DPTR, # DATA_ADDR
            MOV R0, # RAM_ADDR
            MOV R2, # COUNT
     H1:    CLR A
            MOVC A, @ A + DPTR
            MOV @ R0, A
            INC DPTR
            INC R0
            DJNZ R2, H1
            RET
// transfer data from internal RAM to external RAM
COPY_2 :    MOV DPTR, # 0              ; DS89C4X0 1 KB address
            MOV R0, # RAM_ADDR
            MOV R2, # COUNT
     H2 :   MOV A, @ R0                ; get a byte from internal RAM
            MOVX @ DPTR, A             ; store it in 1 KB SRAM of DS89C4X0
            INC DPTR
            INC R0
            DJNZ R2, H2
            RET
// data transfer from 1 KB SRAM to serial port.
```

COPY_COM:

```
            MOV DPTR, # 0           ; DS89C4X0 1 KB address
            MOV R2, # count
    H3:     MOVX A, @ DPTR          ; get a byte from 1 KB SRAM space
            ACALL SERIAL            ; send it to COM port
            INC DPTR
            DJNZ R2, H3
            RET
    // send data to serial port.
    SERIAL: MOV SBUF, A
    H4:     JNB TI, H4
            CLR TI
            RET
    // data in code space
            ORG 400H
    MYBYTE: DB "WELCOME"
            END
```

4.6 STEPPER MOTOR INTERFACING

> **Q. With suitable example and diagram explain interfacing of KB0 with 8051 microcontroller.** **[8 M] [Nov./Dec. 2011]**

Stepper Motor is a device which converts electrical pulses into mechanical movement. Stepper motor is used for position control in applications such as disk drives, dot matrix printers and robotics. Stepper motor consists of a permanent magnet rotor which is also called as the shaft surrounded by a stator. The most common stepper motors have four stator windings that are paired with a center tapped common as shown in Fig. 4.36. This type of stepper motor is commonly called as unipolar stepper motor. The center tap allows a change of current direction in each of two coils when a winding is grounded which changes the polarity of the stator.

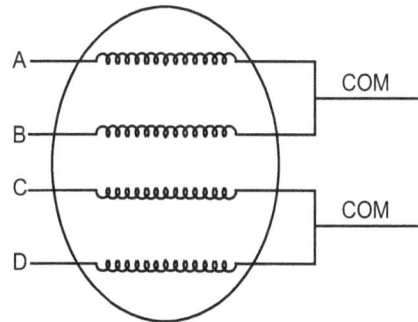

Fig. 4.36 : Stator winding configuration

When a conventional motor shaft runs freely, the stepper motor shaft moves in a fixed repeatable increment which allows one to move it in a precise position. This repeatable fixed movement is possible as a result of basic magnetic theory where poles of the same polarity repels and opposite poles attract. The direction of the rotation is dictated by the stator poles. The stator poles are determined by the current sent through the wire coils. As the direction of current changes, the polarity also changes causing the reverse motion of the rotor. As the sequence of power is applied to each stator winding, the rotor will rotate. There are several widely used sequences where each sequence has a different degree of precision.

Table 4.10 : Shows a 2 phase, 4 step stepping sequence

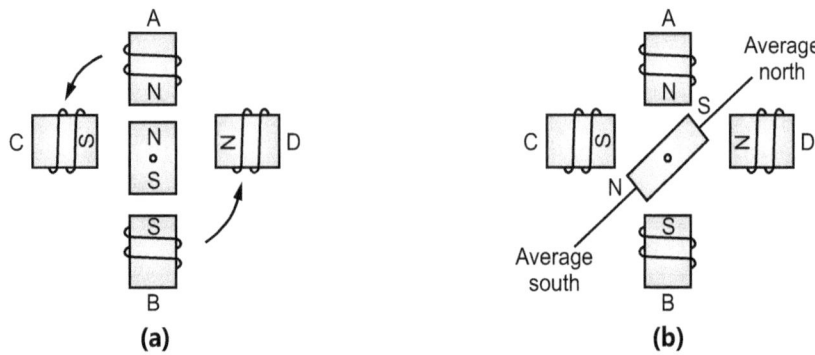

Fig. 4.37 : Rotor Alignment

Table 4.10 : Normal 4 step sequence

Clockwise	Step	Winding A	Winding B	Winding C	Winding D	Counter Clockwise
↓	1	1	0	0	1	↑
	2	1	1	0	0	
	3	0	1	1	0	
	4	0	0	1	1	

4.6.1 Step Angle

The step angle is defined as, the minimum degree of rotation associated with a single step.

Steps per revolution : The total number of steps needed to rotate one complete rotation or 360 degrees.

$$\text{Steps per revolution} = 180 \text{ steps} \times 2 \text{ degrees} = 360°$$

Table 4.11 shows some step angles for various motors.

Table 4.11 : Step angles of stepper motor

Step Angle	Steps per Revolution
0.72	500
1.8	200
2.0	180
2.5	144
5.0	72
7.5	48
15	24

The relation between rpm (revolutions per minute), steps per revolution and steps per second is as follows.

$$\text{Steps per Second} = \frac{\text{rpm} \times \text{Steps per revolution}}{60}$$

Program 4.27

Describe the 8051 connection to the stepper motor and write a code to program to rotate it continuously.

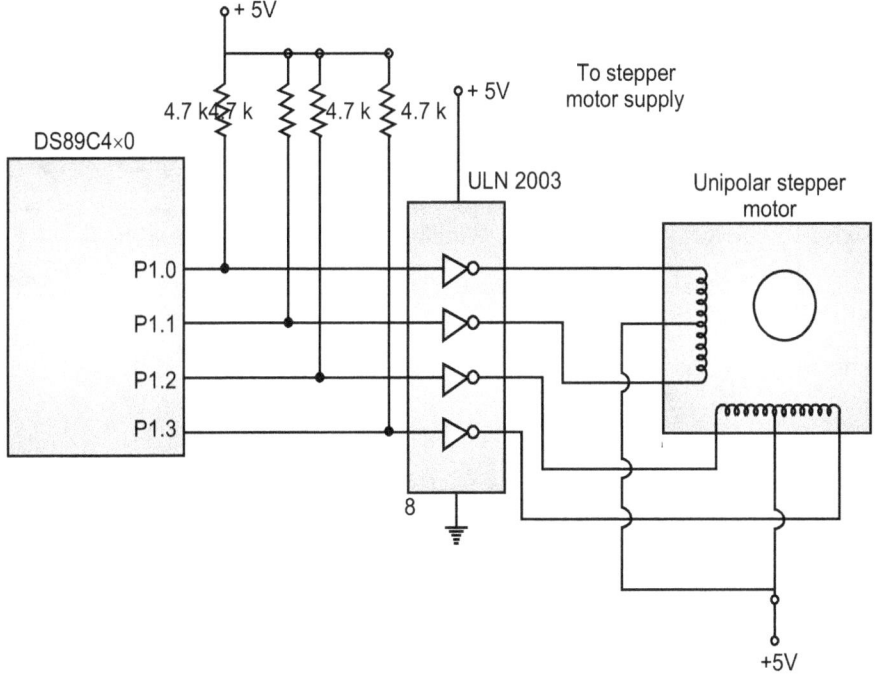

Fig. 4.38 : 8051 connection to stepper motor

Fig. 4.38 shows the 8051 connection to the stepper motor. The four leads of the stator winding are controlled by port 1 bits P1.0 – P1.3. The 8051 does not have sufficient current to drive the stepper motor windings. Hence, a driver like ULN 2003 is required to energize the stator.

Program: MOV A, # 66H
            MOV P1, A
            RR A
            ACALL DELAY
            SJMP BACK
DELAY :   MOV R2, # 100
B1 :   MOV R3, # 255
B2 :   DJNZ R3, B2
            DJNZ R2, B1
            RET

4.6.2 Four Step Sequence and Number of Teeth on Rotor

Table 4.12 shows the 4 step switching sequence since after four steps the same two windings will be 'ON'. After completing every four steps, the rotor moves only one tooth pitch. Therefore in a stepper motor with 200 steps per revolution, the rotor has 50 teeth. The minimum step angle is always a function of the number of teeth on the rotor.

To allow finer resolutions, all stepper motors allow 8-step switching sequence. The 8-step sequence is also called half-stepping. In the 8-step sequence each step is half of the normal step angle. Table 4.12 shows a half stepping sequence.

Table 4.12

Clockwise	Step	Winding A	Winding B	Winding C	Winding D	Anti-Clockwise
↓	1	1	0	0	1	↑
	2	1	0	0	0	
	3	1	1	0	0	
	4	0	1	0	0	
	5	0	1	1	0	
	6	0	0	1	0	
	7	0	0	1	1	
	8	0	0	0	1	

Motor Speed : The motor speed, measured in steps per second is a function of the switching rate. By changing the length of the time delay loop, various rotation speeds can be achieved.

Holding torque : It is defined as the amount of torque, from an external source, required to break away the shaft from its holding position with the motor shaft at standstill or zero rpm condition. The unit of torque is ounce-inch or kg-cm. It is measured with voltage and current applied to the motor.

Wave-drive 4 step sequence : In addition to the 8-step and the 4-step sequences there is another sequence called the wave drive 4 step sequence. Table 4.13 shows the wave drive 4-step sequence.

Table 4.13 : Wave drive 4 step sequence

Clockwise	Step	Winding A	Winding B	Winding C	Winding D	Anti Clockwise
↓	1	1	0	0	0	↑
	2	0	1	0	0	
	3	0	0	1	0	
	4	0	0	0	1	

4.6.3 Unipolar Versus Bipolar Stepper Motor Interface

There are three common types of stepper motor interfacing :
(1) Unipolar, (2) Bipolar, (3) Universal.
They are identified depending on the number of connections to the motor.
- A universal stepper motor has eight connection. The unipolar stepper motor has six connections and the bipolar stepper motor has four connections.
- The universal stepper motor can be configured for all three modes while the unipolar can be either unipolar or bipolar, whereas the bipolar cannot be configured for universal non-unipolar mode.

Table 4.14 shows the selected stepper motor characteristics.

Table 4.14

Part No.	Step angle	Drive system	Volts	Phase resistance	Current
151861 CP	7.5	Unipolar	5 V	9 Ω	550 mA
171601 CP	3.6	Unipolar	7 V	20 Ω	350 mA
164056 CP	7.5	Bipolar	5 V	60 Ω	800 mA

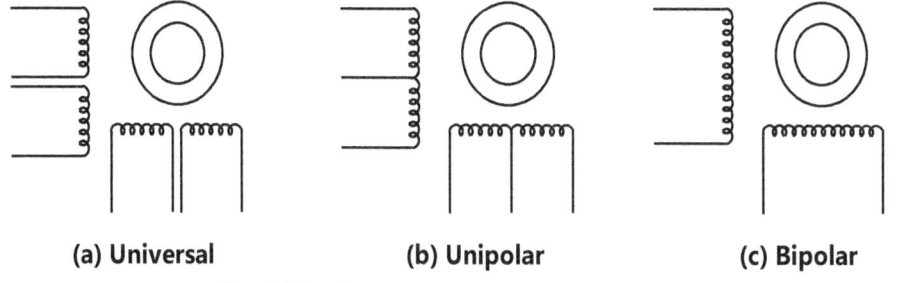

(a) Universal   (b) Unipolar   (c) Bipolar

Fig. 4.39 : Common stepper motor types

Unipolar stepper motors can be controlled using the basic interfacing whereas the bipolar stepper requires H-bridge circuitry. Bipolar stepper motors require a higher operational current than the unipolar.

4.6.4 Using transistors as Drivers

Fig. 4.40 shows an interface to a unipolar stepper motor using transistors. Diodes reduce the back EMF spike created when the coils are energized and de-energized. TIP transistors can be used to supply higher current to the motor. These transistors can accommodate higher voltages and currents.

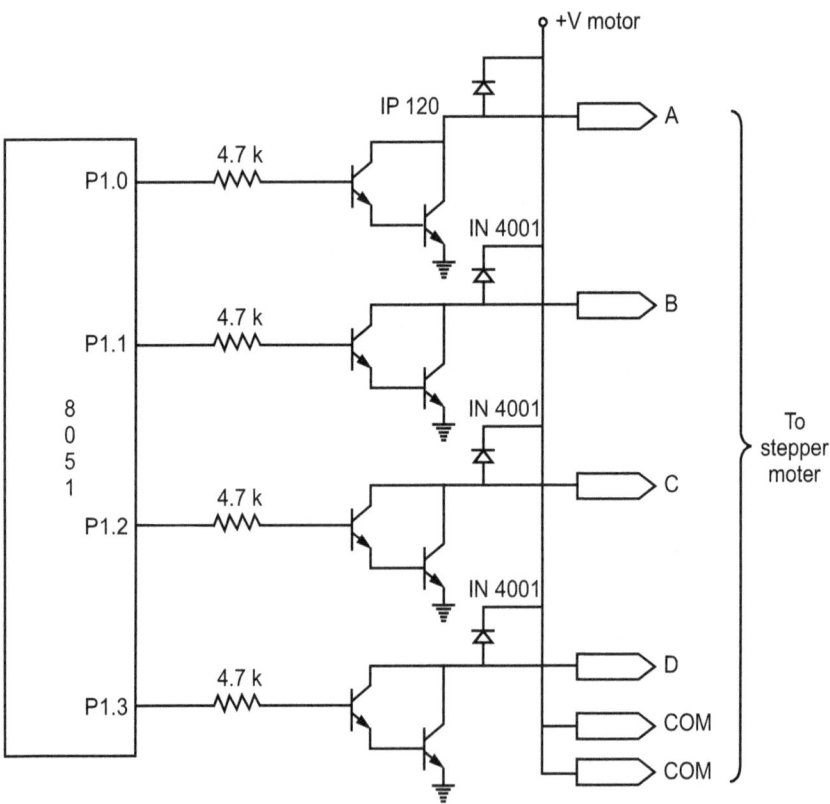

Fig. 4.40 : 8051 connections using transistor drivers for stepper motor

4.6.5 Controlling Stepper Motor Via Optoisolator

The optoisolators are widely used to isolate the stepper motor's EMF voltage and keep it always from damaging the microcontroller system. Fig. 4.41 shows the stepper motor controller using optoisolator.

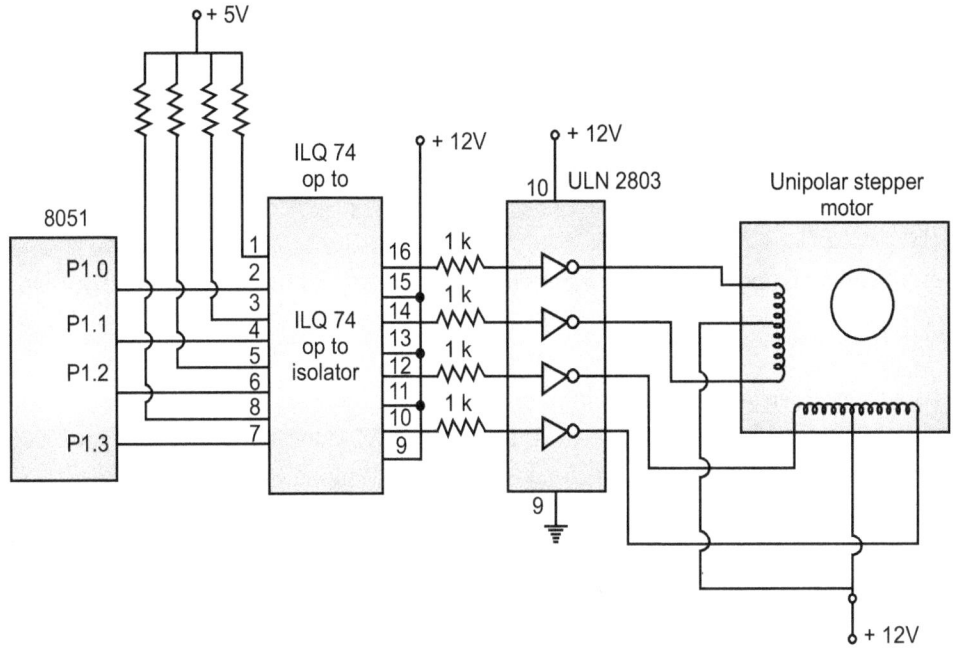

Fig. 4.41 : Controlling stepper motor using optoisolator

Program 4.28

Write an assembly language program to monitor the status of a switch which is connected to pin P2.5 and perform the following operations.
(a) If SW = 0, the stepper motor moves clockwise.
(b) If SW = 1, the stepper motor moves anticlockwise.

Solution: ORG 0000H

	SET B P2.5	// making P2.5 an input port
	MOV A, # 66H	// starting phase value
	MOV P1, A	// send to port 1
REP :	JNB P2.5, CW	// check switch result
	RR A	// rotate right
	ACALL DELAY	call delay
	MOV P1, A	write value to port 1
	SJMP REP	Repeat
CW :	RL A	rotate left
	ACALL DELAY	call delay
	MOV P1, A	// write value to port 1
	SJMP REP	repeat
DELAY :	MOV R2, # 200	

B1 :	MOV R3, # 300
B2 :	DJNZ R3, B2
	DJNZ R2, B1
	RET
	END

Program 4.29

Write an assembly language program to rotate the stepper motor continuously using.
(1) Clockwise using the wave drive 4-step sequence.
(2) Clockwise using the half-step 8-step sequence.
Use the sequence values saved in program ROM locations.

Solution : Case (1) : The sequence values are saved in ROM locations starting from 1000H.

	ORG 0000H
MAIN :	MOV R0, # 04
	MOV DPTR, # 1000H
TURN :	CLR, A
	MOV C A, @ A + DPTR
	MOV P1, A
	ACALL DELAY
	INC DPTR
	DJNZ R0, TURN
	SJMP MAIN
	ORG 1000H
	DB 8, 4, 2, 1
	END

Case (2) : For this, the sequence values are saved in ROM locations starting from 2000H.

	ORG 0000H
MAIN :	MOV R0, # 8
	MOV DPTR, # 2000H
REPT :	CLR A
	MOV C A, @ A + DPTR
	MOV P1, A
	ACALL DELAY
	INC DPTR
	DJNZ R0, REPT
	SJMP MAIN
	ORG 2000H
	DB 09, 08, 0CH, 04 06, 02, 03, 01
	END

4.6.6 Stepper Motor Control with 8051 C [May/June 2010]

Q. A switch is connected to P2.7. Write a C program to monitor the status of switch and perform the following : [8 M] [May/June 2010]
(i) If SW = 0, the stepper motor moves clockwise.
(ii) If SW = 1, the stepper motor moves counter clockwise.

Program 4.30

A switch is connected to pin P2.7. Write a C program to monitor the status of SW and perform the following.
(a) If SW = 0, the stepper motor moves clockwise.
(b) If SW = 1, the stepper motor moves anticlockwise.

Solution :

```c
# include <reg51.h>
Sbit SW = P2^7;
void main ( )
{
  SW = 1;
  while (1)
  {
    if (SW == 0)
    {
      P1 = 0X66;
      MSDELAY (100);
      P1 = 0XCC;
      MSDELAY (100);
      P1 = 0X99;
      MSDelay (100);
      P1 = 0X33;
      MSDelay (100);
    }
    else
    {
      P1 = 0X66;
      MSDelay (100);
      P1 = 0X33;
      MSDelay (100)'
```

```
        P1 = 0X99;
        MSDelay (100);
        P1 = 0XCC;
        MSDelay (100);
      }
    }
  }
  void MSDelay (unsigned int value)
  {
    unsigned int a, b;
    for (a =0; a < 1275; a++)
    for (b = 0; b < value; b++);
  }
```

4.7 RTC INTERFACING

Q. Explain interfacing of RTC 12887 with 8051 microcontroller.
[8 M] [May/June 2010]

The real time clock (RTC) is a widely used device that provides accurate time and data for many applications. The RTC chip uses an internal battery, which keeps the time and date even when the power is OFF. The most widely used RTC chip is the DS12887 from Dallas Semiconductor/Maxim corporation. This chip is found in the vast majority of X86 PCs :

(1) It uses an internal lithium battery to keep operating for over 10 years in the absence of external power.

(2) It keeps track of seconds, minutes, hours, days, days of week, date, month, and year with leap-year compensation valid upto year 2100.

(3) It supports both 12 hour and 24 hour clock modes with AM and PM in the 12 hour mode.

(4) It also supports the daylight saving time option.

(5) It uses CMOS technology to keep the power consumption low.

(6) It has a total of 128 bytes of non-volatile RAM.

(7) It uses 14 bytes of RAM for clock/calendar and control registers and the other 114 bytes of RAM are for general purpose data storage.

4.7.1 Pin Descriptions

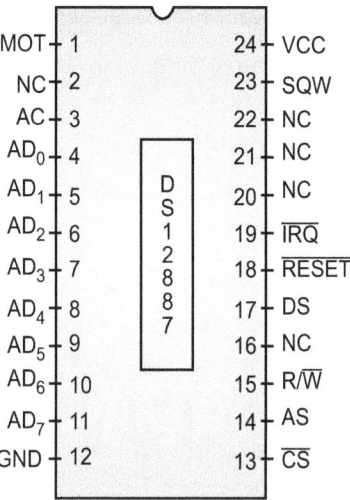

Fig. 4.42

MOT : This is an input pin used to choose between Motorola and Intel microcontroller bus timings. For Intel timing it is connected to GND.

AD_0 – AD_7 : The multiplexed address/data pins provide both addresses and data to the chip. Addresses are latched into the DS12887 on the falling edge of the AS (ALE) signal. AD_0 – AD_7 of the DS12887 are connected directly to P0 of the 8051. There is no need of external latch like 74XX373 because the DS12887 provides the latch internally. To access DS12887 MOVX instruction is used.

$\overline{CS}$ (Chip Select) : This is an active low signal $\overline{CS}$ must be low to access the chip during the read ($\overline{RD}$) and write ($\overline{WR}$) cycle time of Intel timing. $\overline{CS}$ works only when external V_{CC} is connected, when V_{CC} falls below 4.25V, the chip select input is internally forced to an inactive level regardless of the value of CS at the input pin. This is called the write-protected state.

AS (ALE) : AS (address strobe) is an input pin. On the falling edge it will cause the addresses to be latched into the DS12887. The AS pin is used for demultiplexing the address and data and is connected to the ALE pin of the 8051 chip.

$R/\overline{W}$: When MOT = GND for the Intel timing, the $R/\overline{W}$ pin is called the $\overline{WR}$ (write) signal and is connected to the WR pin of the 8051.

DS (Data Strobe) : When MOT = GND for Intel timing, the DS pin is called the $\overline{RD}$ (read) signal and is connected to the RD pin of the 8051.

RESET : It is the active low input pin. In most of the application the reset pin is connected to the V_{CC} pin. When $\overline{RESET} = 0$ it will cause the reset of the IRQ and clearing of the SQW pin.

IRQ : Interrupt request is an active low output pin. To use $\overline{IRQ}$ the interrupt enable bits in register B must be set high.

SQW : This is an output pin. Using this pin the DS12887 is programmed to provide upto 15 different square waves. The square wave is set by programming register A.

4.7.2 Address Map of DS12887

It has total of 128 bytes of RAM space with address 00 to 7FH. The first 10 locations are kept aside for RTC values of time, calendar and alarm data. The next four types are used for the control and status registers. They are registers A, B, C and D and are located at addresses 10 – 13. The next 114 bytes from addresses 0EH to 7FH are available for data storage. The entire 128 bytes of RAM are accessible directly for read or write except the following.

1. Registers C and D are read-only.
2. D_7 bit of register A is read only.
3. The high order bit of the seconds byte is read-only.

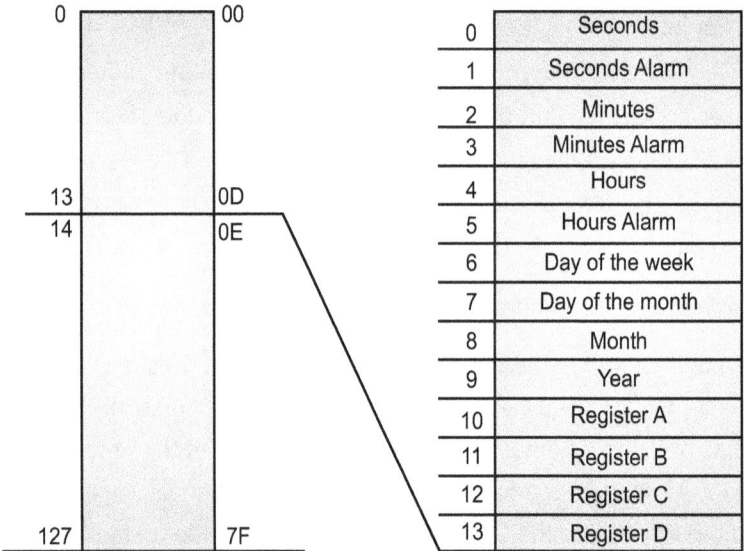

Fig. 4.43 : DS12887 address map

4.7.3 Time, Calender and Alarm Address Locations

The byte address 0 – 9 are set aside for the time, calendar and alarm data. Table 4.15 shows their address locations and modes.

Table 4.15 : DS12887 Address location for Time, Calendar and Alarm

Address Location	Function	Decimal Range	Data Mode Range	
			Binary (Hex)	BCD
0	Seconds	0 – 59	00 – 3B	00 – 59
1	Seconds Alarm	0 – 59	00 – 3B	00 – 59
2	Minutes	0 – 59	00 – 3B	00 – 59
3	Minutes Alarm	0 – 59	00 – 3B	00 – 59
4	Hours, 12 hours mode	1 – 12	01 – 0C AM	01 – 12 AM
	Hours, 12 hours mode	1 – 12	81 – 8C PM	81 – 92 PM
	Hours 24 hours mode	0 – 23	0 – 17	0 – 23
5	Hours alarm, 12 hour	1 – 12	01 – 0C AM	01 – 12 AM
	Hours Alarm 12 hour	1 – 12	81 – 8C PM	81 – 92 PM
6	Day of the week, sun = 1	1 – 7	01 – 07	01 – 07
7	Day of the month	1 – 31	01 – 0F	01 – 31
8	Month	1 – 12	01 – 0C	01 – 12
9	Year	0 – 99	00 – 63	00 – 99

Register A

UIP	DV2	DV1	DV0	RS3	RS2	RS1	RS0

UIP - Update in progress. This is a read-only bit.

DV2   DV1   DV0
0   1   0   will turn on the oscillator.

RS3   RS2   RS1   RS0   provides 14 different frequencies at the SQW pin

RS3	RS2	RS1	RS0	Frequency
0	0	0	0	None
0	0	0	1	256 Hz
0	0	1	0	128 Hz
0	0	1	1	8.192 kHz
0	1	0	0	4.096 kHz
0	1	0	1	2.048 kHz
0	1	1	0	1.024 kHz
0	1	1	1	512 Hz
1	0	0	0	256 Hz (repeat)
1	0	0	1	128 Hz (repeat)
1	0	1	0	64 Hz

1	0	1	1		32 Hz
1	1	0	0		16 Hz
1	1	0	1		8 Hz
1	1	1	0		4 Hz
1	1	1	1		2 Hz

Register B

D_7 D_0

SET	PIE	AIE	UIE	SQWE	DM	24/12	DSW

SET	When SET = 0 clock is counting once per second and time and dates are updated
	When SET = 1 update is prohibited.
PIE	Periodic Interrupt Enable
	If PIE = 1 when generated IRQ pin goes low.
	IRQ becomes a hardware version of the PI bit in register C. The rate of periodic interrupt is given by RS0 – RS3 of register A.
AIE	Alarm Interrupt Enable
	If AIE = 1, the IRQ pin goes low when all three bytes of the real time (hh : mm : ss) are the same as the alarm bytes of hh : mm : ss
	Also, if AIE = 1 the cases of once per second, once per minute and once per hour will make the IRQ pin low.
UIE	The Update-ended Interrupt Enable (UIE)
	It is a read/write bit that enables the update-end flag (UF) bit in Register C to assert IRQ. The $\overline{RESET}$ pin going low or the SET bit going high clears to UIE bit.
SQWE	Square Wave Enable
	If SQWE = 1 the square wave frequency generated by the RS0 – RS3 option of register A will show up on the SQW output pin of the DS12877 chip.
DM	Data Mode : When DM = 0 BCD data format when DM = 1 : Binary (Hex) data format.
24/12	1 for 24 hour mode and 0 for 12 hour mode
DSE	Daylight Saving Enable

Register C

D_7 D_0

IRQF	PF	AF	UF	0	0	0	0

IRQF   1 if PF = PIE or AF = AIE or UF = UIE = 1
PF   Periodic Interrupt Flag (PF)
             It is read only bit that is set to a 1 when an edge is detected on the selected tap of the divider chain. The RS3 through RS0 bits establish the periodic rate. PF is set to 1 independent of the state of the PIE bit. When both PF and PIE are 1's, the IRQ signal is active and sets the IRQF bit. The PF bit is cleared by a $\overline{RESET}$ or a software read of register C.
AF   Alarm Interrupt Flag (AF)
             When AF = 11 when current real time and alarm time matches. When all the three bytes of the real time (yy : mm : dd) are the same as the bytes in alarm time. AF also becomes 1 in cases of once per second, once per minute and once per hour alarm.
UF :   The Update-ended Interrupt Flag (UF) bit is set after each update cycle. When UIE bit is set to 1, the one in UF causes the IRQF bit to be a 1, which asserts the $\overline{IRQ}$ pin. UF is cleared by reading Register C or a $\overline{RESET}$.

Register D

D_7							D_0
VRT	0	0	0	0	0	0	0

VRT   Valid RAM and time bit is set to 1 prior to shipment. This is not writable and always 1 when read.

4.7.4 8051 connections to DS12887

Fig. 4.44 shows how DS12887 is interfaced with 8051.

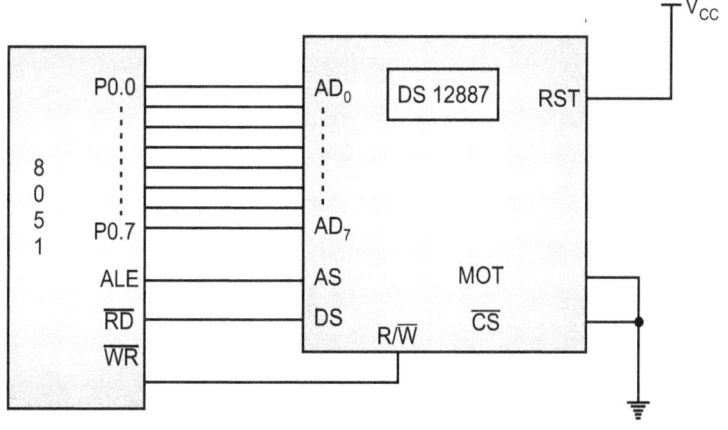

Fig. 4.44 : 8051 connections to DS12887

4.7.5 Setting the Time

To set the time or date, we need to set D_7 of register B to 1. After setting the time and date, we need to make $D_7 = 0$ to ensure that the clock and time are updated. The update occurs once per second.

The following program initializes the clock at 16 : 58 : 55 using the BCD mode and 24 hour clock mode with day light saving time.

Program :

```
    ACALL DELAY_200ms          ; wait 200 ms for RTC to be ready after power-up
// turning on the RTC
    MOV R0, # 0AH              ; Reg A address
    MOV A, # 20H               ; 010 in D6 – D4 to turn on oscillator
    MOV X @ R0, A              ; send it to Reg. A of DS12887
// setting the time mode;
    MOV R0, # 0BH              ' Reg. B address
    MOV A, # 83H               ; BCD 24 hrs, daylight saving D7 = 1, no update
    MOV X @ R0, A              ; send it to Reg B.
// setting the time
    MOV R0, # 0                ; point to seconds address
    MOV A, # 55H               ; seconds = 55
    MOV X @ R0, A              ; set seconds
    MOV R0, # 02               ; point to minutes address
    MOV A # 58H                ; minutes = 58
    MOV X @ R0, A              ; set minutes
    MOV R0, # 04               ; point to hours address
    MOV A, # 16H               ; hours = 16
    MOV X @ R0, A              ; set hours
    MOV R0, # 11               ; Reg. B address
    MOV A, #03                 ; D7 = 0 of reg B to allow update
    MOV X @ R0, A              ; send it to Reg. B
```

Setting the date :

```
// turn ON the RTC
    MOV R0, # 0AH
    MOV A, # 20H
    MOV X @ R0, A
```

```
// setting the time mode
    MOV R0, # 11
    MOV A, # 83H
    MOV X @ R0, A
// setting the date
    MOV R0, # 07              ; load pointer for day of month
    MOV A, # 19H              ; Day = 19H
    MOV X @ R0, A             ; set day of the month
    ACALL DELAY;
    MOV R0, # 08              ; point to month
    MOV A, # 10H              ; 10 = October
    MOV X @ R0, A             ; set month
    ACALL DELAY
    MOV R0, # 09              ; point to year address
    MOV A, # 04               year = 04 for 2004
    MOV X @ R0; A             set year to 2004
    ACALL DELAY
    MOV R0, # 11
    MOV A, # 03
    MOV X @ R0, A
```

4.7.6 RTCs Setting, Reading, Displaying Time and Date

This program is a complete assembly code for setting reading and displaying the time and date. The times and dates are sent to the screen via the serial port after they are converted from BCD to ASCII.

```
// setting time, reading and displaying it
    ORG 0000H
    ACALL DELAY_200ms
// setting serial port for communication
    MOV TMOD, # 20H
    MOV SCON, # 50H
    MOV TH1, # 00FDH
// turn ON the RTC
    MOV R0, # 10
    MOV A, # 20H
    MOV X @ R0, A
```

```
// setting the time mode
    MOV R0, # 11
    MOV A, # 83H
    MOV X @ R0, A
// setting the date
    MOV R0, # 07
    MOV A, # 24H
    MOV X @ R0, A
    ACALL DELAY
    MOV R0, # 08
    MOV A, # 10H
    MOV X @ R0, A
    ACALL DELAY
    MOV R0, # 09
    MOV A, # 04
    MOV X @ R0, A
    ACALL DELAY
    MOV R0, # 11
    MOV A, # 03
    MOV X @ R0, A
    ACALL DELAY
    MOV R0, # 11
    MOV A, # 03
    MOV X @ R0, A
// Read Time (HH : MM : SS) convert it and display it
OV1:  MOV A, # 20H
      ACALL SERIAL
      MOV R0, # 04              ; point to HR location
      MOV X A, @ R0             ; read hours
      ACALL DISPLAY
      MOV A, # 20H
      ACALL SERIAL
      MOV R0, # 2
      MOV X A, @ R0
      ACALL DISPLAY
```

```
        MOV A, # 20H              ; send out space
        ACALL SERIAL
        MOV R0, # 0
        ACALL DISPLAY
        MOV X A, @ R0             ; read seconds
        ACALL DISPLAY
        MOV A, # 0AH              ; send out CR
        ACALL SERIAL
        MOV A, # 0DH              ; send LF
        ACALL SERIAL
        SJMP 0V1
    // Small Delay
DELAY: MOV R7, # 250
D1 :    DJNZ R7, D1
        RET
    // Convert BCD to ASCII and send it to screen.
DISPLAY:
        MOV B, A
        SWAP A
        ANL A, # 0FH
        ORL A, # 30H
        ACALL SERIAL
        MOV A, B
        ANL A, # 0FH
        ORL A, # 30H
        ACALL SERIAL
        RET
SERIAL:
        MOV SBUF, A
        JNB TI, S1
        CLR TI
        RET
        END
    // Read date (YYYY : MM : MM), convert it and display it
```

0V2 :	MOV A, # 20H	; ASCII SPACE
	ACALL SERIAL	
	MOV A, # '2'	; send out 2
	ACALL SERIAL	
	MOV A, # '0'	; send out 0
	ACALL SERIAL	
	MOV R0, # 09	; point to year location
	MOV X A, @ R0	; read year
	ACALL DISPLAY	
	MOV A, # ':'	; send out : for YYYY : MM
	ACALL SERIAL	
	MOV R0, # 08	; point to month location
	MOV A, @ R0	; read month
	ACALL DISPLAY	
	ACALL DELAY	
	MOV A, # ':'	; send out : for mm : dd
	ACALL SERIAL	
	MOV R0, # 07	; point to DAY location
	MOV X A, @ R0	; read day
	ACALL DISPLAY	
	ACALL DELAY	
	MOV A, # ' '	; send out SPACE
	ACALL SERIAL	
	ACALL DELAY	
	MOV A, # ' '	
	ACALL SERIAL	
	ACALL DELAY	
	MOV A, # 0AH	; send out LF
	ACALL SERIAL	
	MOV A, # 0DH	; send CR
	ACALL SERIAL	
	ACALL DELAY	
	LJMP 0V2	; display data forever

4.7.7 DS12887 RTC Programming in C

Program 4.31

Initialization of RTC DS12887 using C.

```c
# include <reg51.h>
# include <absacc.h>
void main ( )
{
    unsigned char i;
    for (i = 0; i < 200; i++)
    XBYTE [0X0A] = 0X20;      // turn on oscillator
    XBYTE [0X0B] = 0X83;      // BCD, 24 hours daylight saving
    XBYTE [0X00] = 0X55;      // second = 55h for BCD
    XBYTE [0X02] = 0X58;      // minute = 58h for BCD
    XBYTE [0X04] = 0X16;      // hour = 16H for BCD
    XBYTE [0X07] = 0X19;      // day = 19h
    XBYTE [0X08] = 0X10;      // month = 10h for October
    XBYTE [0X09] = 0X04;      // year = 04
    XBYTE [0X0B] = 0X03;      // allow update
```

Program 4.32

Write a C program for reading and displaying the time and date.

```c
// Displaying time and date in C.
# include <reg51.h>
# include <absacc.h>
void bcd conv (unsigned i);
void serial (unsigned i);
void main (void)
{
    unsigned char hr, min, sec;
    TMOD = 0X20;
    TH1 = 0XFD;
    SCON = 0X50;
    TR1 = 1;
    while (1)                 // display time forever
```

```c
    {
        hr = XBYTE [4];            // get hour
        bcd conv (hr);             // convert and display
        serial (':');              // send out : to separate
        min = XBYTE [2];           // get minute
        bcd conv (min);            // convert and display
        serial (':');              // send out : to separate
        sec = XBYTE [0];           // get second
        bcd conv (sec);            // convert and display
        serial (0X0D);             // send out CR
        serial (0X0A);             // send out line feed
    }
}
// Convert BCD to ASCII and send it to serial.
void bcd conv (unsigned mybyte)
{
    unsigned char a, b, c;
    a = mybyte & 0X0F;
    a = a|0X30;
    b = mybyte & 0XF0;
    b = b >> 4;
    b = b|0X30;
    serial (b);
    serial (a);
}
// send out one char serially
void serial (unsigned a)
{
    SBUF = a;
    while (TI == 0);
    TI = 0;
}
```

Program 4.33

Write a C program to read and display date.

```
// Read date (YYYY : MM : MM), convert and display
while (1)                    // display data forever
{
    serial ('2');            // send out 2 for 20XX
    serial ('0');            // send out 2 for 20XX
    Yr = XBYTE [9];          // get year
    bcd conv (yr);           // convert and display
    serial (':');            // send out : to separate
    month = XBYTE [8];       // get month
    bcd conv (month);        // convert and display
    serial (':');
    day = XBYTE [7];         // get day
    bcd conv (sec);          // convert and display
    serial (0X0D);           // send out CR
    serial (0X0A);           // send out line feed
}
```

4.7.8 The Alarm and IRQ Output Pin

The alarm interrupt can be programmed to occur at rates of (a) once per day, (b) once per hour, (c) once per minute, (d) once per second.

Once per day alarm :

Table 4.16 shows the address locations 1, 3 and 5 belong to the alarm seconds, alarm minutes and alarm hours respectively. To program the alarm once per day write the desired time for the alarm into the hour, minute and second RAM locations 1, 3 and 5. When all three bytes of hour, minute and second for the real time clock matches the value in the alarm hour, minute and second, the AF (alarm flag) bit in the register C of the DS12887 will go high. To use IRQ pin of the DS12887 for an alarm, the interrupt enable bit for alarm in register B (AIE) must be set high.

Once per hour alarm :

To program the alarm for once per hour, write value 11XXXXX into the alarm hour location of 5 only. value 11XXXXX means any hex value of FCH to FFH. Commonly we use value FFH.

Once per minute alarm :

To program the alarm for once per minute, write value FFH into both the alarm hour and alarm minute locations of 5 and 3.

Once per second alarm :

To program the alarm for once per second, we write value FFH into all three locations of alarm hour, alarm minute and alarm second.

Program 4.34

Write a program (a) to sound the buzzer connected to SQW pin and (b) send the message 'YES' to the serial port once per minute at exactly 8 seconds past the minute. The buzzer will stay on for 7 seconds before it is turned OFF.

Solution : // send HELLO to screen 8 sec past the minute using alarm IRQ.

```
           ORG 0000H
           LJMP MAIN
           ORG 0003H
           LJMP ISR_EX0
           ORG 0100H
MAIN:      MOV IE< # 81H            ; INT0 (EX0) is enabled
           SETB TCON.1              ; make IT EDGE triggered
           MOV TMOD, # 20H
           MOV SCON, # 50H
           MOV TH1, # 00FDH
           SET B TR1
// turning on the RTC
           MOV R0, # 10
           MOV A, # 2DH             ; 010 in D6 - D4 turn ON OSC SQW = 8Hz
           MOV X @ R0, A
// setting the time mode
           MOV R0, # 11
           MOV A, # 83H
           ACALL DELAY
           MOV X @ R0, A
           ACALL DELAY
// setting the alarm time
           MOV R0, # 1
           MOV A, # 08
           MOV X @ R0, A
           MOV R0, # 3
           MOV A, # 0FFH
```

```
        MOV X @ R0, A
        MOV R0, # 5
        MOV A, # 0FFH
        MOV X @ R0, A
        ACALL DELAY
        MOV R0, # 11
        MOV A, # 23H              ; D₇ = 0 to update AIE = 1
        MOV X @ R0, A
    // reading time, serial transfer
SERIAL:
        CLR IE.7
        MOV SBUF, A
B1 :    JNB TI, B1
        CLR TI
        SETB IE.7                 // re-enable the interrupt
        RET
    // ISR to send 'YES' to screen and sound the buzzer.
        ORG 500H
ISR_EX0:
        MOV R0, # 12
        ACALL DELAY
        MOV X A, @ R0
        MOV R0, # 11
        ACALL DELAY
        MOVX A, @ R0
        ACALL DELAY
        SET B ACC.3
        SET B P1.7
        ACALL DELAY
        MOV X @ R0, A
        MOV A, # 'Y'
        ACALL SERIAL
        MOV A, # 'E'
        ACALL SERIAL
        MOV A, # 'S'
        ACALL SERIAL
```

```
ACALL DELAY_1
MOV R0, # 11
ACALL DELAY
MOVX A, @ R0
CLR ACC.3
ACALL DELAY
MOV X @ R0, A
CLAR P1.7
RETI
```

4.7.9 The Periodic Interrupt and IRQ Output Pin

The second source of interrupt is the periodic interrupt flag (PF). It is the part of register C. It will be high at a rate set by RS0 – RS3 bits of register A. This rate is variable from once every 500 ms to once every 122 µs. The PF becomes 1 when an edge is detected for the period. Just like alarm interrupt, the period interrupt can also be directed to the IRQ pin.

To use IRQ, the interrupt enable bits of PIE in register B must be set to 1. If PIE = 1, the IRQ pin goes low periodic interrupt gives the option of sub second interrupts.

Program 4.35

Write a program to send a message to the screen twice per second (2 Hz) using the periodic interrupt with the help of hardware IRQ.

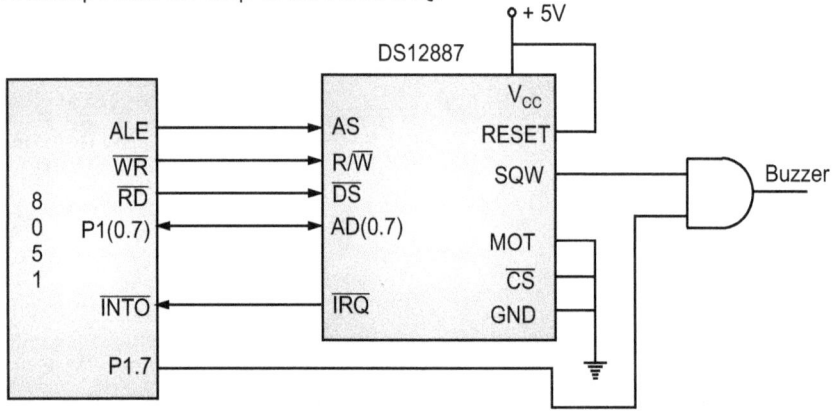

Fig. 4.45 : Using DS12887 IRQ to activate an 8051 interrupt

Program : // Sending "WELCOME" to screen twice per second.
```
ORG 0000H
LJMP START
ORG 0003H
LJMP ISR_EX0
ORG 0100H
```

START: MOV IE, # 81H
    SET B TCON.1
// serial port setting for communication
    MOV TMOD, # 20H
    MOV SCON, # 50H
    MOV TH1, # FDH
    SET B TR1
// turning ON the RTC
    MOV R0, # 10
    MOV A, # 2FH
    MOV X @ R0, A
// setting the time mode
    MOV R0, # 11
    MOV A, # 83H
    ACALL DELAY
    MOV X @ R0, A
    ACALL DELAY
// setting the time
    MOV R0, # 0
    MOV A, # 55H
    MOV X @ R0, A
    MOV R0, # 02
    MOV A, # 56H
    MOV X @ R0, A
    MOV R0, # 04
    MOV A, # 16H
    MOV X @ R0, A
    ACALL DELAY
    MOV R0, # 11
    MOV A, # 43H
    MOV X @ R0, A
// reading time
OV1 : MOV A, # 20H
    ACALL SERIAL
    MOV R0, # 4
    MOV X A, @ R0

```
        ACALL DISPLAY
        MOV A, # 20H
        ACALL SERIAL
        MOV R0, #2
        MOV X A, @ R0
        ACALL DISPLAY
        MOV A, # 20H
        ACALL SERIAL
        MOV R0, # 0
        MOV X A, @ R0
        ACALL DISPLAY
        MOV A, # 0AH
        ACALL SERIAL
        MOV A, # 0DH
        ACALL SERIAL
        SJMP OV1
    // small delay
DELAY :
        MOV R7, # 250
B1 :    DJNZ R7, B1
        RET
    // convert BCD to ASCII and sent it to screen.
DISPLAY :
        MOV B, A
        SWAP A
        ANL A, # 0FH
        ORL A, # 30H
        ACALL SERIAL
        MOV A, B
        ANL A, # 0FH
        ORL A, # 30H
        ACALL SERIAL
        RET
SERIAL :
        CLR IE.7                    // disable INT0
        MOV SBUF, A
```

D1: JNB TI, D1
     CLR TI
     SET B IE.7
     RET
// ISR to send "WELCOME" to screen twice per second.
     ORG 0500H
     ISR_EX0:
     MOV R0, # 12
     ACALL DELAY
     MOV X A, @ R0
     MOV A, # 'W'
     ACALL SERIAL
     MOV A, # 'E'
     ACALL SERIAL
     MOV A, # 'L'
     ACALL SERIAL
     MOV A, # 'C'
     ACALL SERIAL
     MOV A, # 'O'
     ACALL SERIAL
     MOV A, # 'M'
     ACALL SERIAL
     MOV A, # 'E'
     ACALL SERIAL
     RETI

4.8 DC MOTOR CONTROL AND PWM

Q. Explain DC motor control using 8051.   [8 M] [May/June 2010]

A DC motor is used to convert electrical pulses into mechanical movement. If the +ve and −ve leads are connected to a DC voltage source, then the DC motor moves in one direction. If we reverse the polarity, we can change the direction of rotation. For example, small fans used to 0001 the CPU uses DC motor. Stepper motor moves in steps whereas DC motor moves continuously. The speed of DC motor is indicated in rpm (revolutions per minute). The DC motor has two rpms. (i) no load rpm, (ii) loaded rpm. No load rpm is given in the manufacturer's data sheet. It may be from a few thousand to ten's of thousands. The rpm is reduced during movement of the load.

The nominal voltage is the voltage for that motor under normal conditions and can be from 1 to 150 V, depending on the motor. As the voltage is increased, the rpm also increases. As the load increases, the rpm is decreased, until the current or voltage provided to the motor is increased. When the voltage is fixed, as the load increases the current (power) consumption of a DC motor is increased. If we overload the motor it will stall and damage the motor due to generation of heat by high current consumption.

The direction of the DC motor rotation is changed with the help of relays or some specially designed chips.

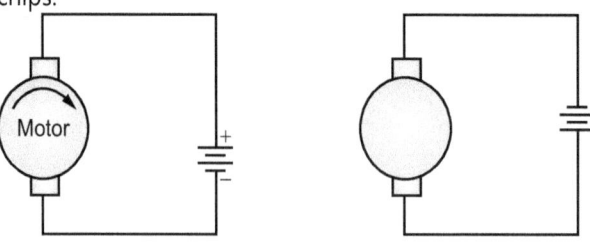

Fig. 4.46 : DC Motor rotation

Fig. 4.46 shows the DC motor rotation for clockwise (CW) and anticlockwise (CCW) rotations.

Table 4.16 : Selected DC Motor Characteristics

Part No.	Nominal volts	Volt range	Current	RPM	Torque
154915 CP	3V	1.5 – 3V	0.070 A	5200	4.0 g-cm
154923 CP	3V	1.5 – 3V	0.240 A	16000	8.3 g-cm
177498 CP	4.5V	3 – 14V	0.150 A	10300	33.3 g-cm
181411 CP	5V	3 – 14V	0.470 A	10000	18.8 g-cm

Fig. 4.46 shows the connection of an H-Bridge using simple switches. All the switches are open which does not allow the motor to turn.

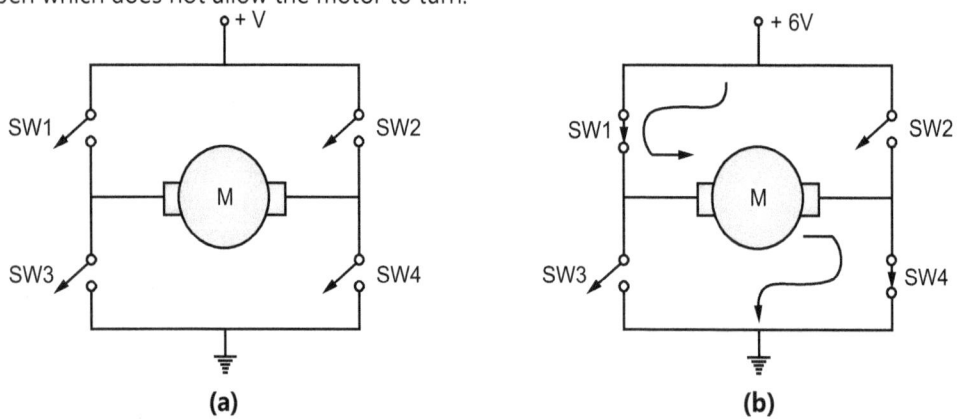

Fig. 4.47 : H-bridge motor configuration

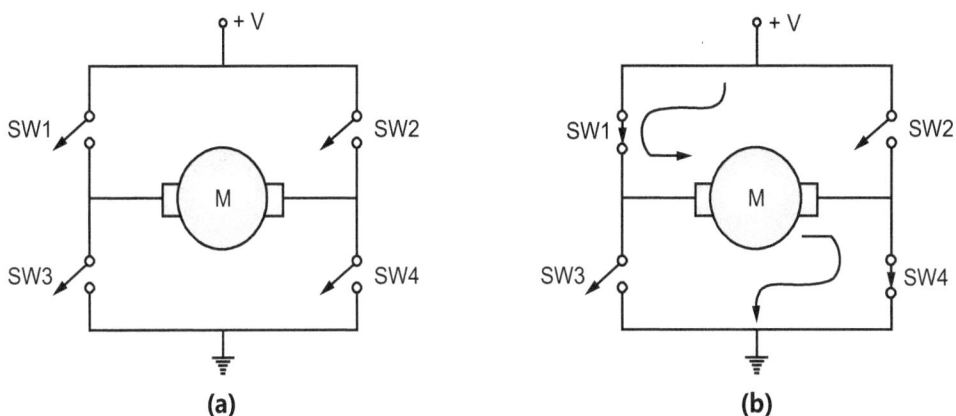

Fig. 4.48 : H-bridge motor clockwise configuration

Fig. 4.48 shows the switch configuration for turning the motor is clockwise direction. Switches 1 and 4 are closed to pass the current through the motor.

Fig. 4.49 shows the switch configuration for turning the motor in anticlockwise direction. Switches 2 and 3 are closed to pass the current through the motor.

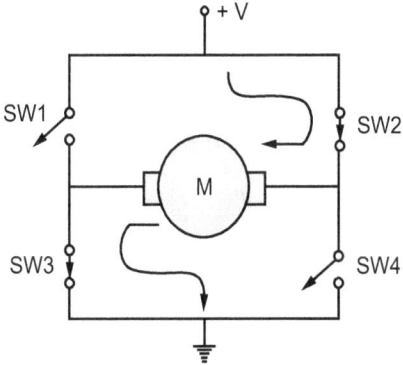

Fig. 4.49 : H-bridge motor for anticlockwise direction

Table 4.17 : Logic configurations for the H-bridge design

Motor Operation	SW1	SW2	SW3	SW4
OFF	Open	Open	Open	Open
Clockwise	Closed	Open	Open	Closed
Anticlockwise	Open	Closed	Closed	Open
Invalid	Closed	Closed	Closed	Closed

H-bridge control can be created using relays, transistors or a single IC solution such as the L293 - using relays and transistors, invalid configurations must not occur.

4.8.1 Pulse Width Modulation (PWM)

The speed of the motor depends on the three factors : (a) load (b) current (c) voltage.

For a fixed load, the steady speed of a motor can be maintained by using pulse width modulation (PWM). By changing the width of the pulse applied to the DC motor, we can increase or decrease the amount of power provided to the motor. Therefore, motor speed can be increased or decreased.

The voltage has a fixed amplitude but it has a variable duty cycle. That means wider the pulse, higher the speed. Therefore PWM circuitry are embedded in the microcontroller chip. The proper register are loaded with the high and low values of the desired pulses and the rest is taken care by the microcontroller. This saves the lot of time to do another things. If PWM is used externally, we have to generate various duty cycle pulses using software, so most of the microcontroller time is wasted.

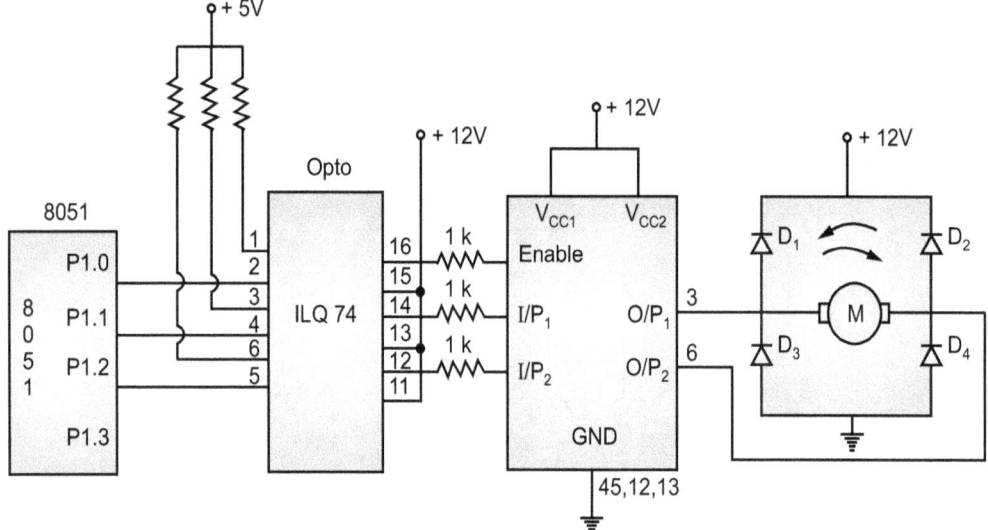

Fig. 4.50 : Bidirectional motor control using L293 chip

Program 4.36

Write a program to monitor the status of SW and perform the following :
(a) If SW = 0, the DC motor moves clockwise.
(b) If SW = 1, the DC motor moves anticlockwise.
Add a switch to pin P2.5.

Solution : ORG 0000H
START : CLR P1.0
        CLR P1.1
        CLR P1.2
        SET B P2.5

MONITOR:

    SET B P1.0   ; enable the chip

    JNB P2.5, clockwise

    CLR P1.1   ; turn the motor anticlockwise

    SET B P1.2

    SJMP MONITOR

CLOCKWISE :

    SEBT P1.1

    CLR P1.2   ; turn motor clockwise

    SJMP, monitor

    END

4.8.2 DC Motor Control with Optoisolator

8051 is protected from EMI created by motor brushes by using an optoisolator and a separate power supply. Fig. 4.51 shows optoisolators for controlling single direction motor. If we separate the power supplies of the motor and logic, then there is less possibility of damage to the control, circuitry.

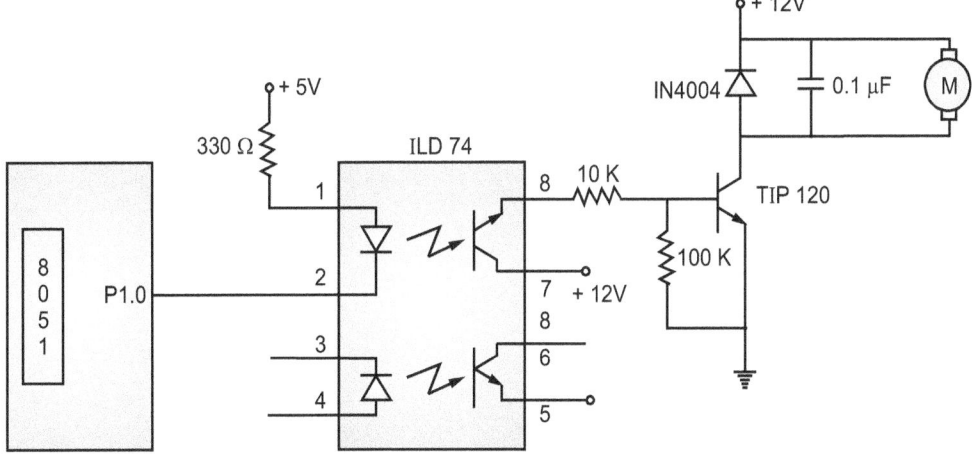

Fig. 4.51 : DC motor control using a Darlington transistor

Protection of the control circuitry is provided by the optoisolator. The motor and 8051 use separate power supplies. The separation of power supplies allows the use of high voltage motors. To reduce the EMI created by the motor a decoupling capacitor is connected across the motor.

Fig. 4.52 shows the connection of MOSFET transistor. The optoisolator protects the 8051 from EMI. The zener diode is used for the transistor to reduce gate voltage below the maximum value.

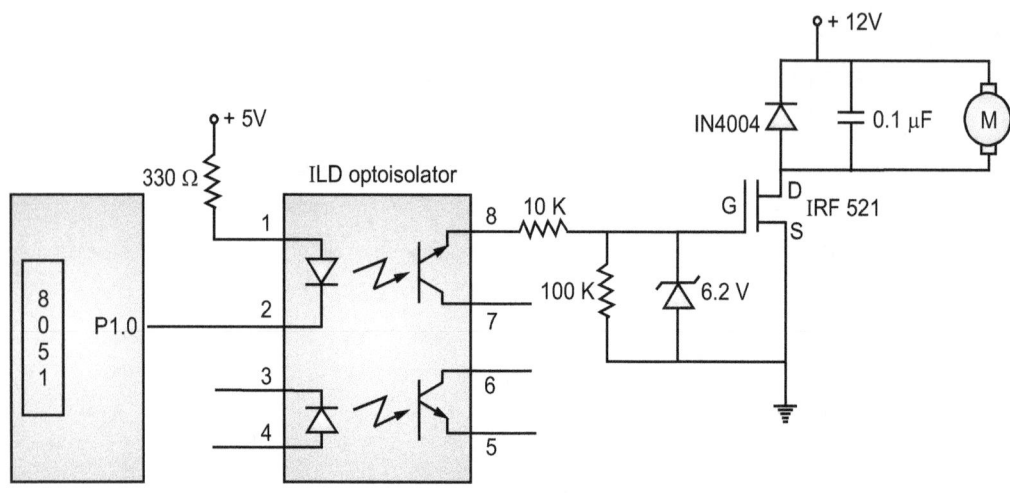

Fig. 4.52 : DC motor connection using a MOSFET transistor

Program 4.37

Refer to the DC motor connection of Fig. 4.52 to the 8051 of this Fig., a switch SW is connected to pin 3.2, which is the INT0 pin. Write a program

(a) Normally the motor runs with a 33% duty cycle.

(b) When INT0 is activated, the motor runs with 10% duty cycle for a short duration.

Solution: ORG 0000H

  LJMP START

// ISR for interrupt INT0

  ORG 0003H

  SJMP FIRST

// main program for initialization

  ORG 0030H

START :	MOV IE, # 81H	; enable INT0
HERE :	SETB, P1.0	
	MOV R0, # 33	; P1.0 set for 33% time
	ACALL DELAY	
	CLR P1.0	
	MOV R0, # 67	; P1.0 cleared for 67% time
	ACALL DELAY	
	SJMP HERE	

// ISR for INT0

FIRST : MOV R5, # 0FFH

```
S1:     SET B, P1.0
        MOV R0, # 10            P1.0 set for 10% time
        ACALL DELAY
        CLR P1.0
        MOV R0, # 90            P1.0 cleared for 90% time
        ACALL DELAY
        DJNZ R5, S1             ; exit from ISR when R5 = 0
        RETI
    // subroutine named DELAY
DELAY :
RPT1 :  MOV  R1, # 20
RPT2 :  MOV  R2, # 100
RPT3 :  DJNZ R2, RPT3
        DJNZ R1, RPT2
        DJNZ R0, RPT1
        RET
        END
```

4.8.3 DC Motor Control and PWM using C

Program 4.38

Write a C program to monitor the status of SW and perform the following :

(a) If SW = 0, the DC motor moves clockwise.

(b) If SW = 1, the DC motor moves anticlockwise.

A switch is connected to pin P2.5.

Solution :

```
# include <reg51.h>
Sbit SW = P2^5;
Sbit ENABLE = P1^0;
Sbit MTR_1 = P1^1;
Sbit MTR_2 = P1^2;
void main ( )
{
  SW = 1;
  ENABLE = 0;
  MTR_1 = 0;
  MTR_2 = 0;
```

```
    while (1)
    {
      ENABLE = 1;
      if (SW == 1)
      {
        MTR_0 = 1;
        MTR_1 = 0;
      }
      else
      {
        MTR_0 = 0;
        MTR_1 = 1;
      }
    }
}
```

Program 4.39

Write a C program to monitor the status of SW and perform the following :
(a) If SW = 0, the DC motor moves with 50% duty cycle pulse.
(b) If SW = 1, the DC motor moves with 25% duty cycle pulse.

Solution :

```
# include <reg51.h>
Sbit SW = P2^5;
Sbit MTR = P1^0;
void MSDelay (unsigned int value);
void main ( )
{
  SW = 1;
  MTR = 0;
  while (1)
  {
    If (SW == 1)
    {
      MTR = 1;
      MSDelay (25);
      MTR = 0;
```

```
      MSDelay (75);
    }
    else
    {
      MTR = 1;
      MSDelay (50)'
      MTR = 0;
      MSDelay (50);
    }
  }
}
void MSDelay (unsigned int value)
{
  unsigned char a, b;
  for (a = 0; a < 1275; a++)
  for (b = 0; <value; b++)
}
```

Program 4.40

Two switches are connected to pins P2.0 and P2.1. Write a C program to monitor the status of both switches and perform the following.

SW2 (P2-7)	SW1 (P2-6)	
0	0	DC motor moves slowly (25% duty cycle)
0	1	DC motor moves moderately (50% D.C.)
1	0	DC motor moves fast (75% D.C.)
1	1	DC motor moves very fast (100% D.C.)

Solution :

```
# include <reg51.h>
Sbit MTR = P^0;
void MSDelay (unsigned int value);
void main ( )
{
  unsigned char x
  P2 = 0XFF
  x = P2;
  x = x & 0X03;
```

```
MTR = 0;
while (1)
{
  switch (x)
  {
    Case (0) :
    {
      MTR = 1;
      MSDelay (25);
      MTR = 0;
      MSDelay (75);
      break;
    }
    Case (1) :
    {
      MTR = 1;
      MSDelay (50);
      MTR = 0;
      MSDelay (50);
      break;
    }
    Case (2) :
    {
      MTR = 1;
      MSDelay (75);
      MTR = 0;
      MSDelay (25);
      break;
    }
    default :
      MTR = 1;
  }
 }
}
```

Chapter - 5

REAL TIME OPERATING SYSTEM

5.1 REAL TIME OPERATING CONCEPTS

The operating system need to meet goals are perfection, correctness, portability, interoperability and providing a common set of that interfaces for the system as well as orderly access and control when managing the process.

The OS structure consists of kernel and other service functions. The OS enables an application run on the system hardware. The OS is the middle layer between the application software and system hardware. An OS includes following structural units:

- Kernel with file management and device management as part of the kernel in the given operating system. OR
- Kernel without file management and device management as the part of the kernel in the given OS and any other needed functions not provided for at the kernel level.

The kernel is the basic structural unit of any OS in which the memory space of the functions, data and stack are protected from access by any call other than the system call. It can be defined as a secured unit of an OS that operates in the supervisory mode while the remaining part of the application software operates in the user mode.

The kernel has management functions for processes, resources, ISRs, ISTs, files, device drivers and IO subsystems and network subsystems. The memory or device and file management functions may be outside the kernel in a given OS, especially in an operating system.

5.1.1 SERVICES PROVIDED BY AN OPERATING SYSTEM

Q. Explain different services offered by RTOS. **[May, June 2010]**

Every computing device needs a piece of software to interact with the hardware. This software is the operating system (OS). In case of a desktop, each job is called as a process and in an embedded system; each job is called a task. Each task needs memory and needs to access IO devices. Managing these multiple tasks is done by the operating system. The OS has to do the following functions:

- Process/Task management.
- Memory management.

- Input/output management including managing the file system.
- Provide services to the applications.
- Provide a user interface so that the user need not be concerned about the underlying hardware details.

Based on the capabilities, operating systems are divided into different categories:
- Single tasking OS versus Multitasking OS.
- Single user OS versus Multi-user OS.
- Command driven OS versus GUI-based OS.

In single tasking OS, only one task is carried out at a time. In multitasking OS, multiple tasks can be run simultaneously. MS DOS is a single tasking OS. Windows and UNIX are multitasking OS.

In a single user OS, only one user can use the system at a time. In a multiuser system, multiple users can share the system simultaneously. In a multitasking system, the application run by each user gets a small slice of time. This is known as time sharing. MS DOS and WINDOWS are single user OS. UNIX is a multiuser OS.

An important function of the OS is to provide an interface to the user to access the computer's resources. The user has to give instructions to the computer to carry out various tasks. One method of giving these instructions is to give commands such as "COPY x.c y.c" through the keyboard. Operating system working on commands are said to be command driven. MS DOS is a command driven OS. On the other hand, the OS can provide a GUI such as in windows operating systems and give instructions through mouse-clicks. This is a GUI driven OS.

Difference between Conventional OS and Embedded OS:

Table 5.1

Conventional OS	Embedded OS
1. In conventional OS there is a difference between operating system and application software.	1. In Embedded OS everything is a single piece of the code.
2. Used for multi document interface.	2. Used for single document interface.
3. It performs many jobs at a time.	3. Performs specific job.
4. These type of OS requires large memory.	4. It requires less memory.
5. Jobs are known as processes.	5. Jobs are known as Tasks.
6. Upgradation is easy.	6. Need to change the system for upgradation.
7. Examples are Windows 98, XP, Vista etc.	7. Examples are RTLinux, RTOS.

In Embedded Systems, the OS provides the same services as in desktop computers. However, as compared to desktops, embedded systems have special requirements.

5.1.2 Requirements of Embedded System

- **Reliability:** The OS in an embedded system has to be very reliable.
- **Multitasking with time constraints:** Embedded systems needs to support multitasking. All operating systems used in embedded systems support this feature. Desktop operating systems do not support real time requirements where as embedded systems must meet definite deadlines for some tasks.
- **Small footprint:** The memory occupied by the operating system is known as footprint. The footprint should be small for an embedded OS.
- **Support diskless systems:** Unlike the desktop computers embedded systems may not have secondary storage such as hard disk. The embedded OS alongwith application software will reside on a memory chip. However, if the application demands a file system, you can create a small file system on the flash memory.
- **Portability:** A variety of processors are available for developing embedded systems so, the important requirement of embedded system is portability.
- **Scalability:** The embedded operating systems may be used on an 8-bit micro controller or a powerful 64-bit microprocessor. So, scalability is important for embedded OS.
- **Support for standard API Application** software is developed using the Application Programming Interface (API) of the operating system. API is a set of function calls. An application developed for one OS may not be portable to another OS. To achieve portability IEEE standardized the API called Portable Operating System Interface (POSIX). Operating Systems used in embedded systems must comply with this standard.

5.2 ARCHITECTURE OF EMBEDDED OPERATING SYSTEMS

To meet the above requirements, the embedded operating systems need to have mechanisms to manage the tasks and to make the tasks communicate with one another. While developing embedded software, these steps must be followed:

- Identify the tasks and assign priorities to each task.
- Identify the time critical tasks.
- Schedule the tasks in such a way that all the tasks are completed and the tasks which are time critical, meet the deadlines.
- Work out when to send interrupts to the processor.
- Identify the shared resources and work out mechanisms for sharing the resource by multiple tasks.
- Work out the strategies for inter task communication.
- Keeping track of the time.

An embedded operating system performs all these activities.

Tasks: The work to be done by an embedded system is divided into number of tasks. Each task competes for the CPU time independently. Each task will have its own stack area. Each task runs forever and hence it is implemented as an infinite loop as in the code segment. Each task is assigned a priority. Generally, an operating system can support 256 priority levels.

Task scheduling: Since only one CPU has to handle multiple tasks, the tasks have to share the CPU time in a disciplined manner so that one task does not get lot of time while others wait for unduly long time. Important time critical tasks have to be given highest priority and a mechanism for deciding which task will get the CPU time next, has to be worked out. This is known as *'task scheduling'*. An operating system in which the time required to execute a task can be estimated is called a *deterministic operating system*. One should be able to determine the worst case timing for completing a task.

Context Switching: Suppose, a low priority task is presently being run by the processor but a high priority task has to run. In this case, the CPU will be interrupted through an interrupt signal. The CPU will save the current task's information in a stack and run the high priority task. The mechanism of storing the current CPU registers in a stack to run the other task is known as *context switching*.

Mutual Exclusion: Different tasks may have to share same resources. Tasks should maintain discipline to share the resources. Ensuring that two or more tasks access a shared resource without corrupting the data is called *mutual exclusion*. Embedded systems provide disciplined access to shared resources through special objects such as mutexes and semaphores. Mutexes and semaphores are like 'keys' to access a resource and release the key.

Inter-task Communication: Tasks may need to exchange data among themselves. For instance, a task may write some data to a file and another task need to read that data. This mechanism is known as *inter-task communication*. The task which has to read the data has to obtain information of the data written by the other task or not. So, the two tasks have to synchronize their activities. Special Kernel objects such as mailboxes, message queues, pipes, status registers and event flags are used to achieve inter-task communication and inter-task synchronization.

Memory Management: The memory of an embedded system is shared by a number of tasks. So, memory management is the important service provided by the OS.

Timer Services: The operating system needs to keep track of the time for activities such as the time for which a particular task is running, the time for which a task can wait for a shared resource. The OS also provides the timer services.

In addition to the application tasks, the kernel has to run its own system tasks with its own priorities. One important system task is the idle task. If no other task is running, the idle task is executed.

The kernel is the heart of the operating system. The software in an embedded system can be divided into the operating system and the application software. The middle layer, the Application Programming Interface (API), is used to write the application software. API provides the function calls, to access the operating system services.

The operating system consists of:
- Kernel
- Device Manager
- Networking Protocol Software
- Libraries
- File System (optional)

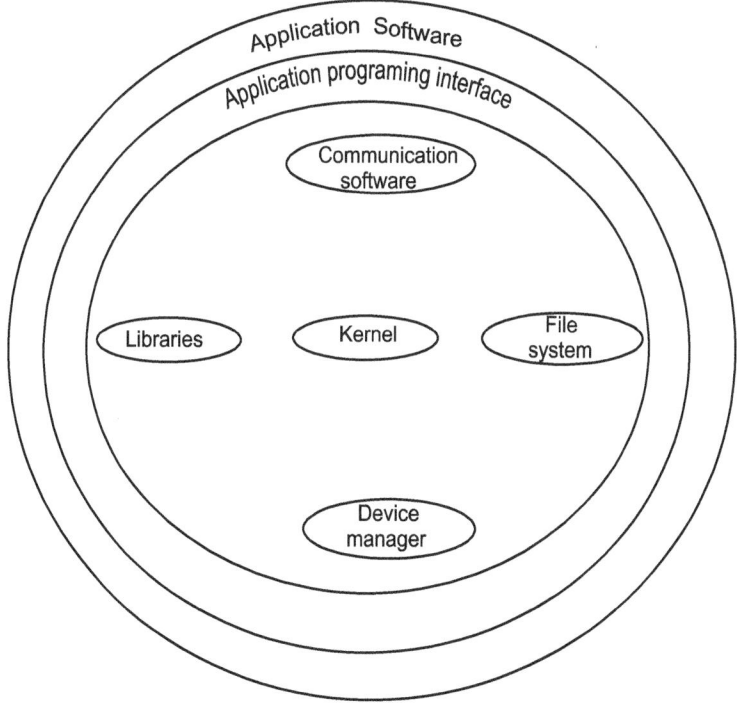

Fig. 5.1: Software architecture of an embedded system

- **Kernel:**

  Kernel manages the tasks to achieve the desired performance of the embedded system. To manage the tasks, the important requirements are to schedule the tasks and to provide inter-task communication facilities. To achieve these two requirements, kernel objects are defined such as tasks, mutexes, ISRs, events, message boxes, mail-boxes, pipes and timers. Kernel provides the memory management services, time management services, interrupt handling services and device management services.

- **Device manager:**

  The IO devices are used to send or receive data from the embedded system. The OS manages the IO devices through interrupts and device drivers. Device driver provides the necessary interface between the application and the hardware.

- **Communication software:**

  If the embedded system has communication interfaces such as Ethernet, USB etc., the upper layer protocols such as TCP/IP stack need to be integrated with the OS. Then the embedded system can be network-enabled.

- **Libraries:**

  The operating system may have some C/C++ library files in object code, which can be used through the API calls.

- **File System:**

  Most of the embedded systems do not have a secondary storage such as floppy disk. In such cases, the ROM is used to store the program. If a file system is required, a small file system can be developed on flash memory. Some embedded systems use a secondary storage just for booting.

5.2.1 Monolithic Kernel and Microkernel

Q. List different types of kernel services. Explain any one in detail.   [May, June 2013]

Monolithic Kernel:

In monolithic kernel architecture, all kernel services run in the kernel space. Here all kernel modules run within the same memory space under a single kernel thread. The tight internal integration of kernel modules in monolithic kernel architecture allows the effective utilization as the low level features of the underlying system. The major drawback of monolithic kernel is that any error or failure in any one of the kernel module leads to the crashing of the entire kernel applications. LINUX, SOLARIS, MS-DOS, Kernels are examples of monolithic kernel.

Microkernel:

The microkernel design incorporates only the essential set of operating system into the kernel. The rest of the operating system services are implemented in program known as *servers* which runs in user space. This provides a highly modular design. Memory management, process management, timer system and interrupt handlers are essential services which forms the part of the microkernel. MACH, QNX are examples for microkernel.

5.2.2 Categories of Embedded Operating System

Operating systems used in embedded systems can be broadly classified as follows:
- Non-real time embedded operating systems.
- Real time operating systems.
- Mobile/Handheld operating systems.

The non-real time operating systems have a small footprint but they are not suitable for hard real time applications. Examples are Embedded Linux, Embedded NT and WINDOWS XP Embedded. These operating systems are used in consumer appliances such as DVD player, Set Top Boxes etc. which are soft real time embedded systems.

The real time operating systems are suitable for hard real time embedded applications. Examples are QNX Neutrino, VxWorks, RT Linux, MicroCOS II and OS/9.

The operating systems used in mobile devices such as palmtops, PDAs, Smart Phones are known as mobile/handheld operating systems. Palm OS, Symbian OS, Windows CE are the major OSs in this category. Embedded Linux, VxWorks, OS/9 are also now being used in handheld computers.

5.3 ARCHITECTURE OF THE KERNEL

Q. Write short note on: RTOS Kernel architecture	[May, June 2013]
Q. List different kernel services	[Nov., Dec. 2011]

The various Kernel objects are:
- Task
- Task Scheduler
- Interrupt Service Routines
- Semaphores
- Mutexes
- Mailboxes
- Message Queues

- Pipes
- Event Registers
- Signals
- Timers

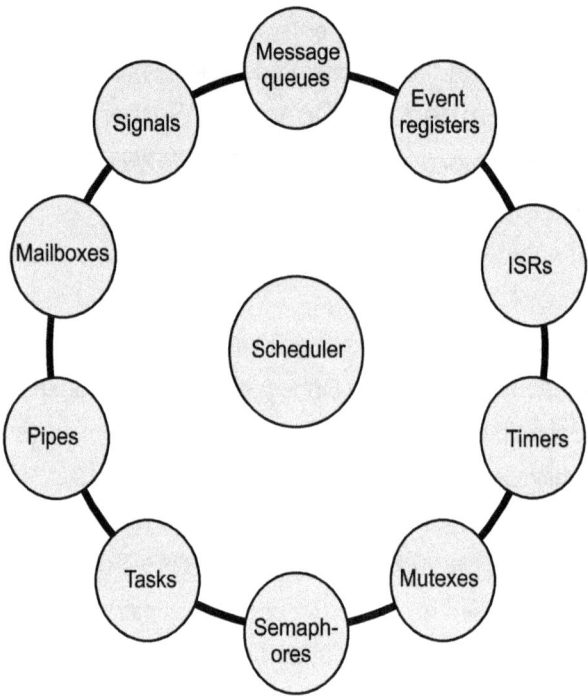

Fig. 5.2: Kernel objects

The embedded software consists of the operating system and the application software. The services provided by the operating system are accessed through the Application Programming Interface (API) to develop application software. The API is a set of function calls using which you can access the various objects and the services provided by the kernel.

The API of the operating system gives the function calls to manage these objects. The syntax of each function call may differ from one operating system to another.

5.3.1 Tasks and Task Schedulers

> **Q. Write short note on: Schedule management for multiple tasks by an RTOS**
> **[May, June 2013]**

The embedded software consists of number of tasks. These tasks include the operating system tasks as well as the application-specific tasks. Each task in an embedded system is implemented as an infinite loop. The task object consists of its name, a unique ID, a priority, a stack and a task control block that contains all the information related to each task.

In addition to the tasks required for the application software, the kernel has its own system tasks with priorities. These tasks are:
- Start-up task, which is executed when the operating system starts.
- Exception handling task to handle the exceptions.
- Logging task, to log the various system messages.
- Idle task, which will have the lowest priority and will run when there is no other task to run. This task ensures that the CPU is not idle.

Since only one CPU has to handle multiple tasks, the tasks need to share the CPU time in a disciplined manner so that one task get lot of time while others are waiting forever. Therefore, each task has to be assigned a priority and a mechanism for deciding which task will get CPU time next has to be worked out. This is known as *task scheduling*. The object that does this work is the task scheduler. In addition to the CPU time the tasks need to share the system resources such as CPU registers, external memory and input/output devices. Another important requirement is that one task should not corrupt the data of another task. While scheduling the tasks, a number of issues, need to be kept in mind.

Many tasks may make calls to a function. A function that can be used by more than one task without data corruption is called re-entrant function. If data is corrupted when more than one task calls the same function, such a function is called *non-re-entrant* function. If you use global variables, then the function is non-re-entrant.

When you run a task, some portion of the code should not be interrupted. Such code is called *critical section of the code*. Interrupts are disabled before the start of the execution of the code's critical section and enabled after the execution is completed. Kernel objects such as semaphores are used to protect the data.

Every task needs resources such as serial port, keyboard, display or memory locations. These resources may need to be shared, for example; two tasks may like to send data to the display. Resources shared by two or more tasks are called *shared resources*. Tasks should maintain discipline to access shared resources. Semaphores and mutexes are used to share resources with discipline.

Tasks may need to communicate data among themselves. For instance a task writes data into an array and another task has to read the data from that array. Inter-task communication needs to be achieved through special mechanism such as mailboxes, message queues, pipes, event registers and signals.

The kernel of the operating system manages the tasks keeping in view the restrictions imposed.

5.3.2 Task States

A task can be in one of the following states.
- Running state.
- Wait state.
- Ready to run state.

(i) Running state:

A task is said to be in running state if it is being executed by the CPU.

(ii) Wait state:

A task is said to be in wait state if it is waiting for another event to occur. For instance, a task may be waiting to get some data from serial port. Even if the CPU is free, the task which is in waiting state cannot be executed till the external event occurs.

(iii) Ready to run state:

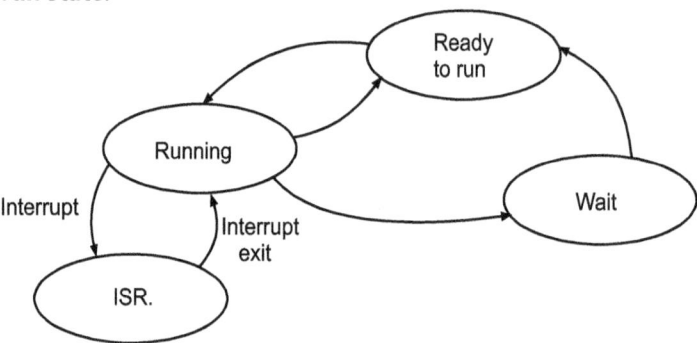

Fig. 5.3: Task and task states

A task is said to be in ready to run state if it is waiting in a queue for the CPU time.

A task which is in wait state can shift to the ready to run state after the external event occurs. Note that it cannot enter directly to the running state. A task which is in ready to run state can enter to the running state. A task in the running state can move to the wait state if it has to wait for an external event to occur; or it can move to the ready to run state if it's job is not completed, but the CPU has to run another task.

A task which is presently running may be interrupted to run an Interrupt Service Routine (ISR) for a short time. After the ISR is executed, the CPU continues to execute the task which is interrupted or the highest priority task which is ready to run. The ISR can do the job of changing the state of a task.

5.3.3 Context Switching

The CPU has to execute one task for some time and then execute another task which is in the queue. Consider the situation when the CPU is executing a low priority task, during which time the CPU registers contain the data corresponding to this task. The CPU now has to take out the low priority task and execute the high priority task.

In this case, the contents of the CPU registers have to be saved before executing the high priority task. The state of the CPU registers when a task is to be pre-empted is called the *context*. Saving the contents of the CPU registers and then loading the new task is called *context switching*.

5.3.4 Types of Scheduler Algorithms

Various scheduling algorithms have been developed to tackle the problem to make the decision for which task has to run. CPU utilization, throughput, turnaround time (TAT), waiting time and response time are the important criteria that need to be considered for the selection of a scheduling algorithm for task scheduling.

- **CPU utilization:**

The scheduling algorithm should always make the CPU utilization high. CPU utilization is a direct measure of how much percentage of the CPU is being utilized.

- **Throughput:**

This gives an indication of the number of processes executed per unit of time. The throughput for a good scheduler should always be higher.

- **Turnaround Time:**

It is the amount of time taken by a process to complete its execution. It includes the time spent by the process for waiting for the main memory, time spent in the ready queue, time spent on completing the I/O operations and the time spent in execution. The TAT should be minimum for a good scheduling algorithm.

- **Waiting Time:**

It is the amount of time spent by a process in the ready queue waiting to get the CPU time for execution. The waiting time should be minimum.

- **Response Time:**

It is the time difference between the submission of a process and the time when the first response is obtained. The response time should be minimum.

Depending upon the requirement of an embedded system, the scheduling algorithm needs to be chosen.

- First-In-First-Out
- Round Robin Algorithm
- Round Robin with Priority
- Shortest Job First
- Non-Preemptive Multitasking
- Preemptive Multitasking

First-In-First-Out (FIFO):

In first-in-first-out scheduling algorithm, the tasks which are ready-to-run are kept in a queue and the CPU serves the tasks on first come first served basis. This scheduling algorithm, shown in Fig. 5.4 is very simple to implement, but not well suited for most applications because it is difficult to estimate the amount of time a task has to wait for being executed. However, this is a good algorithm for an embedded system, it has to perform few small tasks all with small execution times. If there is no time criticality and the number of tasks is small, this algorithm can be implemented.

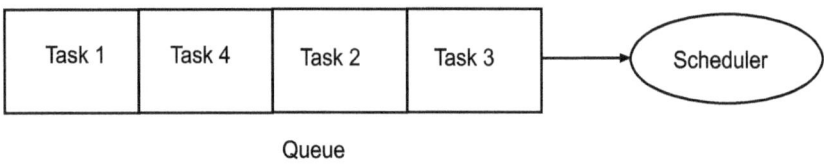

Queue

Fig. 5.4 : First-In-First-Out

Q. Compare the following software architectures:
(i) Round-Robin   (ii) Round-Robin with interrupts.

Round Robin Algorithm:

In round robin algorithm, the kernel allocates a certain amount of time for each task waiting in the queue. The time slice allocated to each task is called quantum. As shown in Fig. 5.5, if three tasks 1, 2 and 3 are waiting in the queue, the CPU first executes task 1 and then task 2 and then task 3 and again task 1.

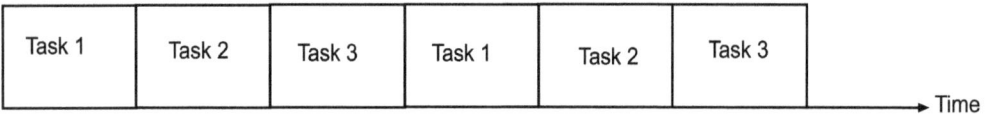

Fig. 5.5: Round robin algorithm

The kernel gives control to the next task if –
- The current task has completed its work within the time slice.
- The current task has no work to do.
- The current task has completed its allocated time slice.

This algorithm is very simple to implement, but note that there are no priorities for any task. All tasks are considered of equal importance. If time-critical operations are not involved then this algorithm will be sufficient. Digital Multimeters and Microwave Ovens use this scheduling algorithm.

Round Robin with Priority:

The round robin algorithm can be slightly modified by assigning priority levels to some or all the tasks. A high priority tasks can interrupt the CPU so that it can be executed. This scheduling algorithm can meet the desired response time for a high priority task. For example, in a bar code scanner, high priority is assigned to the scanning operations. The CPU can execute this task by suspending the task that displays the item/price value. Soft real time systems can use this algorithm.

Shortest Job First:

If the time for each task can be estimated before hand, the CPU can execute the task which takes the least amount of time. Effectively, this is like a priority assignment, the priority being decided by the amount of time - the higher the execution time, the lesser the priority. The advantage of this scheduling algorithm is that a high number of tasks will be executed, but the task with the highest amount of time will have to wait.

The task scheduler is the heart of the operating system. It is the task scheduling algorithm which decides whether the necessary time constraints can be met or not. If the embedded system is a hard-real time system, none of the above scheduling algorithm can be used at all.

The kernels used in embedded systems can implement priority based multitasking scheduling algorithms of two types:

- Non-preemptive multitasking.
- Preemptive multitasking.

Non-preemptive Multitasking:

Assume that you are making a telephone call at a public call office. You need to make many calls, but you see another person waiting. You may make one call, ask the other person to finish his call and then you can make your next call. This is non-preemptive multitasking also known as co-operative multitasking. You are co-operating with the other in the queue.

In non-preemptive multitasking, the tasks co-operate with each other to get their share of the CPU time. Hence, each task has to release the CPU and give control to another task on its own. Each task is given a priority, but the priority has to be respected by the other tasks. If interrupts are enabling, a high priority task can interrupt the running task and make the high priority task ready-to-run. After the ISR is executed, the CPU will continue to execute the low priority task only. And, when the low priority task releases the CPU, the high priority task is executed.

Fig. 5.6 shows the non-preemptive kernel operation. Assume that there are two tasks to be executed - one high priority task and one low priority task. To start with, the high priority task is in waiting state, waiting for an external event to happen, and the low priority task is running. After some time, the high priority task is ready. Using an ISR, the high priority task is moved to ready-to-run state. After the ISR is executed, the low priority will continue to be executed. After some time, the low priority task releases the CPU and then the high priority task gets executed.

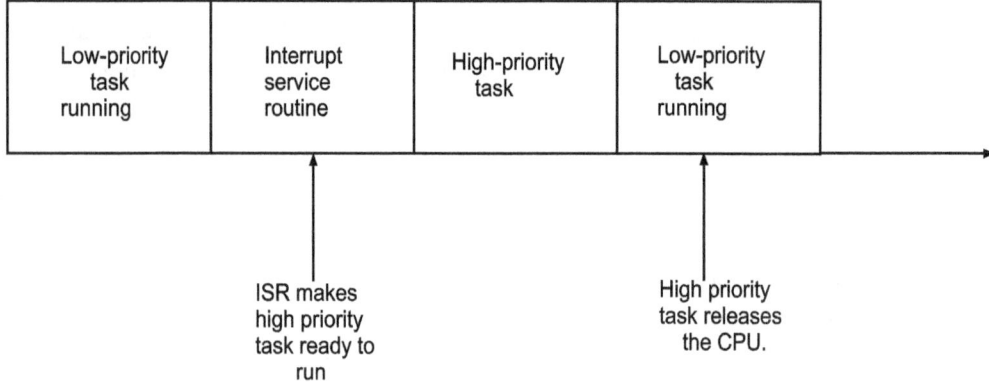

Fig. 5.6: Non-preemptive multitasking

The main disadvantage of non-preemptive multitasking is that a high priority task may have to wait for a long time. Also, it is not possible to determine the exact response times for each of the tasks. So, this type of multitasking is not suitable for embedded real time systems.

Preemptive Multitasking:

In preemptive multitasking the highest priority task is always given the CPU time. If a lower priority task is presently running and a higher priority task is in ready-to-run state, the running task is pre-empted and the higher priority task is executed. This mechanism is shown in Fig. 5.7.

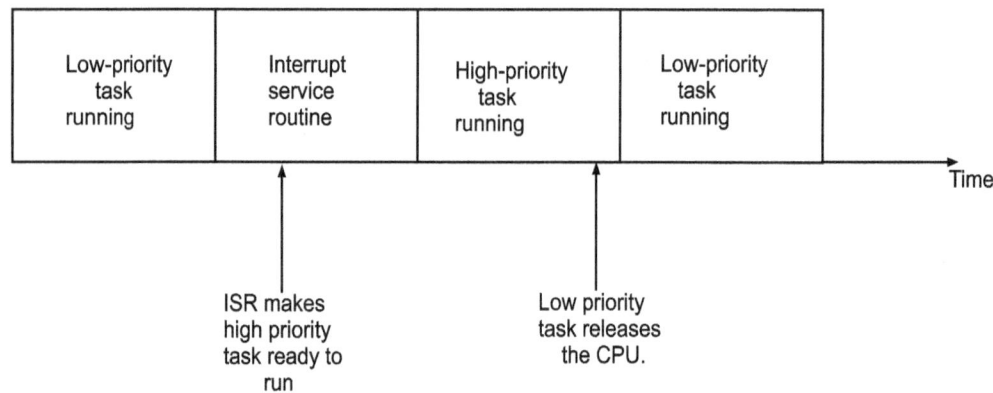

Fig. 5.7: Preemptive multitasking

Consider two tasks - one low priority task and one high priority task. To start with, the low priority task is running as the high priority task is in waiting state, waiting for an external event to occur. After some time, the external event occurs and the high priority tasks now move to ready-to-run state. Through an interrupt, the ISR is executed to move the high priority task from waiting state to ready-to-run state. Then another ISR is executed to put the high priority task in the running state. Again after some time, the high priority task may release the CPU and then the low priority task is executed.

If there are a number of tasks in the ready-to-run state, the task with the highest priority is always given the first chance by the task scheduler.

The main attraction of this scheme is that the execution time of the highest priority task can be calculated and hence the kernel is said to be deterministic. Most of the commercial embedded operating systems use preemptive multitasking to meet real time requirements.

The module within the scheduler that performs context switching is called dispatcher. If ISR makes a system call, the dispatcher is bypassed.

5.4 TASK MANAGEMENT

Priority assignment to a task can be static or dynamic. In static priority assignment, a task will be assigned a priority at the time of creating the task and it remains the same. In dynamic priority assignment, the priority of the task can be changed during execution time. While designing an application, it is not very easy to assign priorities to tasks. A good starting point is the Rate monotonic analysis used for assigning priorities.

While designing an embedded system, you need to make a list of all the tasks. And, then you need to assign priority to each task. Subjectively, we know that some tasks should have high priority. Rate Monotonic Analysis (RMA) provides an answer.

Rate Monotonic Analysis (RMA):

RMA makes the following assumptions:
- Highest priority task will run first, i.e. the priority-based preemptive multitasking is the scheduling algorithm.
- All the tasks run at regular intervals i.e. the tasks are periodic.
- Tasks do not synchronize with each other, i.e. they do not share resources or share data.

In RMA, the priority is proportional to the frequency of execution. If i^{th} task has an execution period of T_i and E_i is it's execution time, E_i / T_i gives the percentage of the CPU time required for execution of ith task. In RMA, the schedulability test indicates how much CPU time is actually utilized by the tasks. If n is the total number of tasks, the equation for schedulability test is given by

$$\sum (E_i/T_i) \leq U(n) = n(2^{1/n} - 1)$$

U(n) is called the utilization factor. The value of number of tasks (n) and the utilization factor for different values of n is given in Table 5.1. If the number of tasks is infinity, then about 70% of the CPU time is utilized.

Table 5.2

n	U(n)
1	1.000
2	0.828
3	0.779
4	0.756
Infinity	0.693

While designing an embedded system, it will be a good idea to start with RMA. List all the tasks, estimate the execution period and execution time, and then calculate the value of U(n). As a thumb rule, ensure that the CPU utilization is not above 70%. Assign priorities based on execution frequency.

Task Management Function Calls:

The various function calls provided by the operating system API for task management are:

- Create a task.
- Delete a task.
- Suspend a task.
- Resume a task.
- Change priority of a task.
- Query a task.

5.5 INTERRUPT SERVICE ROUTINES (ISR)

Q. Illustrate functions, ISRs and tasks. [May, June 2011]

Interrupt is a hardware signal that informs the CPU that an important event has occurred. When interrupt occurs, CPU saves it's context and jumps to the ISR. After ISR processes the event, the CPU returns to the interrupted task in a non-preemptive kernel. In this case of preemptive kernel, highest priority task gets executed.

In real-time operating systems, the interrupt latency, interrupt response time and the interrupt recovery time are very important.

(i) Interrupt latency:

The maximum time for which interrupts are disabled plus time to start the execution of the first instruction in the ISR is called interrupt latency.

(ii) Interrupt response time:

Time between receipt of interrupt signal and starting the code that handles the interrupt is called interrupt response time.

(iii) Interrupt recovery time:

Time required for CPU to return to the interrupted code/ highest priority task is called interrupt recovery time.

In non-preemptive kernel,

> Interrupt recovery time = Time to restore the CPU context + Time to execute the return instruction from the interrupted instruction

In preemptive kernel,

> Interrupt recovery time = Time to check whether a high priority task is ready + Time to restore CPU context of the highest priority task + Time to execute the return instruction from the interrupt instruction

The interrupt latency, interrupt response time and interrupt recovery time are shown in Fig. 5.8.

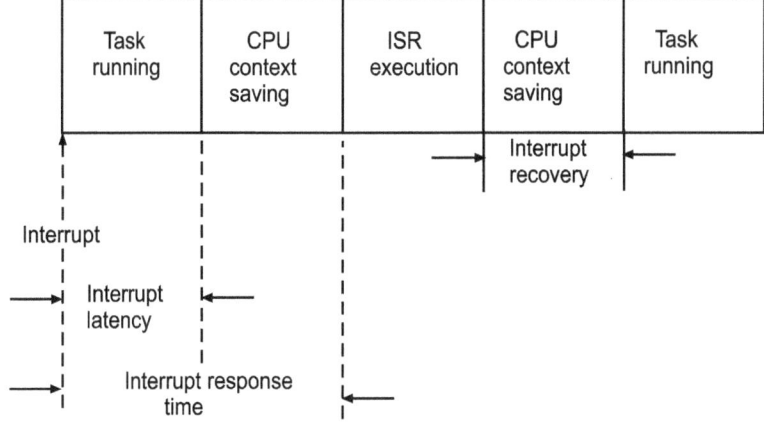

Fig. 5.8: Interrupt service routine times

5.6 SEMAPHORES

Q. Explain different techniques supported by RTOS for inter process communication.
[May, June 2012, 11]

Q. Explain use of semaphore to handle critical section problem. [Nov., Dec. 2011]

When multiple tasks are running two or more tasks may need to share the same resource. Consider a case where two tasks want to write to a display. Assume that task1 wants to display the message and task2 has to display another message. The display is a shared resource and if there is no synchronization between the task, and a garbled message is displayed. To access a shared resource, there should be a mechanism so that there is discipline. This is known as *resource synchronization*.

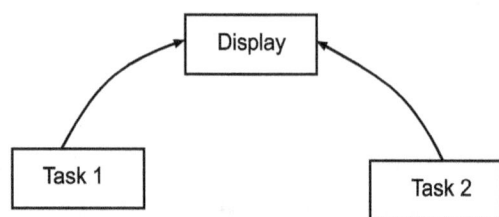

Fig. 5.9: Resource synchronization

Now consider another situation, in this case one task reads the data from an ADC and writes it to memory. Another task reads that data and sends it to a DAC. The read operation takes place only after write operation and it has to be done very fast with minimal time delay. In this case, there should be a mechanism for task1 to inform task2 that it has done its job. This has to be done through a well defined procedure. This is known as *task synchronization*.

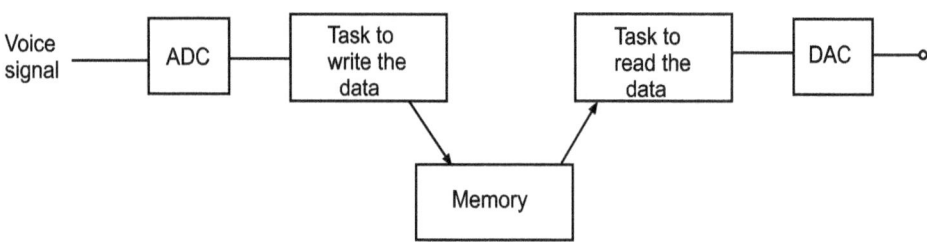

Fig. 5.10: Task synchronization

Semaphore is a kernel object that is used for both resource synchronization and task synchronization. The semaphore is like a key to enter a house and hence the semaphore is represented as a key. If task1 wants to access the printer, it acquires the semaphore, uses the printer and then releases the semaphore. If both the tasks want to access a resource simultaneously, the kernel has to give the semaphore only to one of the task. This allocation may be based on the priority of the task or on first come first served basis. If a number of tasks have to access the same resource then the tasks are kept in a queue and each task can acquire the semaphore one by one.

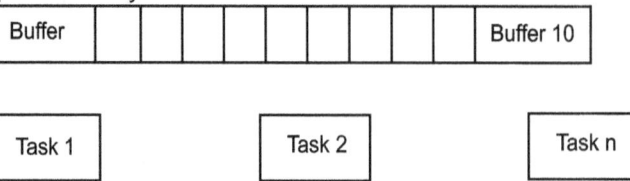

Fig. 5.11: Counting semaphore

Consider another example in which a pool of 10 buffers is available. The buffers need to be shared by a number of tasks. Any task can write to a buffer. A binary semaphore does not work in this case. So, a counting semaphore is used. The initial value of the semaphore is set to zero. Whenever a task acquires the semaphore, the value is decremented by one and whenever a task releases the semaphore, it is incremented by one. When the value is zero, it is an indication that the shared resource is no longer available. A counting semaphore is like having multiple keys to enter a house.

The following are the functions, which are generally provided in an OS, for example, μcos II for the semaphores.

- **OSSemCreate,** a semaphore function to create the semaphore in an event control block (ECB). Initiate it with an initial value.
- **OSSemPost,** a function which sends the semaphore notification to ECB and its value increments on event occurrence.
- **OSSemAccept,** a function which reads and returns the present semaphore value and if it shows occurrence of an event then it takes note of that and decrements that value.
- **OSSemPend,** a function which waits the semaphore from an event and its value decrements on taking note of that event occurrence.
- **OSSemQuery,** a function which queries the semaphore for an event occurrence or non-occurrence by reading its value and returns the present semaphore value and returns pointer to the data structure OSSemData. The semaphore value does not decrease. The OSSemData points to the present value and table of the tasks waiting for the semaphore.

An OS provides the IPC functions create, post, pend, accept and query for using semaphores. The time-out can be provided with pend function arguments. A pointer to error-handling function can also be specified in the arguments.

5.7 MAILBOX

Q. Explain how mailboxes are implemented in RTOS. [May, June 2013, 2011]

A mailbox object is just like your postal mailbox. Someone posts a message in your mailbox and you take out the message. A task can have a mailbox into which others can post a mail. A task or ISR sends the message to the mailbox.

A message mailbox is for an IPC message can be used only by a single destined task. The mailbox message is a message pointer or can be a message. The source is the task that sends the message pointer to a created mailbox. The destination is the place where the OSMBoxPend function waits for the mailbox message and reads it when received.

A mobile phone, LCD display task is an example that uses the message mailboxes as an IPC. In the mailbox, when the time and date message from a clock process arrives, the time is displayed at side corner on top line. When the message from another task to display a phone number arrives, the number is displayed at middle of a line. When the message from another task to display the signal strength at antenna is arrived, it is displayed at the vertical bar on the left.

Another example of using a mailbox is the mailbox for an error-handling task, which handles the different error logins from other tasks. The following may be the provisions at an OS for IPC functions while using the mailbox.
- A task may put into the mailbox only a pointer to the message-block or number of message bytes as per the OS provisioning.
- There are three types of the mailbox provisions.

A queue may be assumed a special case of a mailbox with provisions for multiple messages or message pointers. An OS can provide for queue from which a read can be on a FIFO basis or alternatively an OS can provide for the multiple mailbox messages with each message having a priority parameter. The read can then only be on priority basis in case mailbox message has multiple messages with priority assigned to high priority ones. Even if the messages are inserted in a different priority, the deletion is as per the assigned priority parameter.

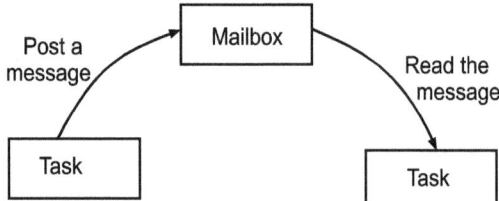

Fig. 5.12: Inter-task synchronization in mailbox

An OS may be provided for mailbox and queue separately. A mailbox will permit one message pointer per box and the queue will permit multiple messages or message pointers. μcos II RTOS is an example of such an OS.

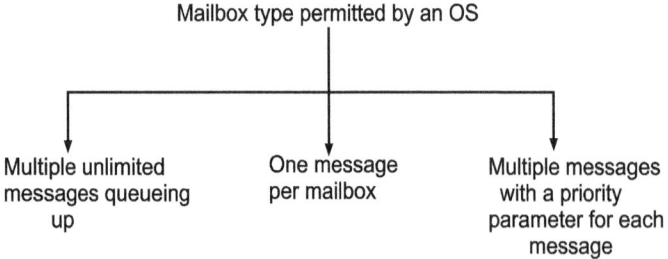

Fig. 5.13: Mailbox type permitted by an OS

The RTOS functions for mailbox used by the tasks are given below:
- **OSMBoxCreate** creates a box and initializes the mailbox contents with a NULL pointer.
- **OSMBoxPost** sends a message to the box.
- **OSMBoxWait(Pend)** waits for a mailbox message, which is read when received.
- **OSMBoxAccept** reads the current message pointer, and after checking the presence yes or no, deletes the mailbox when read.
- **OSMBoxQuery** quarries the mailbox when read.

An ISR can post (but not wait) into the mailbox of a task.

Program

```
#include"includes.h"

static OS_EVENT*mailbox;
char*msg;

char start[1]={'s'};
char stop[1]={'a'};

OS_STK Task1Stack[100];
void LCDDisplay(void*pdata);

OS_STK Task2Stack[56];
void Keyboard (void*pdata);

int main(void)
{
    key_init();
    lcd_init();
    lcd_cmd(0x01);
    lcd_init();
    VPBDIV=0x01;

    lcd_dat(':');
    lcd_cmd(0xc8);
    lcd_dat('K');
```

```c
        lcd_dat('e');
        lcd_dat('y');
        lcd_dat(':');
        OSInit();
        msg=(char)start[0];

        mailbox=OSMboxCreate((char)*msg);

        OSTaskCreate(LCDDisplay,(void*)0, &Task1Stack[100],0);
        OSTaskCreate(Keyboard,(void*)0,&Task2Stack[56],1);
        OSStart();
        return 0;
}

void LCDDisplay(void*pdata)
{
    char*str;
    INT8U err;

timer_init();

while(1)
{
    lcd_cmd(0xc0);
    OSTimeDlyHMSM(0, 0, 2, 0);
    lcd_cmd(0x01);
    lcd_cmd(0x80);
    str= (char*) OSMboxPend(mailbox,0,&err);
    DisplayRow1(str);
    vari++;
    if(vari==0x5b)
    {
     vari=0x41;
    }
}
}
```

```c
void Keyboard(void*pdata)
{

    static INT8U row,col,data;

    while(1)
    {
        OSTimeDlyHMSM(0, 0, 0, 400);
        IOCLR0=0XC0E0;
        while(key_pressed())
        {
            data=ket_dtect();
            row=data/10;
            col=data%10;
            lcd_cmd(0xCC);
            lcd_dat(col+48);
            lcd_dat(col+48);
            if(data==22)
            {
                //msg=(char)stop[0];
                msg="Hello";
                OSMboxPost(mailbox,msg);
            }
            if(data==32)
            {
                msg="Bye";
                OSMboxPost(mailbox,msg);
            }
                while(!(all_key_open()))
                {

                }
        }
    }
}
```

5.8 MESSAGE QUEUES

Message queue can be considered as an array of mailboxes. Some of the applications of message queue are:
- To take the input from a keyboard.
- To display output.
- To read voltages from sensors or transducers.
- Data packet transmission in a network.

In each of these applications, a task or an ISR deposits the message in the message queue. Other tasks can take the messages. Based on your application, the highest priority task or the first task waiting in the queue can take the message.

At the time of creating a queue, the queue is given a name or ID, queue length, sending task waiting list and receiving task waiting list.

A message queue in an IPC has following features:
1. An OS provides for inserting and deleting the message pointers or messages.
2. Each queue for the message or message pointers needs initialization before using functions in kernel for the queue.
3. Each created queue has an ID.
4. Each queue has a user definable size.
5. When an OS call is to insert a message into the queue, the bytes are as per the pointed number of bytes.
6. When a queue becomes full, there is error handling function to handle that.

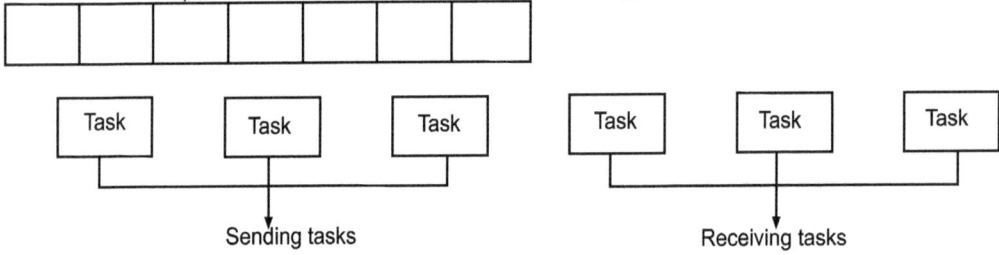

Fig. 5.14: Message queue

The OS functions for a queue, for example, in μcos II can be as follows.
- **OSQCreate** initializes the queue.
- **OSQPost** sends the message into the queue, it can be used by tasks as well as ISRs.
- **OSQPend** waits for a queue message at queue and reads and deletes that when received.
- **OSQAccept** deletes the present message at queue head after checking its presence yes or no and after the deletion the queue head pointer increments.

- **OSQFlush** deletes the messages from queue head to tail. After the flush, the queue head and tail points to Qtop, which is the pointer at start of the queuing.
- **OSQQuery** queries the queue message block but the message is not deleted. The function returns pointer to the message queue. Qhead, if there are the messages in the queue or else returns NULL. It returns a pointer to the structure of the queue data structure for QHEAD, number of queued messages, size and table of tasks waiting for the messages from the queue.
- **OSQPostFront** sends a message to front pointer. Use of the function *QHEAD is made in the following situations. A message is urgent or is of higher priority than all the previously posted messages in the queue.

In certain RTOS, a queue is given select option and option is provided for priority or FIFO. The task having priority if started, deletes the queue message first in case the priority option is selected. The task pending since longer period deletes a queue message first in case the FIFO option is selected.

5.9 PIPES

As shown in Fig. 5.15, a task can be written into a pipe and the other task reads the data that comes out of the pipe. In other words, the output of one task is passed on as input to the other task. Task-to-task or ISR-to-task data transfer can take place using pipes.

Pipes can be used for inter-task communication as shown in Fig. 5.15. One task may send the data packets through one pipe and the other task may send acknowledgements through the other pipe.

Fig. 5.15: Pipes for inter-task communication

In Unix/Linux, we use the pipes as shell commands. The OS pipe functions are unlike message queue functions. The difference is that pipe functions are similar to the ones used for devices such as file.

A message-pipe is a device for inserting (writing) and deleting (reading) between two given interconnected tasks or two sets of tasks. Writing and reading from a pipe is like using a C command, write with a file name to write into a named file, and fread with a file name to read from a named file. Pipes are also like Java PipeInputOutputStreams. Pipe is unidirectional. One thread or task inserts into it and the other one deletes from it.

The OS functions for pipe are the following.
- **PipeDevCreate** - for creating the pipe device.
- **Open( )** - for opening the device to enable its use from beginning of its allocated buffer.
- **Connect( )** - for connecting a thread or task inserting bytes to the thread or task deleting bytes from the pipe.
- **Write( )** - for inserting (writing) from the bottom of the empty memory space in the buffer allotted to it.
- **Read( )** - for deleting (reading) from the pipe from the bottom of the unread memory spaces in the buffer filled after writing into the pipe.
- **Close( )** - for closing the device.

A function is for initialization and creating a pipe. It defines pipe ID, length, maximum length and initial values of two pointers. These are *PFRONT and *PBACK for pipe message destination and pipe message source memory locations, respectively.

Program

```c
#include "includes.h"
#include "edutech.h"
static OS_EVENT *queue;

char*msg;
void*queue[1];
INT8U size=1;
OS_STK Task1Stack[100];
void LCDDisplay(void *pdata);
OS_STK Task2Stack[56];
void keyboard(void *pdata);
int main(void)
{
    key_init();
    lcd_init();
    lcd_cmd(0x01);
    lcd_init();
    VPBDIV = 0x01;
    lcd_cmd(0xC8);
    lcd_dat('K');
    lcd_dat('e');
```

```
   lcd_dat('y');
   lcd_dat(':');
   OSInit();

   Queue=OSQCreate(&queue,size);
   OSTaskCreate(LCDDisplay,(void*)0,&Task1Stack[99],0);

   OSTaskCreate(Keyboard, (void*)0,&Task2Stack[55],1)
   OSStart();
   return0;
}
void LCDDisplay(void*pdata)
{
   char str;
   INT8U err;

   timer_init();

   while(1)
   {
   lcd_cmd(0xc0);
   OSTimeDlyHMSM(0, 0, 2, 0);
   lcd_cmd(0x80);
   str=OSQPend(Queue,0,&err);\lcd_dat(str);
   }
}
void keyboard(void*pdata)
{
   static INT8U row,col,data;
   while(1)
   {
     OSTimeDlyHMSM(0, 0, 0, 300);
     IOCLR0=0XC0E0;

     while(key_pressed())
```

```
{
    data=key_detect();
    row=data/10;
    col=data%10;
    lcd_cmd(0xCC);
    lcd_dat(row+48);
    lcd_dat(col+48);

    if(data==00)
    {
      msg= 'H';
      OSQPost(queue,msg);
    }
    if(data==10)
    {
      msg='B';
      OSQPost(Queue,msg);
    }
    while(!(all_key_open()))
    {
    }
  }
 }
}
```

5.10 EVENTS

In case of IPC, there is wait for only one semaphore post event or mailbox message-posting event. Provision of event functions in an OS offers an advantage that there can be wait for more than one event and the events can also be from the different tasks or ISRs.

The event-functions enable OS actions after a group of events. The OS event functions can be understood as follows.

There is an event register. It has 8 or 16 or 32 event-flags, which form the groups. Each bit of the group in the register corresponds to one event flag in a set of flags.

An event register creates using an OS function, OSEventCreate( ). An event register can be divided into groups, each group assigned to different tasks. An OS function, OSEventQuery( ) queries an event register to find the event register existence and its contents. An event register deletes using an OS function, OSEventDelete( ).

Each event sets one of the bits at the event register using the SET(eventflag) function. Event flag in the register can be set by an ISR or task. CLEAR(eventflag) clears the flag in the event register. An event flag can be cleared by an ISR or task.

A task can use the WAIT-ALL function for the occurrences of setting all the event flags in a group. The task can use WAIT-ANY function for an occurrence of setting of any of the event flags in a group.

5.11 TIMER FUNCTIONS

A real time clock (hardware timer timeout) in the system interrupts the system with each tick, which occurs a number of times in 1 second. An interrupt on a tick can be called SysClkIntr (system real-time clock timer interrupts). An OS provides a number of OS timer functions. These functions use SysClkIntr interrupts on the clock ticks.

The periodic SysClkIntr interrupts on this tick. Following are the steps:
- Before servicing of SysClkIntr, the context of presently running task or thread saves on the TCB data structure.
- SysClkIntr service routine calls the OS.
- The OS finds the new messages or IPCs, which are received from the system call by the OS event control blocks for IPC functions.
- The OS either selects the same task or selects a new task or thread in case of pre-emptive scheduling and switches the context to the new one.
- After return from the interrupt, the new task runs from the code, which was blocked from running earlier.

Each OS has a function for defining the OS ticks per second, which defines generation of the SysClkIntr interrupts and which in turn provides the timer functions of the OS. The function thus defines the SysClkIntr interrupt intervals after initiating the ticks. The functions thus also define the period after which the system calls the ISR on the SysClkIntr interrupts and switches to the OS supervisory mode functions.

The number of ticks if made large, then the frequent running of the OS codes to be run on SysClkIntr interrupt takes place because the context switching to the supervisory mode takes place too frequently. The number of ticks, if made small, the total time spent on SysClkIntr interrupts per second reduces, but then system time accuracy for the OS timer functions becomes small.

μCOS-II Functions for Timer:
- **OS_TICK_PER_SEC**
  Defines the number of system clock ticks per second, which is also the number of SysClkIntr interrupts per second.

- **OS_TickInit( )**
  Initiate the clock ticks in the system and SysClkIntr interrupts.
- **OS Time Delay( )**
  Delay the task executing this function.
- **Os Time Delay Resume( )**
  Resume the delayed task.
- **OS Time Set( )**
  Set the system clock tick count value. Os Time Set(1000) sets the count = 1000. OS Time Set (0) sets the count = 0. After each SysClkintr and clock tick the count increments by one.
- **Os Time Get( )**
  Get the system clock-tick's count value.
- OSSemPend( )
  Wait for the semaphore release and Sem value becomes 1 for the period as per twait. If semaphore get released in this period, then take it and task proceeds further after decrementing the Sem value to 0, else after twait defined period, the task code proceeds with no further wait. If twait = 100, then wait for 100 system clock ticks. The Sem Err points to the error.
- **OSMBoxpend( )**
  Wait for the mailbox message for the period as per twait, if mailbox is posted the message then take it and the task proceeds further, else after twait defined period, the task code proceeds further. If twait=100, then wait for 100 system clock-ticks. The MBoxErr points to the error.

5.12 SIGNALS

Signals can be passed to indicate an event. However, many RTOS do not support it then, and their use is discouraged. Again, in shell commands, the signals are sent to kill a process. Consider the following command.

$kill-9 879:

This is a command to send a signal to a process with a process ID of 879. When the signal is received, the process is terminated.

An important application of the signals is to handle exceptions. A signal reports an error during the running of a task and then lets the scheduler initiate an error-handling process or function or task. An error-handling signal handler handles the different error login of other tasks. The device driver functions also use the signals to call the handlers(ISRs).

The following are the signal related IPC functions, which are generally not provided in the RTOS such as µcos-II and provided in RTOS such as VxWorks or OS such as Unix and Linux.
- SigHandler( ) – To create a signal handler corresponding to a signal identified by the signal number and define a pointer to the signal context. The signal context saves the registers on signal.
- Connect – An interrupt vector to a signal number, with signaled handler function and signal handler arguments. The interrupt vector provides the PC value for the signal-handler function address.
- A function Signal( ) to send a signal identified by a number in the argument to a task.
- Mask the signal.
- Unmask the signal
- Ignore the signal.

5.13 MEMORY MANAGEMENT

When a process is created, the memory manager allocates the memory addresses to it by mapping the process space. Threads of a process share the memory space of the process.

The memory manager of the OS has to be secure, robust and well protected. There must be control such that there are no memory leaks and stack overflows. Memory leaks mean attempts to write in the memory block not allocated to a process or data structure. Stack overflow means that the stack exceeds the allocated memory block(s) when there is no provision for additional stack space.

Memory Managing Strategy for a System:

Fixed blocks allocation:

Memory address space is divided into blocks with processes having small address spaces getting a lesser number of blocks and processes with big address spaces getting a larger number of blocks.

Dynamic blocks allocation:

Memory address space is divided into fixed blocks as above and then later the memory manager later allocates variable size blocks dynamically allocated from a free list of memory blocks of description table at the different computation phases of a process.

Dynamic page allocation:

Memory has fixed sized blocks called pages and the memory manager MMU allocates the pages dynamically with a page descriptor table.

Dynamic data memory allocation:

The manager allocates memory dynamically to different data structures like the nodes of a list, queues and stacks.

Dynamic address relocation:

The manager dynamically allocates the addresses initially bound to the relative addresses. It adds the relative address to address with relocation register. The memory manager now dynamically changes only the contents of relocation register. It also takes into account a limit-defining register so that the relocated addresses are within the limit of available addresses. This is also called run-time dynamic address binding.

Multiprocessor memory allocation:

The memory adopts an allocation strategy either shared with light coupling between two or more processors or shared with loose coupling or multisegmented allocations.

Memory protection to OS function:

Memory protection to the OS functions means that the system call and function call in user space are distinct. The OS function code, data and stack are in the protected memory area. It means that when a user function call attempts to write or read in the exclusively memory space allocated to the OS functions, it is blocked and the system generates an error. The memory of kernel function is distinct and can be addressed only by the system calls. The memory space is called *kernel space*.

Memory protection among the task:

Memory protection to the tasks means that a task function call cannot attempt to write or read in the exclusive area of memory space allocated to another task. The protection increases the memory requirement for each task and also the execution time of the code of the task.

The memory manager manages the following:
- Use of memory address space by a process.
- Specific mechanisms to share the memory space.
- Specific mechanisms to restrict sharing of a given space.
- Optimization of the access periods of a memory by using an hierarchy of memories (external secondary magnetic and optical memories).

The memory manager allocates memory to the processes and manages it with appropriate protection. There may be static or dynamic allocations of memory. The manager optimizes the memory needs and memory utilization. An RTOS may disable the support to the dynamic block allocations, MMU support to the dynamic page allocation and dynamic binding as this increases the latency of servicing the tasks and ISRs. An RTOS may or may not support memory protection in order to reduce the latency and memory needs of the processes.

5.14 OVERVIEW OF RTOS

A complex multitasking embedded system design requires:
- Integrated development environment.
- Task functions in embedded C or embedded C++.
- Real time clock based hardware and software timers.
- Schedulers.
- Device drivers and device managers.
- Functions for Inter Process Communications (IPC) using the signals, event flag group, semaphore-handling functions and functions for the queues, mailboxes, pipes and sockets.
- Additional functions for example TCP/IP or USB or Bluetooth or Wi-Fi or IrDA and GUIs.
- Functions for Error and exception handling.
- Testing and system debugging software to test RTOS as well as developed embedded applications.

5.14.1 General Features of RTOS

The RTOS's have the following features in general:
- Basic kernel functions and scheduling; pre-emptive or pre-emptive and time slicing.
- Priority definitions for the tasks and IST.
- Priority inheritance feature with option of priority ceiling feature.
- Limit for number of tasks.
- Task synchronization and IPC functions.
- IDE having editor, platform builder, GUI and graphics software, complier, debugging and host target support tools in it.
- Device imaging tool and device drivers.
- Support to the clock, time and timer functions, POSIX, asynchronous IOs, memory allocation and deallocation system, file systems, flash systems, number of processors, TCP/IP network, wireless and bus protocols, development environment with JAVA and componentization (reusable modules for different functions), which leads to small footprint.
- To Support number of processor architectures.

5.14.2 Types of RTOSes

Following are the types of RTOSes:
- **In-House Developed RTOS**

  In-house RTOS has the codes written for the specific need and application or product. It customizes the in-house design needs. Generally In-House RTOS is used by a small-level application developer or a big research and development company.

- **Broad-based Commercial RTOS**

  There are also readily available broad-based commercial RTOS packages. They offer the following advantages.
  1. Availability of off the shelf, thoroughly tested and debugged RTOS functions.
  2. Inbuilt several development tools. These development tools consist of tools for the source-code engineering, testing, simulating and debugging. When designing a mission critical real-time application, lack of appropriate error-handling capability or an appropriate RTOS or a testing and debugging tool causes data loss. Even may cause hardware loss.
  3. Supports many processor architectures. For e.g. ARM as well as X86, MIPS and SuperH.
  4. Supports development of GUIs in the system.
  5. Supports many devices, graphics, network connectivity protocols and file systems.
  6. Supports device software optimization (DSO). It is a recently developed concept in a few RTOSes.
  7. Availability of error and exceptional handling functions, which can be ported directly as these are already well tested by thousands of users.
  8. It simplifies the coding process to a great extent for a developer and also helps in building a product fast; it helps in building robust and bug-free software by thorough testing and simulation before embedding the codes into the hardware.
  9. Reduces large amount of development time for RTOS tools and in-house documentation.
  10. Reduces maintenance cost.
  11. Reduces cost of keeping in-house engineers.

- **General Purposes OS with RTOS**

  Embedded Linux or Windows XP are general purpose OS. They are not componentized. Footprint (the code that goes as ROM image) is not reducible. The tasks are not assignable priorities. They offer powerful GUIs, rich multimedia interfaces and have low cost.

  The general purpose OS can be used in combination with the RTOS functions. For example; RT Linux is a real time kernel over the Linux kernel. Another example is windows XP Embedded for X86 architecture.

- **Special Focus RTOS**

  This is used with specific processors such as ARM or 8051 or DSP, for e.g. OSEK for automotives or Symbian OS for the mobile phones.

5.15 VxWORKS

VxWorks is a real-time operating system made and sold by Wind River Systems of Alameda, California, USA. Intel acquired Wind River Systems on July 17, 2009.

VxWorks is a high performance, Unix like, Scalable RTOS and supports ARM, ColdFire, MIPS, Pentium, Intel, X-Scale, SuperH and other popular processors for Embedded System design. VxWorks RTOS design is hierarchical and is for hard real-time applications. It supports kernel mode execution of tasks for fast execution of application codes.

VxWorks is supported with powerful development tools that make it easy and efficient to use. It also supports many advanced processor architectures, Device Software Optimization (DSO), which is to be a new methodology that enables the development and the running of the device software faster, better and more reliable.

VxWorks is designed for use in embedded systems. Unlike "self-hosting" systems such as Unix, VxWorks development is done on a "host" machine running Linux, Unix, or Microsoft Windows, cross-compiling target software to run on various "target" CPU architectures. VxWorks 6.x is it's latest version.

5.15.1 Key Features of Vx Works OS

The key features of the current OS are:

- Multitasking kernel with preemptive as well as round-robin scheduling and fast interrupt response.
- Native 64-bit operating system (only one 64-bit architecture supported: Intel 64). Data model: LP64.
- User-mode applications ("Real-Time Processes", or RTP) isolated from other user-mode applications as well as the kernel via memory protection mechanisms.
- SMP and AMP support.
- Fast, flexible inter-process communication including TIPC.
- Error handling framework.
- Binary, counting, and mutual exclusion semaphores with priority inheritance.
- Local and distributed message queues.
- POSIX PSE52 certified conformance in user-mode execution environment.
- File systems: High Reliability File System (HRFS), FAT-based file system (DOSFS), Network File System (NFS).
- IPv6 networking stack.

5.15.2 Tornado (Development Environment for VxWorks 5.x releases)

Tornado is an Integrated development environment (IDE) for software cross-development targeting VxWorks 5.x.
- Tornado consists of the following elements:
- VxWorks 5.x target operating system.
- Application-building tools (cross-compiler and associated programs).
- An integrated development environment (IDE) that facilitates managing and building projects, establishing host-target communication, and running, debugging, and monitoring VxWorks applications.
- VxWorks simulator (VxSim).

5.15.3 Workbench (Development Environment for VxWorks 6.x releases)

Workbench replaced Tornado IDE for VxWorks 6.x. The Wind River Workbench is now built on Eclipse technology. Workbench is also the IDE for the Wind River Linux and On-Chip Debugging product lines.

Workbench for VxWorks consists of the following elements:
- Eclipse framework and Eclipse (CDT) project.
- Project and Build System.
- Wind River Compiler and Wind River GNU Compiler.
- Debugger.
- Wind River Host Shell and Kernel Shell for VxWorks.
- VxWorks Kernel Configurator.
- Target file system configuration tools.
- Run-time analysis tools.
- VxWorks simulator (VxSim).

5.16 RT LINUX

Q. Write short note on: RT Linux [May, June 2010]

There are two different versions of RTLinux: RTLinux/Pro and RTLinux/Open.

RTLinux/Open is available on the web. The main (only) developer of this version was FSMLabs and stops its development in 2nd quarter of 2001. RTLinux/Pro is available for a free from FSMLabs and the license is non-GPL.

5.16.1 Architecture Overview

There are two approaches to provide real-time performance in a Linux system:
1. Improving the Linux kernel preemption.
2. Adding a new software layer beneath Linux kernel with full control of interrupts and processor key features.

These two approaches are known as *"preemption improvement"* and *"interrupt abstraction"* respectively. This second approach is the one used by RTLinux.

RTLinux is a small, fast operating system, following the POSIX 1003.13 "minimal realtime operating system" standard.

RTLinux adds a layer of virtual hardware between the standard Linux kernel and the computer hardware (see Fig. 5.16). As far as the standard Linux kernel is concerned, this new layer appears to be the actual hardware. RTLinux implements a complete and predictable RTOS with no interference from the non-real-time Linux. The RTLinux threads are executed directly by a fixed-priority scheduler. The whole Linux kernel, and all the normal Linux processes, are managed by the RTLinux scheduler as the background task. This way, it is possible to have a complete general purpose operating system running on top of a small predictable RTOS.

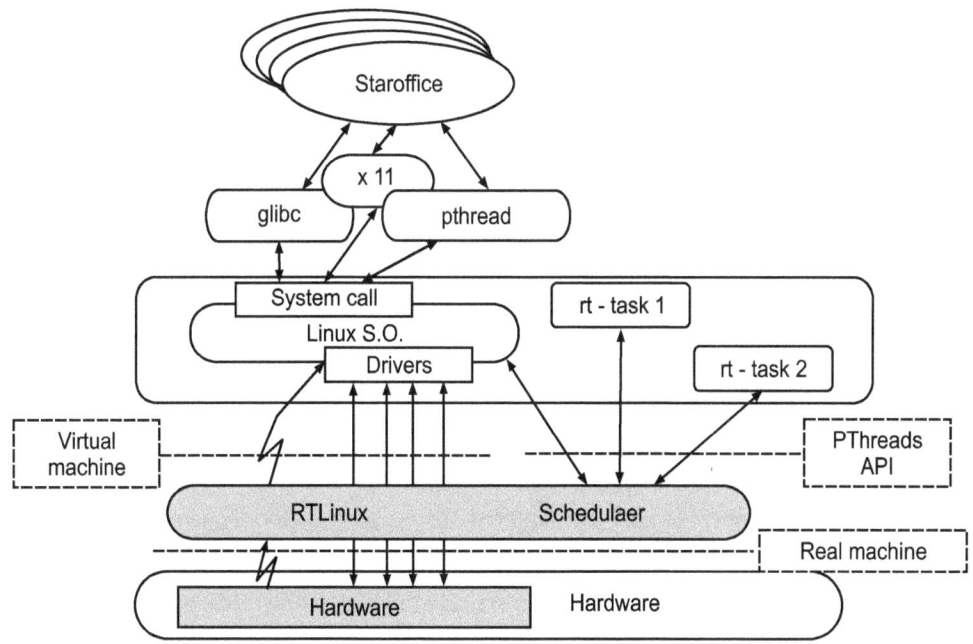

Fig. 5.16: RTLinux layer architecture

There are three main modifications done to the Linux kernel in order to virtualize the hardware so that RTLinux can take full control of the machine: The RTLinux layer takes direct control of all the hardware interrupts, interrupts that are not controlled by real-time threads are forwarded to the Linux upper level; RTLinux also takes the control of the timer hardware (8254 and APIC when available) and implements a virtual timer to Linux; and the last modification done to Linux to remove the basic control of the hardware from Linux is to replace all the cli and sti (disable and enable interrupt flag) function calls from the Linux kernel so that Linux can no make a real disable but a virtual interrupt disable. These modifications are quiet complex and tricky, but do not require large code (Linux) modifications.

RTLinux provides an execution environment "below" the Linux kernel. One consequence of this is that real-time threads cannot use Linux services because deadlock or system inconsistencies may happen. To overcome this problem, the real-time system has to be divided into two separated layers: the hard real-time layer, executed on top of RTLinux, and the soft real-time, executed as normal Linux processes. Several mechanisms (FIFO, shared memory) can be used to communicate threads in both layers.

The two layer approach is a useful method to provide hard real-time while having all the features of a desktop operating system. It decouples the mechanism of the real-time kernel from the mechanism of the general purpose Linux kernel so that each system can be optimized independently.

5.16.2 Hardware Characteristics

Supported processors:
    i386, PPC, ARM (StrongARM/iPAQ).

Supported multi processor:
    It is available for i386 architectures.

5.16.3 Process Management

Scheduling Policy:
    There are three scheduling policies available: SCHED_FIFO, SCHED_SPORADIC SCHED_EDF. SCHED_FIFO is a fixed priority scheduling and threads with the same priority are scheduled in FIFO order. SCHED_SPORADIC an implementation of the sporadic server used to run a periodic activities. SCHED_EDF implements a dynamic priority scheduling policy the EDF (Earliest Deadline First). Each thread has a fixed priority and a deadline. Threads are sorted by priority, but same priority threads are scheduled according to the EDF policy.

Periodic Threads:
    The system provides special system calls to implement periodic threads. pthread_make_periodic_np( ) and pthread_wait_np( ).

Range of Priorities and Maximum Number of Threads:

Minimum and maximum priority is 0 and 1000000 respectively. There is no limit in the number of running threads, but the scheduling cost is proportional to the number of threads. Current scheduler code is designed to handle efficiently a low number of threads (around 10).

Thread Creation and Deletion:

It provides all the POSIX Thread termination facilities and also some extensions to remove termitate threads easier.

A thread can terminate itself by calling pthread_exit( ) function. pthread_ join( ) suspend the execution of the calling thread until the target thread terminates. To implement this behaviour, when a thread exits, the system do not delete the supporting data until other thread has joined. The system also provides the pthread_detach( ) function to indicate that the target thread will not be joined and the system support data can be reclaimed as soon as the thread exits.

A thread can request the cancellation (termination) of other thread: pthread_cancel( ). The thread that receives the cancellation request, depending on the cancelability state, can do one of the following action:

- PTHREAD_CANCEL_DISABLE: The cancel request is ignored.
- PTHREAD_CANCEL_DEFERRED: The thread will be canceled but only at some safe points.
- PTHREAD_CANCEL_ASYNCHRONOUS:The thread is canceled immediately.

A thread can install cancellation cleanup handlers: pthread_cleanup_push( ) and pthread_cleanup_pop( ). The cleanup handlers are called when the thread exits, is canceled or the handler is removed.

pthread_delete_np( ) function can be used to termintate inmediately a thread and can be used instead of the pair: pthread_cancel( )/pthread_join( ).

5.16.4 Memory Management

Protected Address Spaces:

Although RTLinux is designed to run in processors with MMU, all the application threads and the RTLinux kernel run in the same address space. There is no memory protection between threads and the kernel and also between threads themselves.

From the point of view of memory management, RTLinux is the guest operating system of the Linux Kernel. The Linux kernel has the whole control of the memory.

Dynamic Memory Allocation:

RTLinux do not provide dynamic memory allocation nor use it internally. The main argument is that dynamic memory allocation is not predictable if implemented efficiently. The Real-Time goal of predictability is usually achieved by preallocating most of the resources the threads will use at run time.

It is possible to allocate all the memory that each thread will require before the threads are created.

5.16.5 Inter-Process Communication

Semaphores:

POSIX REALTIME semaphores are fully implemented: sem_init( ), sem_destroy( ), sem_ getvalue( ), sem_post( ), sem_trywait( ) and sem_wait( ). These are counting semaphores.

Mutex:

RTLinux supports the POSIX pthread_mutex_ family of functions: pthread_mutex_init( ), pthread_mutex_destroy( ), pthread_mutex_lock( ), pthread_mutex_trylock( ) and pthread_mutex_unlock( ). As well as all the supporting, pthread_mutexattr_... like, functions to handle mutex creation attributes.

The supported mutex types are:
- PTHREAD_MUTEX_NORMAL: The default POSIX mutex.
- PTHREAD_MUTEX_SPINLOCK_NP: Provides a interface to spin-locks used to synchronize the execution in multiprocessor systems.
- The supported mutex protocols are:
- PTHREAD_PRIO_NONE: No priority control is performed on locking and unlocking.
- PTHREAD_PRIO_PROTECT: Immediate priority inheritance. The thread that locks the mutex inherits the priority ceiling of the semaphore, and returns to the original priority when the unlocks the mutex.

Priority Inversion Control:

Mutex provide immediate priority inheritance.

Messages Queues:

There is no message queues available.

Mailboxes:

There is no mailboxes.

Shared Memory:

Shared memory is provided with a non-POSIX interface called mbuff. Since all threads are executed in the kernel address space (rtlinux threads share by default all the memory), this sharing memory mechanism is used to communicate rtlinux threads and normal linux processes.

Both execution environments, RTLinux and Linux, have the same mbuff API.

Following the idea that not dynamic memory allocation can be requested during normal system execution, allocation and releasing functions can not be used from RTLinux threads, only at module loading or by linux processes.

FIFOs:

RTLinux provide a single IPC called FIFO. It is First-In-First-Out queues that can be read from and written to by Linux processes and RTLinux threads. FIFOs are uni-directional - you can use a pair of FIFOs for bi-directional data exchange.

5.16.6 Time and Timers

Time Resolution:

Time is measured in nano-seconds. Two different data structures are used to measure time: POSIX structure:

```
struct timespec {
  time_t tv_sec; /* seconds */
  long tv_nsec; /* nanoseconds */
};
```

and RTLinux specific:

```
typedef long long hrtime_t; /* Nano seconds */
```

RTLinux use the highest resolution that the underlying hardware provides.

Currently supported clocks are:

- CLOCK_MONOTONIC: This POSIX clock runs at a steady rate, and is never adjusted or reset.
- CLOCK_REALTIME: This is the standard POSIX real time clock. Currently, it is the same as CLOCK_MONOTONIC.
- CLOCK_RTL_SCHED: The clock that the scheduler uses for task scheduling, it is the best hardware clock.
    - The following clocks are architecture-dependent. They are not normally found in user programs.
- CLOCK_8254: Used on non-APIC x86 machines for scheduling. Its frequency is 1193180 Hz.
- CLOCK_APIC: Used on SMP x86 machines and single processor equipped with local APIC. This clock ticks at the same frequency than the internal processor clock. If the processor is clocked at 1 GHz or higher, then this clock has a resolution smaller than 1 nano-second.

User Timers:

There is no user timers. There is only one timer handler per hardware timer, which is associated with the interrupt handler. When the scheduler module is loaded, the scheduler takes the control of the timer and no other thread can use the timer.

The only timing facility that a thread can use being a periodic thread.

Facilities to add new hardware timers

The internal structure of the source code is prepared to add new timer drivers easily. There is a struct rtl_clock similar to the device driver structure used to register UNIX device drivers.

5.16.7 Driver Programming

Interrupts

RTLinux defines two types of interrupts: Soft and Hard Interrupts.

Hard Interrupts the one originated directly by the real hardware. There is very little system interference in the service of these interrupts, therefore the interrupt latency is almost only limited by the performance of the underlying hardware. Since these handlers are executed at the RTLinux level, it is not possible to call linux services. Interrupt handlers are installed and uninstalled with rtl_request_irq( ) and rtl_free_irq( ) functions.

Soft interrupts are normal Linux kernel interrupts, in the sense that the interrupt handlers are executed by the Linux kernel thread. The latency of this interrupts are the same than that of a normal linux, i.e., no realtime. On the other hand, is possible to use all the facilities of the linux kernel. The following functions are used to manage this kind of interrupts: rtl_get_soft_irq( ) and rtl_free_soft_irq( ).

It is possible to generate interrupts from RTLinux to Linux with the function: rtl_global_pend_irq. Also, by using the POSIX signal mechanism is possible to send signals (which are received like soft interrupts) to the linux thread.

Low Level Programming:

Since RTLinux threads are executed in kernel address space and processor mode, it is possible to use all the reserved processor instructions directly. To direct access io ports in ISA bus: rtl_inb, rtl_inb_p, and the outb counterparts. To access physical memory (devices located at the PCI bus) it is possible to use ioremap( ) function at thread initialization and then access the device through the returned pointer.

5.16.8 Network

A separate module called RTnet provides the drivers (only two network drivers are supported) and the protocols (IP, ARP, UDP and ICMP) over Ethernet. The API is quiet similar to the sockets API: rt_socket( ), rt_connect( ), rt_sendmsg( ), etc. Current version of RTnet only works with Linux kernel version 2.2.x.

Also several CAN drivers are available.

5.16.9 Filesystems

The module rtl_posixio.o implements the /dev filesystem. It provides unix like (open( ), read( ), write( ) ...) functions to access device driver services, and drivers can be registered with the function: rtl_register_rtldev().

Current implementation provides the following devices: /dev/rtf, /dev/mem and /dev/ttyS.

RTLinux do not provide any block device nor regular filesystem implementation. Since the background RTLinux process is the Linux kernel, RTLinux designers choose not to include non-realtime features that are already available and usable.

5.16.10 Trace and Debug

Logic debug:

Source level debugging using GDB directly from the same machine that is running the system. The debugging target system (RTLinux) and the host system (where GDB is running) are communicated with FIFOS.

It is possible to debug periodic threads (gdb command **info threads**) in the usual way: step by step, break points, inspect variable values etc. Multiprocessor systems can be debugged. Also is possible to use graphical front-ends like: DDD, gvd, xxgdb, insight.

Timing debug

An optional tracer module can be included in the system. The tracer will register all the relevant system events and user-defined ones.

The built-in set of events includes RTLinux interrupt handlers entry and exit, scheduler entry and exit, spin-lock acquiring and freeing, context switches, interrupts disabling and enabling. It is possible to attach an arbitrary 32-bit value to each event record. The current value of instruction pointer is also logged with each event.

Events are grouped into classes. It is possible to select logging of events of any combination of different classes during runtime.

Events are logged in circular buffers located in shared memory, where a user-space program can collect and store in disk. This logging mechanism causes a minimal interference.

5.17 QNX

QNX is a commercial Unix-like real-time operating system, aimed primarily at the embedded systems market. The product was originally developed by Canadian company, QNX Software Systems, which was later acquired by Canadian BlackBerry-producer Research In Motion.

5.17.1 Description

As a microkernel-based OS, QNX is based on the idea of running most of the OS in the form of a number of small tasks, known as servers. This differs from the more traditional monolithic kernel, in which the operating system is a single very large program composed of a huge number of "parts" with special abilities. In the case of QNX, the use of a microkernel allows users (developers) to turn off any functionality they do not require, without having to change the OS itself; instead, those servers are simply not run.

The system is quite small, with earlier versions fitting on a single floppy disk.

QNX Neutrino (2001) has been ported to a number of platforms and now runs on practically any modern CPU that is used in the embedded market. This includes the PowerPC, x86 family, MIPS, SH-4 and the closely related family of ARM, StrongARM and XScale CPUs. QNX offers a license for non-commercial users.

The BlackBerry Playbook tablet computer designed by Research In Motion uses a version of QNX as the primary operating system.

5.17.2 Technology

The QNX kernel contains only CPU scheduling, interprocess communication, interrupt redirection and timers. Everything else runs as a user process, including a special process known as 'proc' which performs process creation, and memory management by operating in conjunction with the microkernel. This is made possible by two key mechanisms - subroutine-call type interprocess communication, and a boot loader which can load an image containing not only the kernel but any desired collection of user programs and shared libraries. There are no device drivers in the kernel. The network stack is based on NetBSD code. Along with its support for its own, native, device drivers, QNX supports its legacy, io-net manager server, and the network drivers ported from NetBSD.

QNX interprocess communication consists of sending a message from one process to another and waiting for a reply. This is a single operation, called MsgSend. The message is copied, by the kernel, from the address space of the sending process to that of the receiving process. If the receiving process is waiting for the message, control of the CPU is transferred at the same time, without a pass through the CPU scheduler. Thus, sending a message to another process and waiting for a reply does not result in "losing one's turn" for the CPU. This tight integration between message passing and CPU scheduling is one of the key mechanisms that makes QNX message passing broadly usable. Most UNIX and Linux interprocess communication mechanisms lack this tight integration, although an implementation of QNX-type messaging for Linux does exist.

Due to the microkernel architecture, QNX is also a distributed operating system. Dan Dodge and Peter van der Veen hold a patent based on the QNX operating system's distributed processing features known commercially as Transparent Distributed Processing.

All I/O operations, file system operations, and network operations were meant to work through this mechanism, and the data transferred was copied during message passing. Later versions of QNX reduce the number of separate processes and integrate the network stack and other function blocks into single applications for performance reasons.

Message handling is prioritized by thread priority. Since I/O requests are performed using message passing, high priority threads receive I/O service before low priority threads, an essential feature in a hard real-time system.

The boot loader, is the other key component of the minimal microkernel system. As user programs can be built into the boot image, the set of device drivers and support libraries needed for startup need not be, and are not, in the kernel. Even such functions as program loading are not in the kernel, but instead are in shared user-space libraries loaded as part of the boot image. It is possible to put an entire boot image into ROM, which is used for diskless embedded systems.

Neutrino supports symmetric multiprocessing and bound multiprocessing (BMP), which is QNX's term for being able to lock selected threads to selected CPUs. BMP is used to improve cache hitting and to ease the migration of non-SMP safe applications to multi-processor computers.

Neutrino supports strict priority-preemptive scheduling and adaptive partition scheduling (APS). APS guarantees minimum CPU percentages to selected groups of threads, even though others may have higher priority. The adaptive partition scheduler is still strictly priority-preemptive when the system is underloaded. It can also be configured to run a selected set of critical threads strictly real-time, even when the system is overloaded.

5.17.3 Transparent Distributed Processing

Transparent Distributed Processing, or TDP, is the name that the QNX operating system uses to refer to its network distributed architecture. Since QNX is a microkernel, it is inherently network distributable, so TDP actually boils down to a protocol module that plugs in to the QNX networking stack. This protocol module (known as qnet) links the microkernels across the network together, so that operating system services are accessed using exactly the same mechanism without regard to the computer node on which they reside.

APPENDIX

Embedded Systems (Elective 1)

Time : 3 Hours　　　　　　　　　　　　　　　　　　　　　　　　Max. Marks : 100

N.B. (i) Attempt any three questions from each section.
(ii) Use separate answer sheet for each section.
(iii) Draw appropriate diagram wherever necessary.

MAY/JUNE 2013

Section (A)

Q.1. (a) Explain the criteria used for choosing a microcontroller for embedded application. [8 M]
(b) Explain RAM space allocation and register banks in 8051 microcontroller. [8 M]

Q.2. (a) Explain bit addressability features of 8051 for I/O ports. [8 M]
(b) Write a 8051 C program to convert FAH (1111 1010) to decimal and display the decimal digits on ports P0, P1 and P2. [8 M]

Q.3. (a) Explain the use of SWAP instruction of 8051 microcontroller. [8 M]
(b) Explain program status word register of 8051 in detail. [8 M]

Q.4. (a) Explain the following instructions of 8051 : [8 M]
(i) CJNE,　(ii) CPLA.
(b) What is register bank? Why 8051 supports multiple register banks? How 8051 switches between these banks? [8 M]

Q.5. (a) Write short notes on any three : [18 M]
(i) Bitwise operators,　(ii) X86 PC embedded applications,　(iii) Delay generation using loops of 8051 timer,　(iv) Checksum bytes in ROM.

Section (B)

Q.6. (a) What is the significance of SCON register of 8051? Explain all the bits of SCON register of 8051. [8 M]
(b) Explain the role of TI and RI flags of 8051 for serial communications. [8 M]

Q.7. (a) Explain how mail boxes are implemented in RTOS. [8 M]
(b) Explain the interfacing of ADC 0808 with 8051 microcontroller. [8 M]

Q.8. (a) Explain memory address decoding techniques with suitable example. [8 M]
(b) Explain different interrupts in 8051. Also explain how to set up interrupt priority. [8 M]

Q.9. (a) Explain LCD interfacing with 8051 microcontroller. [8 M]
(b) List differential types of Kernel services. Explain any one in detail. [8 M]

Q.10. Write short notes on (any three) : [18 M]
(a) RTC 12887.
(b) Stepper motor interfacing.
(c) MOVX instruction for external RAM data.
(d) RTOS Kernel architecture.

MAY/JUNE 2012

Section (A)

Q.1. (a) Explain stacks in 8051 with suitable example. [8 M]
(b) Draw and explain block diagram of 8051. [8 M]

Q.2. (a) Explain bit addressability for I/O ports of 8051. [8 M]
(b) Draw and explain the role of TMOD and TCON register of 8051, while programming 8051 microcontroller for embedded applications. [8 M]

Q.3. (a) Assume that 1 MHz external clock is being fed into pin TI(P3.5). Write a C program for counter 1, mode on port P1. Start count from 00H. [8 M]
(b) Explain the following instructions of 8051 : [8 M]
(i) RR, (ii) RL, (iii) RRC, (iv) RLC.

Q.4. (a) Assume LEDs are connected to bits P_1 and P_2 write an 8051 C program that shows the count from 00 to FFH (0000 0000 to 1111 1111) on the LEDs. [8 M]
(b) What is register bank and why multiple register banks are supported in 8051. Also explain how to switch among these banks. [8 M]

Q.5. Write short notes on (any three) : [18 M]
(a) SWAP instruction of 8051.
(b) Compare features of microcontroller with microprocessor.
(c) PSW of 8051.
(d) Watchdog timer.

Section (B)

Q.6. (a) Explain memory address decoding technique with suitable example. [8 M]
(b) Explain how TI and RI flags are used in 8051. [8 M]

Q.7. Compare edge triggered interrupts with level triggered interrupts. Illustrate how 8051 differentiates in these two. [8 M]

Q.8. (a) Explain with suitable diagram interfacing of KBO with 8051 microcontroller. [8 M]
(b) With a suitable diagram interfacing and programming of DAC 0808 with 8051 microcontroller. [8 M]

EMBEDDED SYSTEMS (BAMU)   APPENDIX

Q.9. (a) Explain different techniques supported by RTOS for interprocess communication.
                                                                       [8 M]
     (b) Explain use of SBUF and SCON registers of 8051 for serial communication. **[8 M]**

Q.10. Write short notes on (any three):   **[18 M]**
     (a) Schedule management for multiple tasks by an RTOS.
     (b) Virtual sockets.
     (c) Setting interrupt priority with IP register of 8051.
     (d) RTOS Kernel Architecture.

NOVEMBER/DECEMBER 2011

Section (A)

Q.1. (a) Explain in brief criteria for choosing a microcontroller.   **[8 M]**
     (b) Draw and explain ROM memory map in 8051 family.   **[8 M]**

Q.2. (a) Explain dual role of port 2 with suitable diagram.   **[8 M]**
     (b) Explain different 'C' data types used for programming 8051 microcontroller. **[8 M]**

Q.3. (a) Explain bit addressability of RAM of 8051.   **[8 M]**
     (b) Write a 8051 C program to convert 1111 1101 (FDH) to decimal and display the
         digit on port P0, P1 and P2.   **[8 M]**

Q.4. (a) Compare and explain LCALL and ACALL instruction.   **[8 M]**
     (b) Explain the following instructions of 8051 (any two):   **[8 M]**
         (i) AND, (ii) CPLA, (iii) CJNE

Q.5. (a) Write short notes on (any three):   **[18 M]**
         (i) Flag register of 8051.
         (ii) RAM data space vs Code data space of 8051.
         (iii) Conversion of packed BCD to ASCII.
     (b) Compare delay generation using:
         (i) Simple for loop.
         (ii) Using 8051 timer.

Section (B)

Q.6. (a) Explain all bits of SCON register of 8051.   **[8 M]**
     (b) Explain different types of semiconductor memories.   **[8 M]**

Q.7. (a) Explain use of EI register of 8051 of enable and disable interrupts. **[8 M]**
     (b) Illustrate with suitable example the use of MOVX instruction for external RAM.
                                                                       [8 M]

Q.8. (a) With suitable example and diagram explain interfacing of KB0 with 8051 microcontroller. [8 M]

(b) Write a C program to move the stepper motor clockwise. The base address of 4000H for 8255. Draw interfacing diagram also. [8 M]

Q.9. (a) Explain use of semaphore to handle critical section problem. [8 M]

(b) List different Kernel services. [8 M]

Q.10. Write short notes on (any three) : [18 M]

(a) Priority inversion problem.

(b) RTC - 12887.

(c) Setting interrupt priority with IP register of 8051.

(d) Compare edge triggered interrupts with level triggered interrupts.

MAY/JUNE 2011

Section (A)

Q.1. (a) Compare microcontroller with general purpose microprocessor. [8 M]

(b) Explain RAM space allocation and register banks in 8051. [8 M]

Q.2. (a) Explain PSW register of 8051 in detail. [8 M]

(b) Explain the concept of system-on-chip (SOC) with suitable example. [8 M]

Q.3. (a) Explain how CALL instruction uses stack. [8 M]

(b) Write an 8051 C program to get a byte of data from P1, wait 1/2 second and then send it to P2. [8 M]

Q.4. (a) Write a 8051 C program to toggle all the bits of port P1 continuously with same delay. [8 M]

(b) Explain importance of TI and RI flags of 8051 for serial communication. [8 M]

Q.5. Write short notes on (any three) : [18 M]

(a) Checksum byte in ROM.

(b) X86 PC embedded applications.

(c) Watchdog timer.

(d) Different addressing modes of 8051.

Section (B)

Q.6. (a) Explain use of SBUF and SCON register of 8051 for serial communication. [8 M]

(b) Write a C program that continuously gets a single bit data from P1.7 and sends it to P1.0 in the main, while simultaneously creating :

(i) a square wave of 200 m second period on P2.5.

(ii) sending letter A to serial port. Using timer - 0 to create square wave. Assume XTAL = 11.0592 MHz. Use 9600 baud rate. [8 M]

Q.7. (a) Explain different types of semiconductor memories. **[8 M]**
(b) Explain in brief different techniques supported by RTOS for interprocess communication. **[8 M]**

Q.8. (a) Explain with suitable diagram, interfacing of LCD with 8051 microcontroller. **[8 M]**
(b) With suitable diagram explain interfacing and programming of ADC0808 with 8051 microcontroller. **[8 M]**

Q.9. (a) Illustrate functions, ISRs and tasks **[8 M]**
(b) Explain how mail boxes are implemented. **[8 M]**

Q.10. Write short notes on (any three) : **[18 M]**
(a) Remote Procedure Call (RPC).
(b) File system organization and implementation.
(c) Doubling baud rate of 8051 data transmission of Kernel services.

MAY/JUNE 2010

Section (A)

Q.1. (a) Explain 8051 register banks and stacks with suitable example. **[8 M]**
(b) Compare and contrast microprocessor based systems with microcontroller based systems. **[8 M]**

Q.2. (a) Explain different C data types used for programming 8051 microcontroller. **[8 M]**
(b) Write an 8051 C program to calculate the checksum byte for the 4-byte of hex data. : 25H, 62H, 3FH, 52H **[8 M]**

Q.3. (a) Explain with suitable example mode 1 and mode 2 programming of 8051 timers. **[8 M]**
(b) Assume that a 60Hz clock is being feed into pin T_0 (P3.4). Write a C program for counter 0 is mode 2 (8 bit auto reload) to display the seconds and minutes on P1 and P2 respectively. **[8 M]**

Q.4. (a) Explain data serialization using 8051 C with suitable example. **[8 M]**
(b) Draw pin diagram of 8051 microcontroller and explain the function of the following pins : **[8 M]**
(i) $\frac{\overline{EA}}{VPP}$, (ii) $\overline{INT0}$ and $\overline{INT0}$, (iii) XTAL1 and XTAL2, (iv) RST

Q.5. Write short notes on (any three) : **[18 M]**
(a) Flag register of 8051.
(b) 8051 addressing modes.
(c) RAM data space versus code data space.
(d) Special Function Registers (SFR).
(e) Interrupts in 8051.

Section (B)

Q.6. (a) Explain different methods of memory address decoding used for interfacing memory with 8051 microcontroller. **[8 M]**

(b) What is serial communication? Explain asynchronous serial communication with suitable diagram. **[8 M]**

Q.7. (a) Explain interfacing of ADC 0804 with 8051 microcontroller. Also give timing diagram of ADC 0804. **[8 M]**

(b) A switch is connected to P2.7. Write a C program to monitor the status of switch and perform the following:
  (i) If SW = 0, the stepper motor moves clockwise.
  (ii) If SW = 1, the stepper motor moves counter clockwise.

Q.8. (a) Explain different services offered by RTOS. **[8 M]**

(b) With suitable diagram explain interfacing of LCD with 8051 microcontroller. **[8 M]**

Q.9. (a) Explain DC motor control using 8051. **[8 M]**

(b) Explain interfacing of RTC 12887 with 8051 microcontroller. **[8 M]**

Q.10. Write short notes on (any three): **[18 M]**
  (a) RT linux.
  (b) PWM.
  (c) DAC interfacing.
  (d) Semiconductor memories.
  (e) Keyboard interfacing with 8051.

www.ingramcontent.com/pod-product-compliance
Lightning Source LLC
Chambersburg PA
CBHW082037230426
43670CB00016B/2681